Dr Taylor of Norwich
1694 — 1761

'That great man, Dr Taylor of Norwich'
John Wesley

'Dr Taylor of Norwich, a divine who yielded to few in
command of temper, benevolent feeling, and deep
acquaintance with the Hebrew and Greek Scriptures'
Adam Clarke

Dr Taylor of Norwich

Wesley's Arch-heretic

G. T. Eddy

EPWORTH PRESS

British Library Cataloguing in Publication data

A catalogue record for this book is available from the British Library

0 7162 0568 8

First published in 2003
by Epworth Press
4 John Wesley Road
Werrington
Peterborough PE4 7ZP

Typeset by Regent Typesetting, London
and printed in Great Britain
by Biddles Ltd, www.biddles.co.uk

To the memory of my dear wife
Joyce
who gave so much support and encouragement
but did not live to see the work completed

Contents

Preface

The chance gift of an old book, which proved to be a first edition of John Wesley's treatise on Original Sin, first led me to look at that work, which had been on my shelves for years in the 1830 edition of Wesley's Works. Then an invitation to read a paper to the East Anglia branch of the Wesley Historical Society brought to mind the long ministry of Dr John Taylor in Norwich, where he opened the splendid Octagon meeting house in May 1756. It was Taylor's attack on that doctrine that had moved Wesley to write his defence of it. This suggested a suitable subject for the paper, which was read in that beautiful building by courtesy of the minister and congregation. But the study thus begun seemed to merit further pursuit.

References to Taylor occur, naturally, in books devoted to Wesley and his theology. These are numerous, and their number grows, especially in America, where the very large Methodist connexion, with its colleges and universities, ensures a perennial interest in the thought of its founder. But the tendency among Methodist writers has been to follow his lead in their assessment of Taylor, and in particular, to accept Wesley's view that he had successfully defended the doctrine of Original Sin against Taylor's attack upon it. It is difficult to avoid the impression that judgements have often been formed without any direct acquaintance with Taylor's own works. Writers tend to approach him with an uncriticized assumption that they are dealing with a dangerous heretic who hastened the decline of Dissent into a barren rationalism fatal to evangelical religion. One notable and honourable exception among early Methodists is Adam Clarke,

who in his own great Commentary, when he came to the Epistle
to the Romans, borrowed from Taylor, with an acknowledgement couched in glowing terms.[1] His contemporaries more com-
monly dismiss Taylor with such epithets as 'Arian', 'Socinian',
and the like.

Volume by volume, with majestic deliberation, the Works of
John Wesley are being republished in the handsome and scholarly Bicentennial edition, and some time in this new century his
rejoinder to Dr Taylor's treatise on Original Sin will appear with
introduction and notes. It must be admitted to be one of Wesley's
major theological writings, and has even sometimes been said to
be his greatest. Whether the modern editors will be more critical
of it than were earlier generations of Methodist scholars we have
yet to see; but the imminence of its republication offers an occasion to take a fresh look at the whole controversy, and to accord
to Dr Taylor and his writings the courtesy of an unprejudiced
appraisal. Such a study reveals him as a very significant figure
in his own right, and a powerful adversary, by no means to be
dismissed as Wesley's ignominiously defeated antagonist in a
forgotten controversy.

No monograph on John Taylor has been published for several
generations, though he is one of the many Dissenting divines
accorded a very full entry in the *Dictionary of National
Biography*. He is frequently mentioned in studies of eighteenth-
century Dissent and kindred subjects, and receives more extensive treatment in an essay by Professor Alan P. F. Sell entitled ' "A
Little Friendly Light": The Candour of Bourn, Taylor and Tow-
good'.[2] There seems to be room for a modern study of the life and
works of this remarkable man.

Methodists have continued to sing John Wesley's gospel in his
brother Charles's hymns these two centuries and more. Despite
Wesley's fears, it is not endangered by taking a less prejudiced
look at Taylor, the man and his writings. At worst this may lead
to the discovery that at some points Taylor had a much better
case than Wesley could bring himself to admit; and that there are
not a few matters on which even 'the people called Methodists'
today are more likely to agree with Taylor than with their

founder and his early followers. Among the most important of these is the doctrine of Original Sin,[3] which will accordingly receive a good deal of attention in the following pages; and there are others, such as the understanding of childhood, marriage and family life, upon which that baleful doctrine has had most unfortunate effects, ever since Augustine imposed it on Western theology. Taylor certainly contributed hugely to the loosening of its hold. 'For this relief, much thanks.'

Acknowledgements

To Mr David Elvidge of King's Lynn and the East Anglia Wesley Historical Society I owe the initial impulse to this study, and the circulation of its first fruits in their typescript journal, no. 68. Foremost among those to whom I am indebted for encouragement in its further development are Dr John Vickers of the Wesley Historical Society, and Dr Ralph Waller, Principal of Harris Manchester College, Oxford, where there is a considerable archive relating to Dr Taylor. I am indebted to the former librarian of that college, Margaret Sarosi, the present librarian Sue Killoran, and especially to their assistant Joyce Meakin, for their willing response to all my requests. Professor Clyde Binfield of Sheffield University and Professor Alan P. F. Sell of Milton Keynes have replied most kindly to my inquiries. I am especially grateful to the late Dr P. O'Brien of Wigan not only for his interest and for complimentary copies of his two books relating to the Warrington story, but for bringing to my notice the existence of the eighteen letters of John Taylor preserved in the archive of the Central Library, Lancaster, here printed as Appendix V. For the supply of photocopies of those letters, and consent to their publication, I am indebted to the county archivist; also to the archivist of Lincolnshire County Council, and the Revd Simon Whitcombe, Rector of Woodhall Spa, for information about Kirkstead; and to staff in Nottingham University library for access to the Castle Gate Church Book. For much of the material in Chapter 3 relating to Kirkstead and the Disney family I am especially indebted to Miss Ruth Tinley, who not only guided me to the sources of information, but obtained photocopies of the relevant pages. I am grateful to the Revd Jack Burton for a photocopy of his account of the Octagon, and for help with the illustrations; and to Miss Aureol Hughes for inquiries in the Norwich record office. The Revd Amos Cresswell has supplied my want of classical Greek where Taylor shows his command of it. To Dr John A. Newton and the Revd Gerald M. Burt of the Epworth Press publications committee, and to Dr Waller and Dr Vickers I am indebted for reading the manuscript, noting errors, offering wise comments, and encouraging its publication. To Dr Vickers I am especially grateful for much expert practical advice and technical guidance, for the benefit of his literally encyclopedic knowledge of Methodist historical and contemporary sources, and not least for undertaking the compilation of the index.

For the supply of illustrations, and permission to use them, thanks are due to the following:

- Harris Manchester College for the copy of Taylor's advertisement for the Hebrew Concordance; and for their portrait of Dr Taylor.
- Dr Lesley Smith for the photograph of that portrait reproduced on the book cover.
- The Bodleian Library, University of Oxford, for the engraved portrait of Dr Taylor from Vol. II of his Hebrew Concordance, (Fol. Godw. 50, 51).
- The congregation of the Octagon Unitarian chapel, Norwich, for pictures of it from their brochure.
- Lancashire County Council Central Library, Lancaster, for the photocopy of Taylor's letter of April 16, 1754.

I

Christians, and Only Christians

John Taylor was at the zenith of a distinguished career when he climbed the pulpit stairs on 12 May 1756, to preach the sermon at the opening of the Octagon, the beautiful new meeting house in Colegate, Norwich. Only the previous month, he had received the diploma of the degree of Doctor of Divinity, conferred in January by the University of Glasgow in recognition of his monumental achievement, the great Hebrew Concordance published two years earlier. He was the author of a number of biblical and theological works that were widely read, one in particular not only in these islands but in New England and on the continent of Europe. Their rational approach, combined with strong belief in the inspiration of Scripture, found ready acceptance among his liberal-minded contemporaries, not least in the Church of England. He was on cordial terms with Thomas Hayter, Bishop of Norwich, during the last twelve years of his residence there, and corresponded with Edmund Law, later Bishop of Carlisle, as well as with such eminent scholars as Benjamin Kennicott (1718–83), later to become the leading Hebrew Old Testament scholar of his generation, and Johann David Michaelis of Gottingen (1717–91), another theologian with a deep interest in that field; but his doctrinal conclusions were anathema to orthodox Calvinists, and even to such Arminians as the great evangelist John Wesley.

Both the building and the sermon express the spirit and religion of this remarkable man. The Octagon stands to this day, a monument to former glories, still used for worship by a Unitarian congregation. Its building had been undertaken when it became necessary to replace an older meeting place on the same site. This was to prove the last important event in the preacher's ministry in Norwich, for little more than a year later he was called away to give the benefit of his great learning and fame to a new venture in Dissenting education, the Warrington Academy. The style of the Octagon is classical, the interior beautifully proportioned and very light. A gallery round all eight sides, supported by elegant Corinthian columns which continue upward to the arched ceiling, completes an auditorium focused on the pulpit. The preaching of the Word of God is clearly central; but the atmosphere is ordered, rational, moderate. It is very easy to imagine that eighteenth-century congregation of well-established business and professional men with their families as they gathered to hear their greatly respected and indeed beloved pastor at its opening.

The sermon,[1] of the generous length expected in those days, is so expressive of the outlook of the preacher that it will serve well to introduce him to us. His text is from Haggai chapter 2, which relates to the rebuilding of the Temple in Jerusalem, verse 9: 'The glory of this latter house shall be greater than of the former, saith the LORD of hosts: and in this place will I give peace, saith the LORD of hosts.' Close student of the Old Testament that he was, he takes note of the historical occasion of the prophecy. The second Temple then about to be dedicated could in no way compare with Solomon's in outward splendour, so its 'glory' could only be 'greater' by reason of God's promise: 'In this place will I give peace; meaning, more especially, the Gospel, which by our Lord, the Messiah, was first preached, and in his blood established, in the land of Judea.' Dr Taylor then proceeds, in the methodical manner of those days, to enumerate the several 'blessings' comprised in this 'peace'. First is 'Peace with God, or reconciliation with him as our God in the everlasting Covenant'. Next, 'Peace and comfort in our own breasts, from the sense of pardoning mercy, and from a consciousness of our being truly directed in our tempers and conversation'. While any evangelical Calvinist or Arminian might assent to the former, the latter point under this head is a far cry from Toplady's 'Nothing in my hand

I bring', and signals a major area of disagreement between Taylor and his critics.

Vigorous controversialist though he could be, however, his next head is a sincere expression of his tolerant spirit: 'The Gospel, on the part of the universal Father, is a declaration of peace on earth, and goodwill towards men, and is intended to produce corresponding affections of Benevolence in our hearts.' This is to extend to all mankind: 'But we are under stronger obligations to those that stand in a nearer situation, I mean to our fellow-Christians; such especially as are not involved in the grand apostasy.' (The good doctor has no time for 'Popery'!) He continues:

> We are *Christians*, and only *Christians*; and we consider all our fellow-Protestants of every denomination in the same light; only as *Christians*; and cordially embrace them all in affection and charity as such. Whatever peculiar tenets they may hold, or in what respects soever they may differ from us, such tenets and such differences we consider not as affecting their Christian character and profession in general. Notwithstanding such peculiarities, we allow they may be good Christians, and as good Christians as ourselves. And therefore upon these just and extensive principles we deny communion to none of our fellow Protestants; we refuse communion, upon the same catholic foundation, with none of them. From the Church of England we do indeed dissent, but not as enemies, seeking her destruction; but as real friends, wishing her the most perfect establishment and prosperity.

Do we catch in that last sentence an echo of the long lost hope of a 'Comprehension' that Baxter and others had cherished, and that set 'Presbyterians' apart from 'Independents' a century before? By 1756 it had settled down, for Taylor and those who thought as he did, into a comfortably friendly relationship between them and the latitudinarians in the established church. He goes on to say that we are all liable to mistakes, and that therefore unanimity is not to be expected:

But though we cannot unite in opinions or modes of worship, we may very amicably agree, and be sufficiently united in spirit, in love, or charity, which is the very highest degree of perfection to which religion can be raised here below, and which the apostle very justly terms *the bond of perfectness.*

Such sentiments will seem natural, almost commonplace, in these ecumenical days, but they were still far from the minds of many at that time. Taylor's contemporary, John Wesley, had used remarkably similar language six years earlier, in part I of his sermon on 'The Catholic Spirit', and in the closing paragraphs of his *Letter to a Roman Catholic*. Both he and Taylor were echoing the pleas of Richard Baxter in the previous century.[2] But Wesley, as we shall see, proved to be one of Taylor's most determined opponents.

Two further heads remain. The fourth is 'Peace in a civic sense'. Here Taylor's sentiments show how far the militancy of the old Puritans had settled down, in such a congregation as sat before the preacher that day in May, into a socially-at-ease Nonconformity. He pays warm tribute to the toleration enjoyed under the Hanoverians, not least in 'this ancient and honourable city', where 'many members of this Society have gained the reputation of very worthy and useful citizens'. We have come a long way from the harsh times that followed the great ejection of 1662. The sermon concludes with a fifth and last exhortation to 'Peace among ourselves', which calls for mutual respect and tolerance of differences, and above all, says Taylor, 'Let no man affect to rule or dictate.'

It may seem strange that one who could not only express, but sincerely hold and live by such eirenic principles, should nevertheless have become the object of extreme vituperation and even hatred. But those were hard-hitting times among the protagonists of the different theological persuasions, and though Taylor, to his great credit, did not descend to the scorn and personal abuse he met with from some of his attackers, he was forthright in controversy. He struck hard and with devastating effect at some of the most cherished beliefs of others, and they believed it their duty to counter-attack no less vigorously. Such terms as 'heretic' and 'deist' were the small shot of the conflict. Wesley described Taylor's teaching as 'poison' and 'far more dangerous than open Deism itself'.[3] But the Protestant underworld could descend to far lower depths than that. Taylor's great-grandson mentions 'a pamphlet by a fellow-citizen' which he says 'exceeded perhaps any publication that ever appeared in virulence and abuse'.[4] No doubt this refers to a pseudonymous attack by Grantham Killingworth, a Baptist, writing in the character of a Quaker, 'M. Adamson', against Taylor's claim in his sermon to be Christian without party label. It is said that Taylor was sometimes even the object of verbal abuse in the street, with such remarks as 'There goes the arch-heretic!'

The weirdest of all the attacks upon Taylor is a booklet of a score of pages entitled *The Arians' and Socinians' Monitor*, by 'Antisocinus'. This was at first published with no other indication of authorship, but later editions carry on the title page the name of John MacGowan,[5] the Baptist minister of Devonshire Square chapel, London. The earliest edition, printed in London 'for the Author, and sold by J. Johnson, Bookseller and Stationer, opposite the Monument', is dated 'MDCCLXI', the year of Taylor's death; but the title-page speaks of him as having died 'some years ago', and within the text, Taylor's shade speaks of 'about seven years ago, a little before I died', so either the author was ill-informed or the title-page is wrongly dated.

The tract purports to be the narration of 'a Vision that a young Socinian Teacher lately had, in which he saw, in the most exquisite Torments, his Tutor, who died some Years ago, and had from his own mouth the fearful Relation of what befell him at and after his death'. What this was may readily be guessed. The author describes how one evening, still possessed by blind faith in reason, and full of contempt for 'the glorious doctrines of the everlasting gospel', he took a walk through pleasant wooded country. Reflecting on the satisfactions of reason and its superiority to bigotry in religion, he did not at first notice how surroundings were at every step growing more and more blasted and sinister, until at last he found himself at the very mouth of

Hell. There, sure enough, was his former tutor, Dr Taylor, writhing and tossing on the lake of fire, and loudly lamenting the errors that had brought upon him this terrible judgement:

> In the midst of all, I beheld one person, who stood for some time on the suphurous billows surrounded by an enraged company, who with red-hot irons, kept pushing against him. Deep despair and wild distraction lowered on his condemned countenance. He raved; he foamed; he wrestled! and then sunk down in final despair, while the direful floods of omnipotent vengeance rolled upon him

Needless to say, he now sees the truth of the doctrines he had attacked, and earnestly presses upon his former pupil the need to recant before it is too late, and to warn the many others whom he has misled along with him. In a nice touch, the Doctor makes it clear that this solicitude arises from concern, not for their fate, but his own: with every batch of new arrivals, it seems, his torments are increased! He launches upon a defence of the doctrines he had once attacked. The young man returns home, rereads his tutor's works, which he now sees to be heretical, and burns them. He does not immediately carry out the task of warning others, however, and it takes a visitation by Taylor's ghost to spur him to action.

The market for such lurid nonsense is attested by successive editions, through to at least a twelfth dated 1883. Taylor's grandson mentions one illustrated with a frontispiece, showing the dire scene described within. One can only suppose that stuff of this kind supplied, for a readership denied the pleasures of theatre-going and novel-reading, the thrills their neighbours got from 'Murder in the Red Barn', and the like. But the appetite for it attests the virulence of the bigotry bred by the crude theology of some populist preachers. We are hearing echoes of the terrifying hellfire preaching of men like MacGowan, as Taylor in Hell warns his erstwhile pupil to avoid his own terrible fate:

> As for me, my fate is unalterably fixed, the die is cast, my loss

is irreparable, and my afflictions remediless . . . The irre-
vocable doom is past, my tree is fallen, and in Hell it must lie
burning, but never be consumed! Dying, but never dead!

The fault for which he must thus suffer eternally is unorthodoxy:

> You say that the Deity of Christ is subordinate; but believe me,
> if ever you are so unhappy as to see him in the terrible manner
> in which I beheld him on the judgement seat, you will have
> done with talking of subordinacy in the Godhead. His terrors,
> the awful terrors of omnipotence, will pierce you through with
> infinite sorrow . . . Is not this Infinite vengeance that I sustain?
> Is not this Almighty wrath that rolls in incessant floods upon
> me? Yet this is the very wrath and vengeance of the Saviour
> whom I denied. Nothing less than Omnipotence could thus
> torment, and along with the torment, convey sustaining
> strength. Is he a creature? No, verily, this is uncreated indig-
> nation that falls upon me.

No less crude is the 'orthodox' theology the tormented spirit
then proceeds to inculcate into his hearer, with its emphasis on
'imputed righteousness', and its naive substitutionary view of the
work of Christ. A modern reader is likely to be either bored or
disgusted by such stuff; yet something like it was preached to
many a congregation, as the widespread and violent reaction to
Taylor's teaching clearly shows.

The very crudity and horror of such preaching serves to expose
the ill effects of some of the doctrines taught by more respected
theologians and preachers, which Taylor had exposed to criticism. Among these weightier opponents the most important
were Isaac Watts and John Wesley in England, and Jonathan
Edwards in New England. In later chapters, we shall examine
their criticisms of Taylor's teachings. Wesley's attack, in particular, calls for consideration because the Methodist movement
deriving from his evangelistic enterprise ensures a continuing
interest in its founder's theology, and keeps his works in print in
Britain and America. Thus Taylor is most widely known today

through the writings of one of his opponents, rather than through his own statement of his case. It will be the aim of this study to make a fairer assessment of the man and his work, by means of such a delineation of Dr Taylor himself as the available materials allow, and an account and reappraisal of his major works.

Wishley though Disparing

Beyond the bare facts that his father was a timber merchant and adhered to the established church, while his mother was a Dissenter, there is very little information about John Taylor's childhood. We are told that 'The arms borne by the family were, *Sab. a Lion, passant, reg.*',[1] but this by no means implies aristocratic lineage, and no great significance seems to attach to it. He was born in Scotforth, in the parish of Lancaster, in 1694, but at what point in the life of the family is not recorded. It seems he had two sisters, Catherine and Janet, but no brother.[2] His character may be thought to exhibit the sort of self-confidence shown by only sons of devoted mothers, especially if any sisters are similarly admiring. But in default of evidence, it is idle to speculate about the influences on his childhood. There is a suggestion that his father must have been a tolerant and indeed a generous man, to have been willing to put him to school in a Dissenting academy, with a view to the ministry; but it must also be remembered that such academies offered a liberal education, and were not infrequently chosen for that reason even by Anglican families. As one of his descendants notes in the margin of Taylor's *Life*, his contemporary, Thomas Secker, Bishop of Bristol, and then Archbishop of Canterbury, was also educated at first in a Dissenting Academy. So too were Bishop Butler and many who achieved distinction in other fields.

It was clearly in the Dissenting congregation that the boy's own religion was grounded, and like many a lad sitting next to his mother at worship, he evidently formed an early impression of the dignity and worth of the ministerial office, and began to aspire to it. A note written in the following century attests this early attraction:

> The following memorandum is extracted from his pocket book, in his handwriting whilst he was a student:
> 'I have always from my first acquaintance with the holy office been desirous to engage in it, if such a thing might possibly be, and when it seemed at the greatest distance from me, I could not but cast a wishley, though a disparing look upon it, and at present, blessed be God, I think I could refuse the greatest Honours, Preferment and Pleasure, if proposed as temptations to make me drop my present resolutions . . .'[3]

According to his great-grandsons, he was 'scarcely fourteen' when he entered Whitehaven Academy. He had already acquired the proficiency in Latin that was essential to anyone aspiring to scholarship in those days. His later towering achievements in the study of the languages of the Bible rested upon a foundation of excellent classical learning. He had, we are told, 'in early life committed to memory, and faithfully retained, almost all the most beautiful passages and striking descriptions in the Greek and Roman Poets, and could repeat them with an exactness and propriety that was amazing'.[4] Thus when he entered the academy of Thomas Dixon he would be well able to profit by the instruction, though given in Latin. Such was the practice in the Dissenting academies, as in the universities. It was only later, in his Academy at Northampton, that Doddridge led the way in using English as the medium of instruction.

Whitehaven at that date was a busy little port for trade with northern Ireland. The Dissenting congregation in the town had been formed by Presbyterians originating from that country. In 1705 they called to their pulpit Thomas Dixon from Colchester, where he had ministered briefly on completing his training at Manchester Academy. Like many learned Nonconformist ministers, besides his preaching and pastoral care of the congregation he established an academy, mainly, though not exclusively, for the education of young men preparing for the ministry. 'Academy' is a word that suggests something rather grand, but in fact these Dissenting academies were usually on a very small scale, little more in numbers than an enlarged family: a word which is often used in informal references to their activities. One may imagine about a dozen adolescent youths boarding in a large house, with their tutor's wife as surrogate mother. From 1709, just about the time Taylor was enrolled, Dixon employed John Barclay to teach mathematics; but the rest of the wide curriculum he taught himself. Besides classics, the Bible in its original languages, and theology, this included the works of Locke and an introduction to the 'natural philosophy' (science) that was becoming ever more important in the thought of that age. Three volumes of a student's notes have survived, which, though not Taylor's own, give a remarkable picture of some of the studies in which he was engaged. One volume covers the several branches of mathematics; another, in Latin, is an introduction to astronomy; and the third contains extracts from the Fathers, and such writers as Locke, Limborch, Newton and Bishop Burnet. Obviously these reflect reading guided by the tutor, whose own personal library was the only one available to the students. Such an ambitious programme, especially when taught by one or two men, however learned, has been criticized as necessarily superficial; but in fact, the achievements of some of those trained under it show that it could lay the foundation of scholarship equal to any in its day.[5] The liberality and scope of such an education compares favourably with the studies at the two English universities; where, moreover, the examinations were sometimes very perfunctory, compared with the system of testing used in the academies. Scottish universities at this date were more modern in their outlook, and it was the grant of their degrees to English Nonconformists, excluded from Oxford and Cambridge by the religious tests, that validated the achievements of these small and often struggling institutions.[6] Dixon himself was granted the degree of MA *honoris causa* by the University of Edinburgh in 1709. It may have been at Whitehaven, or only later, after he had removed with his academy to Bolton, that he added a medical practice to his other commitments. He obtained the degree of MD from the same university. How one man could sustain three such demanding roles

defeats imagination, and it is hardly surprising that his congregation at Bolton looked for a successor with fewer irons in the fire.

For those formative middle years of his adolescence, then,
young John Taylor was under the tuition and daily guidance of
Thomas Dixon. He showed early promise of his later eminence
in the study of Hebrew by compiling for himself a grammar of
that language, at the age of 18. Such were the skills he was
acquiring; but what was the theological outlook, the underlying
belief that Dixon would impart to his young charges? Was it
Calvinistic orthodoxy, or were the seeds of Taylor's later views
sown even here?

We are sometimes told that Taylor was orthodox until about
the time of his move to Norwich, when he read Clarke's
Scripture Doctrine of the Trinity. John Wesley, to whom Taylor
and his teachings were anathema, says, 'For some years he was
an earnest Calvinist; but afterwards, judging he could not get far
enough from that melancholy system, he ran not only into
Arianism, but into the very dregs of Socinianism.'[7] It seems most
unlikely, however, that the tuition at Whitehaven would confirm
the pupils in dogmatic Calvinism, even though by comparison
with later developments, in which Taylor played an important
part, it may have been orthodox enough. Dixon is described as
'an advanced disciple of the Baxterian school'. He was one of
those more liberal-minded Dissenting divines who, beginning
from Baxter's confidence in Scripture as the rule of faith, without
the guidance of 'man-made' schemes, were moving, under the
influence of Limborch and Locke, further and further from the
'melancholy system' enshrined in the Westminster Confession.
'Dixon himself', says Michael Watts, 'was a Baxterian, but the
Baxterian of one generation was likely to foster the Arians or
Socinians of the next, and Dixon numbered among his students
George Benson . . . John Taylor . . . and Caleb Rotheram.'[8] It
does not seem probable that he turned out his young pupil 'an
earnest Calvinist'; more likely, at this stage, like his mentor, 'an
advanced Baxterian', but one for whom that position proved to
be a staging post. His study of Samuel Clarke's book with the
Norwich congregation was undoubtedly a further, and impor-

tant, stage along that road, but in a direction in which he was already travelling, not a dramatic reversal.

The course at Whitehaven took four years, and presumably it was upon its completion that Taylor moved to Findern Academy, near Derby, to perfect his training for the ministry under Thomas Hill (1680–1720), the son of an ejected minister. There is an amusing glimpse of Hill, and a reminder of the difficulties for Nonconformist education under the Test Acts, especially in the reign of Queen Anne. Hill was arraigned before the magistrates for keeping a school, but the case was dismissed after he gave the following account of it: 'I board young men; I advise them what books to read; and when they apply to me for information on anything they do not understand, I inform them.'[9] This is obviously a fairly minimalist account of his activities, if not 'economical with the truth'. We know of some of the text books studied: Baxter's *End to Doctrinal Controversies* for theology; and the works of Le Clerc, Rohault and Fromenius in logic, natural philosophy and metaphysics.

Hill's enthusiasm for the classical languages is attested by his publication of a small collection of Psalms rendered in Latin and Greek verse for his pupils to sing. These were not of his own composition, but a selection mainly from the work of the eminent Scottish Reformer, George Buchanan (1506–82), who was highly esteemed for his skill in Latin verse. The little book, 3 inches by 5½, bears the date 1715, just in time for Taylor to possess one and join in its use. His own love of the classics must have been greatly encouraged and fostered by such a tutor. This very copy is now in the rare books section of the British Library.[10] To handle it, and imagine the young men singing these settings, is to receive a powerful impression of the intellectual rigour and disciplined devotion of such an academy. But is there also a hint of the pedantry that may have been a factor in Taylor's later difficulties at Warrington?

In 1716, his training completed, Taylor was offered the pastorate of a small Dissenting congregation in Lincolnshire, and sought ordination. Among the Independents, this would have taken place in the congregation that called him; but the

Presbyterian mode was by 'the laying on of hands of the presby-
tery'. Even in England under Cromwell, the Presbyterians had
never established the complete system adopted in Scotland, but
their ordinations retained this sense that the local church is not,
as the Independents held, complete in itself, and able to call and
commission its own ministry. Thus it was not in Lincolnshire
that Taylor was ordained, but by ministers in Derbyshire, consti-
tuting, in high Presbyterian terms, a 'classis':

> In several of the Northern counties the attempt was still made,
> in the early part of the 18th century, to keep up a semblance of
> Presbyterian discipline. Although the congregations were, for
> the most part, independent in their church government, the
> ministers of the several counties retained in their hands the
> right of admitting candidates for the ministry, and ordaining
> them when approved by themselves, and, after their election,
> by a congregation. The Dissenting interest was never otherwise
> than feeble in Lincolnshire; and, in order to procure ordina-
> tion, Mr Taylor made application to the ministers of Derby.
> The ordination took place April 11, 1716, perhaps at Chester-
> field . . .[11]

The testing of candidates for ordination was very rigorous.
The Presbyterian ministers attached great importance to sound
learning, and candidates were subjected to a searching examination in the classical and biblical languages, and in philosophy
and divinity. Taylor was also required to propose and defend a
thesis in Latin. Candidates were of course examined closely as to
their personal integrity and fitness, attested by testimonials from
those among whom they had already exercised some ministry;
and they were required to give an account of their motives in
seeking orders, and of their call. This must obviously have
included some indication of their personal faith. The controversy
about requiring subscription to a creed or confession, and the
historic Salters' Hall decision of 1719 against such tests, was still
three years in the future; but evidently no signature or consent to
any formula was demanded of Taylor.

Thanks to a legal wrangle in the next century, we have from

his great-grandson some record of this event. When, in the nine-teenth century, many congregations had become fully Unitarian, their right to the enjoyment of their meeting houses was chal-lenged on the ground that these had been founded upon a differ-ent basis of faith. In the debates over the Dissenters' Chapels Bill of 1844, it became necessary to show that in fact no doctrinal tests were imposed upon such congregations by their trust deeds or their history. It was in support of this contention that Taylor's great-grandsons republished their ancestor's life and selections of his writings, including a copy of his certificate of ordination, and Taylor's own account of the statement of faith he made on that occasion. This is adduced to demonstrate that no affirmation of loyalty to any man-made creed or confession was required of him. It is admitted that this is not a contemporary record, but that he wrote it down afterwards from memory; nevertheless we may be confident that it fairly represents the young man's mind at that solemn moment when he was about to enter upon the ministry towards which, so long before, he had cast 'a wishley though a disparing look'. 'I am fully persuaded', he said, 'of the truth of the holy scriptures, and it has ever been my notion of the Protestant religion, in the abstract, that it regulates itself entirely according to God's word; therefore I am fully persuaded that the Protestant religion is, or should be, the true primitive Christian religion.'[12] In the same spirit, he answers the question, 'Do you promise you will be zealous and faithful in defence of truth and unity against error and schism?'

> I do promise through God's assistance, that I will in a manner consistent with Christian love and charity, maintain the truths of the Gospel, especially such as are beyond controversy deter-mined in the Holy Scriptures, and will strive to inculcate them upon the minds of all with whom I have to do. I will heartily endeavour to propagate Christian charity, and shall see them with real pleasure when I see believers maintain the unity of the Spirit in the bond of peace.[13]

Such was the conviction with which the young minister em-barked upon his first charge.

3

Insensible of their Duty to a Minister

It was no doubt with the high hopes of a newly trained and ordained young minister that Taylor made the journey to the heart of rural Lincolnshire. Those hopes were not to be fulfilled, and it is greatly to his credit that through the years of privation and hard grind that he spent there, he never lost the dedication to scholarly ministry that was eventually to produce such distinguished results.

When Daniel Disney of Swinderby married 'pretty young Katherine', as his brother Gervase calls her, she brought him more than her personal attractions. She was the daughter of Henry Fynes of Kirkstead, Esquire, and heiress to property deriving from the Earl of Lincoln. Poor Katherine died in 1690, aged only 35, and was buried at Swinderby; but through this marriage, Daniel acquired the manor of Kirkstead, with a tiny chapel that was not under episcopal jurisdiction.[1] Kirkstead had been the site of an important Cistercian monastery, colonized by monks from Fountains in Yorkshire, and itself the parent of an abbey at Hovedoya on Oslo Fjord, Norway. After the dissolution, Kirkstead Abbey suffered the usual fate of becoming a source of materials for new building; but one small chapel outside its walls survived intact, and is now recognized as a little gem of twelfth-century architecture.[2]

Daniel Disney belonged to an old family whose name in its original form, d'Isnay, reflects its Norman origin. His grandfather was a strong Puritan, who under the Commonwealth had been active in sequestering Anglican clergy and the estates of Royalists, but who survived the Restoration apparently with little personal loss. He and his family retained their Puritan principles, and a memoir of the life of Daniel's brother Gervase records that they were raised 'constantly under a religious discipline'. Daniel was active in the Dissenting interest, and thus it was that towards the end of the seventeenth century the congregation meeting in the little pre-Reformation chapel came under the care of a Presbyterian minister. Their number can never have been very great, since the chapel interior only measures 42 feet by 19. The first Dissenter to be appointed by Daniel Disney was one Mr Reed. To him John Taylor succeeded in 1715.

For all the architectural beauty that is now recognized in the little chapel, when its new minister arrived there it must have seemed a very humble meeting house indeed. There was a thatched roof over the vault, and the bell hung in a neighbouring oak. Though at the end of the eighteenth century a new owner returned it to Anglican use, the interior survived into the age of photography as it had been in Taylor's day, and a nineteenth-century picture shows the Jacobean pulpit standing in front of the centre lancet in the east wall. Thus we have a very complete picture of the setting for John Taylor's first ministry. The beauty of the Early English Gothic interior would be unlikely to appeal to Taylor, any more than to most of his contemporaries; nor would he feel any sense of spiritual kinship with the monks for whom it was built. In his eyes, their religion was at best a superstitious corruption of Christianity, from which the Reformation itself had brought only incomplete deliverance.

In some respects, Taylor's ministry at Kirkstead resembled that of a parish minister. This little pre-Reformation chapel was outside episcopal jurisdiction, and was in the gift of its patron, who appointed Dissenters, just as earlier owners had appointed ministers of the Church of England. We are told that they buried 'by the established forms', and presumably they conducted baptisms and weddings too, though it can hardly be supposed that they would use the Prayer Book services for these. Thus Taylor's flock, it seems, was not so much a congregation of thoroughgoing Dissenters, rather just the local people gathering in this ancient building, and accepting the parson their squire had chosen for them. He came, as we have seen, after receiving ordination in Derbyshire. It is perhaps not surprising that he did not find them very responsive. No doubt some of them shared, or came to share, his Dissenting principles. There were such in every parish congregation; it is not to be supposed that in 1662 all the worshippers in the parish churches changed their views, any more than they had under the Commonwealth, but only the minority with strong convictions braved the hardships of not conforming, under either regime. The Vicar of Bray had many lay followers; indeed, there must have been a majority, both clerical and lay, who, without the violent changes of religious allegiance lampooned in that song, quietly got on with their Christian life under whichever establishment held sway, without making it a great matter of conscience either to conform or to dissent. But when the chapel reverted to Anglican occupancy at the end of the century, a Dissenting congregation continued in other accommodation. Though no registers have survived, the legal wrangle in the next century over Dissenting congregations' right to their chapels led to the gathering of transcripts from family records. These show that weddings and baptisms were performed there, as was Taylor's own marriage. Lord Hardwicke's Marriage Act, which debarred Dissenters from performing marriages, did not become law until 1753, twenty years after Taylor had left for Norwich.

It seems doubtful whether Daniel Disney was ever much in residence at Kirkstead; he is closely associated with Lincoln, as well as Swinderby. However, he provided the stipend for the minister, on which Taylor found himself hard put to it to make ends meet. In 1726, when he had already been at Kirkstead more than a decade, he received an invitation to Pudsey, near Leeds, which he did not accept. It can hardly have been an attractive one, since he declined it; yet when considering it, he made a note of his reflections which contains the following lugubrious assessment of his situation at Kirkstead: 'I am now amongst a People not only illiterate, but generally sluggish; little addicted to reading, of no ingenuity, and insensible of their Duty to a Minister. My Income is very small, only £25 p.ann.; a great House to repair; Window Money 20/- (?) p.ann. and hard set to get fuel.'[3]

The area, though fertile, is inclined to be marshy. The monks had from time to time complained of their situation. Want of good heating in a somewhat damp area was a source of something more serious than discomfort: the cold winters he endured in that inadequately heated house and fireless study left a legacy of rheumatism that plagued him throughout life, and crippled him in his last years.

In 1717 he married Elizabeth Jenkinson, a widow from nearby Boston. No story of their courtship, or of her earlier life, has come to light. Their marriage took place at Kirkstead on 3 August. She was three or four years his senior. It seems to have been a happy marriage, only ended by their death within a few months of each other forty-four years later. A son and a daughter survived them.

Like many Dissenting ministers and the poorer clergy, he eked out his living by boarding and educating a few boys. There is some evidence that he did not begin this much before 1724, so their married life was already well established before Elizabeth was called upon to be matron to a larger household. His later writings, and his record as a pastor in Norwich, show Taylor as a kindly and understanding man where youth was concerned, though his academic standards were exacting; but the lads must have had an uncomfortable time of it in winter, in that cold house. Such spartan conditions were the common lot of boarding schoolboys then, and long after. There is perhaps a small sign of the penury of those days in the way Taylor used notebooks, of which a number survive among his papers at Harris Manchester College. One of these is dated 1721, and others too must belong to the Kirkstead period. Every inch of paper is covered with very small handwriting, and books originally used for one purpose have spare pages put to other use. It is a reminder that the purchase not only of books, but even of paper, must have been quite a tax upon an income of £25 a year.

Financial strain and overwork were obviously not the only cause of his unhappiness at Kirkstead. His description of his congregation as 'illiterate, sluggish, and insensible of their duty to a minister' indicates clearly enough the gulf between the educational level of a highly trained and very scholarly minister and the ordinary folk of rural Lincolnshire in the early eighteenth century. We must have some sympathy for them as well as for him. Such a pastor as John Bunyan, the converted tinker, in an earlier generation, or the homespun preachers recruited by Wesley decades later, were better able to reach the hearts of humble folk, as the phenomenal success of Methodism was to show, not least in Lincolnshire. Even in this rural spot, however, Taylor did find some intellectual fellowship. He formed a friendship with Philips Glover of Wispington in the same county, who shared his interest in moral philosophy. Glover later wrote *An Enquiry concerning Virtue and Happiness* (1751). This was a subject in which Taylor took a keen interest, and he developed a strong position in regard to it, which became one of the causes of contention with his colleagues at Warrington much later in his life.

Very valuable insight into his situation, interests and pursuits during this period is found in a letter he wrote at this time.[4] It is addressed 'To Mr. Tho. Johnson . . . Mercht in London', who had evidently written to ask for advice about his religious life and studies. As one would expect, Taylor dwells on the value of regular study of Scripture. For this purpose, he thinks, they were already pretty well furnished with the labour of learned and pious men upon the Bible'. What is wanting is 'a practical comment upon the whole Bible, so contrived for the use of families that a chapter may conveniently be read, with the exposition, morning and night, and yet take in the main of what is necessary to enlighten the head and better the heart'. For this kind of family devotion he finds 'Mr Henry . . . quite too large and tedious', so he is himself engaged upon the task of abridging the famous commentary, and has got as far as the Book of Jonah. He is stalled, however, by want of time and money. He cannot afford to buy the later volumes, and feels he can no longer follow his 'former trade of *borrowing*'. Though he cannot yet foresee when it may be printed, he promises, 'The price will be as low as I can bring it; for, if I can therein do any service to the interests of Christ's kingdom, I am not at all solicitous about my own.' This task was never completed, but some of this abridgement survives in manuscript among his papers. The notebook dated 1721 is part of this series, containing the notes on the books of Judges and Ruth, and there are others, on parts of the Pentateuch, the historical books, Job, etc.; but if he had indeed completed his task as far as Jonah, not all is there. Clearly, when he left Kirkstead, he entered upon an altogether more creative period in his life, when the abridgement of the work of another was no longer the best use of his time.

The next paragraph advertises his sideline in taking boys 'to table and teach', and solicits his correspondent's help in finding scholars:

> If you know of any, Mr. Johnson, who would have their children instructed in the language, writing, arithmetick, in a good, wholesome air, in a country retirement, out of the way of the common temptations of the age, where they should in every respect be carefully looked after, and well done to, if you should recommend them to me, I hope, through the blessing of God upon my endeavours, you would never be ashamed of it.

His pleasant rural situation is 'out of the sight or hearing of any thing that's vicious', and his wife 'is particularly well qualified for ordering and encouraging children'.

Next comes a paragraph which, in view of his later involvement in controversy, is of particular interest for the insight it offers into his mind at this time on the vexed question of ministerial orthodoxy and freedom of thought, especially in respect of the Trinity. With obvious reference to the dispute about subscription to statements of faith in the Trinity that led to the famous meeting of London ministers in the Salters' Hall in 1719, he writes:

> As to the unhappy differences among the London ministers, I think I should not have subscribed had I been among them, because I am not satisfied that it is a means sanctified and appointed by God for either finding out or ascertaining the

truth. On the other hand, I am sure it has been grievously abused from the first times of Christianity, to the dividing of Christians, and destroying that love and mutual forbearance which is the distinguishing character of our holy religion, and the only bottom upon which the tranquillity of the church can be rightly settled.[5]

This implies that Taylor was not at this stage himself disposed to deny the doctrine of the Trinity, any more than were many, even most, of the 'non-subscribers'. Like them, he is only cavilling at the use of subscription to a formula of human devising, not found in Scripture, as a test of Christian faith and fitness for ministry. Some years later, he was to write, with reference to the gathering in the Salters' Hall, that their majority resolution against such a requirement 'should always be remembered to their honour, as being the only instance, perhaps, that can be produced out of church history, for many centuries, of any synod of ministers declaring in favour of religious liberty'. A further paragraph of advice to Mr Johnson on suitable reading concludes the letter.

Though he had as yet no published work to his credit, Taylor's reputation must have spread, not only to Pudsey, and the year 1733 brought him deliverance from his uncomfortable situation in the form of an invitation to Norwich. This time he did not refuse. How his rustic congregation felt at losing their very learned minister is not recorded. However 'insensible' they may have seemed, seventeen years of faithful pastorate must surely have forged some bonds of affection and gratitude.

Daniel Disney died in 1734, leaving an endowment to provide a stipend of £30 a year for the maintenance of the Dissenting ministry at Kirkstead. At the end of the century the owner of the property returned the chapel to the occupancy of the Church of England, but a later legal judgement secured the endowment to the Presbyterians. A new chapel was built near Woodhall, where a Unitarian service is still occasionally held: a surviving link with this most distinguished of their former ministers.

4

Doctor Taylor of Norwich

In 1733 Taylor was called to be co-pastor with Peter Finch of the Presbyterian congregation in Norwich, then even more than now one of Britain's leading cities, and a provincial capital. East Anglia was always a stronghold of Puritanism, and after the Restoration this persisted, even to some extent in the Anglican Church itself, where Baxter's associate, Edward Reynolds, became bishop in 1661. The city was remarkable for the number of its medieval churches, of which there were forty within its bounds. Over against the established church there were the Dissenting congregations. The two leading ones that separated from the established church in the seventeenth century have noteworthy architectural representation in the city's two historic Nonconformist buildings, both in Colegate, the Octagon and the Old Meeting. The latter stood for the older and more radical Dissent. Its congregation was heir to that Puritan tradition which was opposed to the church establishment of Charles I, and was offended by the promulgation of the *Book of Sports*. In this Independent tradition, the 'gathered' congregation of believers is held to be the true form of the church. The congregation that was later to build the Octagon, by contrast, was part of the great secession that followed the settlement of 1662, when large numbers of clergy and members who had sought a comprehensive national church found it impossible to accept what was offered, and became Nonconformists. Some of these had hoped for a Presbyterian establishment something like the Church of Scotland; others, like Richard Baxter, had been prepared to settle for a more radically revised liturgy and some form of

episcopacy, shorn of its prelatical features, within a comprehensive national church. Neither aspiration was achieved, even
under the Commonwealth, and after the ejection of 1662, hope
of a 'comprehension' faded, and a broadly Presbyterian ethos
prevailed. In Norwich, the first place of meeting of Dissenters of
this outlook was a building that had been part of the establishment of the Black Friars, whose magnificent church, designed for
preaching to large congregations, survives as St Andrew's Hall.
After the Dissolution one of their smaller buildings had been
used for a time as a granary, and had lost all ecclesiastical character; but when, in 1672, application was made for a licence to
preach in it, this was refused, perhaps because of some lingering
sense of its former association. Nevertheless the Presbyterians
continued to renew its lease and to use it until the passing of the
Toleration Act. They then acquired land on the other side of
the river Wensum, and built a new meeting house, later replaced
on the same site by the Octagon.

   In the confused times from the Restoration to the end of the
seventeenth century, these two forms of Dissent had much common interest, and shared the same Calvinist doctrinal tradition.
The general public tended to use the term 'Presbyterian' of all
without distinction. But under the surface there was an important difference, and like streams at a watershed, they diverged
more and more in the century to come. For a 'gathered church'
the personal faith of each aspirant to membership was all-
important, and such congregations usually required of their
members an assurance both of their orthodoxy and of their
personal religious experience. But for those who had sought a
comprehensive national church, whether or not they might have
been willing to accept a modified form of episcopacy, it was
unrealistic to expect every Tom, Dick and Harry in the parish to
have a fully formed faith, or for all to be able to give an articulate
account of themselves. Even under such a faithful ministry as
Richard Baxter's at Kidderminster, where he had the people
family by family into his house for instruction, and was sometimes rewarded with 'store of lice', he could hardly have expected all such humble folk, or for that matter all the parishioners

of any social level, to produce the sort of testimony that would qualify for membership of an Independent congregation. Assent to the catechism, and a respectable manner of life, would be enough to ensure acceptance in the parish church, however much more they might be exhorted to aspire to.

The hope of a 'comprehension' faded after the Act of Uniformity, though with occasional revivals from time to time; and when it finally expired, those who had cherished it remained Puritan and Calvinist indeed, but with the less exclusive attitude. This undoubtedly made them more open, some would say more vulnerable, to the liberalizing forces that were already at work, and were to become powerful with the advance of the Age of Reason. Dissenters of this type continued to wear the Presbyterian label, but in practice, each congregation was self-governing, save in one respect. As we have already seen in the case of Taylor in Derbyshire, the ministers retained within their own control the perpetuation of the preaching ministry. New ministers were examined and ordained by those of neighbouring churches. During his ministry in Norwich, Taylor himself was involved in such ordinations. One of these took place at Harleston on 11 November 1755, when Isaac Smithson was ordained by Ralph Milner, John Taylor and Thomas Stanton. The charge he delivered on that occasion is preserved among his papers in Harris Manchester College library. He himself has left us an account of the day in a letter to his friend Dr George Benson,[1] of which there will be more to say.

In Norwich, these divergent attitudes were exemplified by the two Dissenting churches in Colegate, the Independent by the Old Meeting,[2] the Presbyterian by the one to which John Taylor came as co-pastor with Peter Finch in 1733. The congregation was large and prosperous enough to be served by two ministers, and to maintain them handsomely. The stipends had recently been increased from £80 to £100 per annum, but despite this, Taylor's predecessor, John Brooke, who had served since 1718, had been unable to make ends meet. He had, it seems, 'a turn for expense too great for his income',[3] and in 1733 he moved to York. The income on which poor Mr Brooke could not manage must have seemed riches indeed to John and Elizabeth. Mr Finch enjoyed an extraordinarily long ministry there, from 1691 to his death at the age of 91 in 1754. It would seem that he remained orthodox, but he must have been tolerant of his younger colleague's questing spirit. He obviously became less and less active in his later years, and an additional minister was engaged as his assistant.[4] To John and Elizabeth the change from the hardships of Kirkstead to the service of this well-established congregation in a fine city must have seemed like Canaan after the wilderness years. Here John's great powers were able to expand and find expression in a series of publications that earned him national and even international repute – or notoriety. These, especially his great Hebrew Concordance, would have done credit to any scholar in a university; Taylor achieved them in the midst of a devoted pastoral and preaching ministry.

'No minister', we are told, 'was more attentive to his other congregational duties than Dr Taylor. He thought it his duty to visit all his people; it was his pleasure to converse with and instruct them.'[5] For testimony to his devotion to the care of the flock we are not entirely dependent on the many such tributes to him that are on record, which are undoubtedly sincere, but may perhaps have the characteristics of farewell speeches and funeral orations, in which only the subject's good qualities are mentioned. Direct evidence of some of his work survives among his papers. While some at least of the notebooks filled with closely written studies of various parts of the Bible are undoubtedly relics of that uncompleted undertaking to abridge Matthew Henry's commentary, they afford a glimpse of the careful Bible teaching in which he engaged. Other papers relate to his work in catechizing the young, for whom he seems to have had an especial care. As younger colleague to the septuagenarian Peter Finch, he would naturally be more likely to be assigned to this part of the work. An attractive feature of his ministry among the younger members of the congregation is his concern for the musical part of the services. He devoted an evening a week to a choir of young people, and put much effort into training them in what he clearly regarded as an important element in public worship. There is a title-page of a book 'Printed by J. Waugh at the Turk's Head in Lombard Street' announcing 'A Collection of Tunes In various Airs adapted to Psalms taken out of Dr Watts's Imitation of David's Psalms With a Scheme for supporting the Spirit and Practice of Psalmody in Congregations To which are prefixed Instructions in the Art of Psalmody By John Taylor For the Use of a Congregation in Norwich'. But what follows is in manuscript: is it as prepared for the printer?

The sermons that survive among his papers are not a representative sample of his regular pulpit ministry, being of the 'occasional' sort: an ordination charge, and several funeral sermons, some on texts indicated by the deceased in their final instructions, to be 'improved' at their obsequies. The sermon at the opening of the Octagon, despite the special occasion, may perhaps be taken as a fairer sample of his style. A memoir by 'a descendant', though published a century later, no doubt faithfully records the impression he left in the memory of those who had heard him regularly:

> As a preacher, he was impressive and dignified. His sermons, nevertheless, were plain and simple; no one of his hearers could listen to them without being warmed by their piety, and animated and instructed by their morality. He possessed in a singular manner the talent of explaining difficult passages of scripture, and placing the sense and meaning of every part in a clear and perspicuous point of view . . . He inspired his congregation with the same liberal views of religion as he himself possessed, and it may be said to be almost entirely owing to his preaching and conversation that the same change in the sentiments of the congregation took place as in his own mind; he may therefore be said to have laid the foundation for that liberality which now prevails in it.[6]

Which is to say that his ministry in Norwich was decisive for that change from the Calvinist orthodoxy which prevailed at the beginning of the century, however much relaxed and moderated, to the outlook often called 'Socinian' or 'Unitarian' but essentially undogmatic, to which that had given way by its end.

The same could doubtless have been said of many of his contemporaries in the ministry; but by his writings and his great
prestige, Taylor's influence extended far beyond his own congregation. That letter of 5 December 1755 to Dr Benson is interesting, not only for its account of the ordination itself, but for the
glimpse it gives us of the changing climate of opinion among
Dissenters of this sort. In unusually exuberant mood, Taylor
describes how the attitude of the congregation changed in the
course of the day. He had arrived fearing that few ministers
would attend, owing to the hostility his liberal views had aroused
among them, but finds that thirteen have turned up, 'all able and
worthy men, and cordial friends'. The 'audience', he records,
'were not prepossessed in our favour, as great pains had been
taken for many years to render us odious all over the country, so
that I reckoned my reputation absolutely irretrievable'; but by
the end of the service they were clamouring for both his charge
and the sermon preached by Ralph Milner to be printed!

Although the complete Presbyterian order, with its regional
and national bodies, had never been fully established, vestiges
of it are seen, not only in the ordination of ministers, but in
sporadic attempts to achieve some sort of unity through associa-
tions of ministers over an area, such as Baxter had sought to promote in Worcestershire during his ministry at Kidderminster.
With the death of Peter Finch the previous year, Taylor was
manifestly in the position he must for all practical purposes have
occupied for some years: that of the senior minister in one of the
most prestigious Presbyterian congregations in England. Add to
this his fame as a Hebraist, biblical scholar and theologian, and
the lustre of the doctorate bestowed that year by the University
of Glasgow, and we see the justice of John Wesley's reference to
him as 'that great man, Dr Taylor of Norwich'. He now exerted
his influence to try to bring about a regional association of
churches through an annual assembly of Dissenting ministers
of Norfolk, Suffolk and Essex, without distinction of doctrine or
church order. A considerable number, of very various shades of
opinion, met at Palgrave on 18 May 1757.[7] But a further meeting
at Colchester the next year proved to be the last. By then Taylor

had already been called away to Warrington, and with the loss of his influence and enthusiasm it would seem that the scheme collapsed.

All these pastoral and regional activities add up to a very full and active ministry; nor did he neglect his own family. His son was growing up, and in an earlier letter to Benson the father exhibits affectionate pride in his 'sober and industrious' character, and his self-taught skill in weaving.[8] His pleasure in becoming a grandfather finds expression in a little publication of his thoughts on the care and upbringing of children, addressed as a letter to his daughter. For most men, there would have been room for no more, but Taylor was no ordinary man. His industry was prodigious. He found at Norwich the time and circumstances that released his powers in a series of publications which were to make him famous as a Hebraist, biblical scholar and influential though controversial theologian, not only in Britain and Ireland but in America and Europe.

5

Dissenting Popery

References to John Taylor sometimes suggest that there was a great change in his belief after his move to Norwich. John Wesley, as we have seen, writing to Sir Harry Trelawney to urge him not to run from one extreme to another, says: 'This was the case with that great man, Dr Taylor of Norwich. For some years he was an earnest Calvinist; but afterwards, judging he could not get far enough from that melancholy system, he ran not only into Arianism, but into the very dregs of Socinianism.'[1] This is a gross exaggeration; Taylor was certainly not a 'Socinian', and what we know of his personality and history suggests a smoother and more gradual progression in his belief. He may indeed, for all we know, have been brought up in the Calvinist creed, but at both Whitehaven and Findern he came under the influence of tutors in the Baxter tradition, who might be described as semi-Arminians. It seems more probable that the influence of Locke and Limborch was upon him from his student days, though how far it carried him from 'that melancholy system' before he left Kirkstead, we can only surmise. What we do know is that early in his ministry at Norwich he studied, and introduced to the congregation, a book which marked an important stage in the development of his belief.

Samuel Clarke (1675–1729) was a native of Norwich, and became chaplain to Bishop Moore of that see. At Cambridge he had come under the influence of Isaac Newton. In 1712 he published *The Scripture-Doctrine of the Trinity*. Its effect seems to have been somewhat similar to that of John Robinson's *Honest to God*, two and a half centuries later.[2] Both books broke upon a public that had become much less secure in orthodox belief than earlier generations. Both upset large numbers of clergy, but demands for episcopal action were in both cases unsuccessful. The lower house of Convocation sought the condemnation of Clarke's book, but the bishops took no severer action than to require him to write no more on the subject. The early eighteenth century had nothing comparable to the modern media of which Robinson made such effective use, but the book had a considerable impact, and continued to be read years after its first appearance. It had already been published more than twenty years when Taylor read it, and sought the consent of his colleague to introduce it to the congregation.

The proposal caused considerable heart-searching, and it was only after prayer and careful thought that Finch and the leaders of the church agreed to it. It was a momentous decision, and undoubtedly marked an important stage in the movement of that Presbyterian congregation towards the Unitarianism that ultimately prevailed. By the end of the eighteenth century, most of the Presbyterian churches in England had either taken the same road or become Independent. We may therefore surmise that the ground was not altogether unprepared. Without doubt there would be strongly orthodox members to whom such teaching was disturbing; but in the two or three generations since the end of the Commonwealth, much greater freedom of thought had become widespread among both Anglicans and Presbyterians. There may well have been members of the congregation who were affected by that movement, and were ready to welcome their new minister's radical ideas. At the very least, the intellectual atmosphere was hospitable to them, and many who until that point had been orthodox, whether uncritically or uneasily, were open to change. Certain it is that Taylor remained at Norwich for the next twenty years, ever more respected and loved. Just how the Norwich congregation accommodated the differences of belief that must have developed there we can only guess. The elderly Peter Finch remained, so far as we know, an orthodox trinitarian to his death, and so must have many of his people; whereas at least some of those who read Samuel Clarke along with Taylor must have come to share their younger minister's opinions. Taylor's frequent insistence on the right, and indeed the duty, of every Christian to study the Scriptures for himself, and to reach his own conclusions, required also a spirit of mutual tolerance and respect that enabled all to worship together and accept the pulpit ministry of both their pastors. What Taylor could not tolerate was intolerance; and it was an affair which he saw as a flagrant instance of that spirit that moved him to his first publication.

The events that aroused his indignation took place in Nottingham.[3] There, as in Norwich and many other towns, two Dissenting congregations represented the two contrasted attitudes: High Pavement was of the Presbyterian, and Castle Gate of the Independent or Congregational tradition. In 1728, the latter was seeking a minister to be assistant to the pastor, Mr Bateson, who is described as 'often under disorder, and Indisposition, as to his state of health'. Their first and most enthusiastic attempt was directed to no less a person than Philip Doddridge. The contemporary record in the Church Book[4] tells an interesting story:

> At the Call and desire of the Congregation the said Mr Doderidge did come and Preach amongst us, with General approbation, and gave encouragement that he would come too us. But at the Same time he did Designe and Endeavour to get himself Fixt into The High Pavement Meeting, which when it came to Light, he left the Town in some Confusion.

It is eloquent testimony to the rising reputation of the young minister that in spite of this embarrassing setback, the Castle Gate congregation tried again:

> Mr Dodridge being disappointed in his expectation of getting in at the High Pavement Meeting, and we haveing had some encouragement to thinke that upon further Application to him, we might Obtain him, in Feb. 1728 [i.e. 1728/9] the Congregation was Calld together on this Affaire, and Unanimously Voated to give him a Second Call, and Messengers were sent forthwith, with a Letter of Invitations from the Church.

Once more Doddridge gave them considerable encouragement to expect a favourable reply, but asked for time to consult his friends in London, and then for further time to confer with 'his Friends at Harbrow and Kibboth'. After all that, he gave 'a positive Denyall to our Repeated Invitation, and his Full Determination NOT to come to us. Which Indeed was very Surprising.'

Indeed it was. This episode is of interest in several ways. It shows that the two traditions were not so mutually exclusive at that time that they might not invite ministers as it were from a common pool. But it also carries more than a hint that Doddridge sniffed the air of Castle Gate, and suspected that High Pavement might be more congenial to him. That Presbyterian congregation, like so many others of that tradition, was evidently less firmly orthodox, and by the end of the century it had become Unitarian. Now Doddridge would generally be regarded as orthodox; but in the famous Academy over which he later presided in Northampton, the teaching was undogmatic. Both sides of disputed questions were laid before the pupils, and they were encouraged to use their own judgement. Among the dogmatically orthodox, Doddridge was suspect; so it is no far-fetched inference to discern, in his treatment of the reiterated invitation to Castle Gate, evidence that he sensed in that congregation a spirit that might cause him difficulty.

Disappointed in their hopes of Doddridge, the congregation suffered further rejections, but eventually called a very different minister. James Sloss came to them from Scotland, where one of their members had come across him, and had ascertained that he might well be prepared to consider favourably a call from Nottingham, if one should be offered. The young man had graduated MA from the University of Glasgow, where he had studied theology under John Simson. That the doctrine of the Trinity is something of a theological minefield Sloss ought to have learnt from his professor's story. Having first written against Samuel Clarke in defence of the orthodox position, Simson was suspected of the opposite error, Sabellianism; but when he sought to clear himself by opposing that, he was accused of having gone over to Clarke's side! All this involved him in trials for heresy in the Church of Scotland, with its strong Calvinist theology. But James Sloss was not a man to hesitate to rush in where angels fear to tread. Even the most convinced trinitarian may think he was somewhat fanatical on that subject. Early in his ministry in Nottingham, he delivered a series of eighteen lectures on it, based on 1 John 5:7, a text which is now universally recognized to be a late interpolation.[5] The story of Erasmus' exclusion of it from the first edition of his Greek New Testament is well known, and even in the mid-eighteenth century there were those who doubted its authenticity; but not Mr Sloss.

If only Philip Doddridge had been his minister, perhaps we should never have heard of Joseph Rawson; but perhaps that is not what he would have wished! He emerges clearly from the record of the affair as a man who had plenty of courage for the fray, and was very determined not to be browbeaten. He and his minister were a well-matched pair. The story has been retold in various places,[6] all dependent on three primary sources: the Church Book of Castle Gate Congregational church, a manuscript account, culminating in the solemn formal excommunication; Joseph Rawson's printed *Narrative*; and James Sloss's rejoinder. Needless to say, the last two do not agree in all particulars. The manuscript Church Book is probably a pretty reliable summary, but it is shorter, and lacks the colourful details of the contestants' accounts.

Joseph Rawson was a member of the Castle Gate church. When the new minister arrived from Scotland, he lodged for a time in Rawson's house. They must surely have had religious conversation during that time, and in view of the temper both displayed later, it is tempting to try to imagine it. However, the trouble did not come to a head until after Sloss had found other accommodation. Poor Rawson then fell on hard times, through the failure of some of his business associates to meet their obligations, and he was helped to compound with his creditors by a friend, to whom therefore he felt much obliged, and with whom he became closely associated. But apparently this friend was of dubious orthodoxy, and Mr Sloss and some of his members began to suspect that Rawson was tarred with the same brush. They therefore demanded of him a statement of his faith, in particular on the subject of the Trinity. Not finding it sufficiently explicit, Mr Sloss put to him, in a series of confrontations, his own formulation of the doctrine, which Rawson parried with vaguer expressions, confined to scriptural language. The Church Book[7] records:

> They gave him another Question, to be answered in any Words, he thought Proper, Provided they came up to a Sound Sense, (To Witt) Whither the Lord Jesus Christ, is the one true Supreame God, The Same with the Father in Nature, and Equall with him in all Divine Perfections, to which he would Give no other answer than in Such Expressions of Scripture as the Arrians take in an unsound Sence, and would not Declare to us, that he took these Expressions in any other Sence, than the Arrians did, and withall still Continued in an Obstinate Refuseing to owne the Supreame Deiteye of God the Son, and his Equality with the Father. And plainly told us, he would give no further Sattisfaction, and that, That was his Finall Answer.

It all ended with Rawson's exclusion from membership and communion with the Castle Gate congregation, and a hint that he might be in more serious trouble. We must remember that to deny the Trinity was still, at that date, a penal offence; but it seems hardly likely that a serious threat was intended. All Nonconformists had good reason to be rather wary of invoking the law. The threat of resort to some sort of civil enforcement seems to have related, not to Rawson's unorthodoxy, but to his stated intention of intruding himself at the Table on the next occasion after he had been excommunicated. He does not appear to have carried out this threat, and it seems that he eventually joined the High Pavement Meeting. The whole episode is an interesting illustration of the widening divergence between the Presbyterians and the Independents. Despite having occupied doctrinally common ground a century earlier, the Presbyterians' less strict requirement of their members had laid them open to liberalizing influences to which the Independents remained resistant. The Church Book records that Rawson was 'Generally Reputed to have drank in the Arian Heresye', and 'Considering how much that Daingerous Error Prevailed in this place, to the great Dishonour of Christianity in Generall, and the Dissenting Interest in Particular, and how Fatall in might prove to this Congregation', they felt constrained to question him closely. The phrase 'in this place' surely points to High Pavement, and it is no great surprise to find the Church Book recording under the date 28 December 1739:

> The Church then Agreed that no person be Received from the High Pavement Congregation as a Member of this Congregation without Giveing in their Experience. Unless they had been Received Members of that Church, before the Reverd Mr Hewes Left that Congregation.[8]

It is not clear how Taylor became interested in the affair. It must have become something of a *cause célèbre*. It moved him to write and publish a booklet entitled *A Narrative of Mr Joseph Rawson's Case, or An Account of several Occurrences relating to the Affair of his being excluded from Communion with the Congregational Church in Nottingham with a Prefatory Discourse in Defence of the Common Rights of Christians*, dated London 1737, and priced six pence. The narrative is Rawson's account of his trials, to which Taylor contributes the *Prefatory Discourse* and the *Defence* etc. These are of special interest for their revelation of Taylor's mind on the subject of orthodoxy and doctrinal tests. In the *Discourse*, he describes three kinds of 'popery', by which he means the illegitimate imposition of dogma not found in Scripture, and its enforcement by persecution. The plain teaching of Scripture, he tells us, was gradually corrupted and overlaid with man-made theology and scholastic elaborations, which were then imposed on people by the use of the secular power and all the apparatus of the Inquisition. This is 'Romish popery', 'suppressing the use of understanding in reli-

gious matters'. The Reformers swept away much of this accre-
tion, but not all. While they abandoned the claim to infallibility,
they went beyond Scripture by formulating their understanding
of the faith in 'Confessions', which they then, where they could,
imposed upon Christians with the aid of the secular authorities.
This is 'Protestant popery'. Against this, there arose the revolt of
the Dissenters, but they too, in spite of their principle that the
Scripture alone is the rule of faith, try to impose particular interpretations of it on members of their congregations, exclude from
communion those who cannot accept them, and even threaten
recourse to the magistrate. This is 'Dissenting popery'. In a
passionate plea for liberty of thought, he asks what is the use of
such liberty, if it is not to be freely exercised, and points out the
paradox that the reformed churches pray for fuller reformation,
yet oppose what they pray for. The dark days, though under a
Protestant regime, when 'People were taught it was their duty to
believe what they could not understand', and 'Worldly Emolu-
ments were annexed to a supposed right Belief, and many
Penalties inflicted upon Recusants', are contrasted with 'the day
when LIBERTY at the *Revolution*, O bright, auspicious Day,
reared up her heavenly Form, and smiled upon our happy Land'.

This preface is followed by Joseph Rawson's *Narrative* and
Taylor's *Defence of the Common Rights of Christians*. In the
Narrative, Sloss appears in a very unfavourable light, showing an
uncompromising determination to nail Rawson down to the
statement that 'Jesus Christ is the one, true, supreme God, the
same with the Father in Nature, and equal with him in all Divine
Perfections'; but we must remember that this is Rawson's story.
He seems to have been a born member of the 'awkward squad';
the Church Book describes his demeanour as 'obstinate' and
'insolent'. But there is a strong whiff of the inquisitor about his
minister. At one point, according to Rawson, Sloss exclaims that
he would not care to appear before the judgement seat alongside
such a blasphemer as Rawson. It is mentioned somewhere that
somebody mutters that he would be more wary of appearing
there with the want of love that is being shown; and there were
four courageous souls who in the end voted against the excom-

munication. Sloss, of course, puts a different gloss on his own remark. One may wonder why Rawson did not just quietly take himself off to High Pavement, with its more liberal attitude – as eventually he did. On the other hand, if he had been a long-standing, and in his own belief loyal, member of his church, one may sympathize with his reluctance to accept ejection. And the story leaves an impression that he enjoyed doing battle with Sloss.

Under Taylor's attack, as we might expect, James Sloss proved a doughty adversary. He responded to Taylor's pamphlet, and Rawson's *Narrative*, with his own account of the case.[9] He too begins with a 'Prefatory Discourse'. As we read it, we think we must have picked up the wrong booklet; are we reading Taylor's tract again by mistake? No: but word for word, paragraph by paragraph, it seems to be the same. Then we begin to notice small differences, that lead to the conclusion, 'This is *Arian Popery.*' A concluding passage, still parallel to Taylor's, warns that it is Arianism, not intolerance, that will, if unchecked, be the ruin of the faith. This Preface is followed by *A Plea for the Right of Religious Societies to Exclude Heretical and Unruly Members.* Next comes Sloss's response to Taylor's *Defence*, and then an exposure of *Falsehoods in Joseph Rawson's Narrative*, and finally, *Observations* on the whole affair. Naturally, Sloss contradicts Rawson's account at several points, and puts it all in a different perspective.

Taylor came back with *A Further Defence of the Common Rights of Christians*, vehemently reasserting his view of the matter. On the first page of his former statement of the case he had asserted the inalienable duty of Christians to use their reason in matters of religion: 'Without an honest use of our natural faculties, any revelation is given in vain.' In response to Sloss's counter-attack, he returns to this theme, and stakes the claim of reason even more eloquently: 'Reason is the light of the whole universe, the perfection of the Divine perfections; without which, the existence of God would be of no use, and his power a blind ungoverned force.' It is absurd and meaningless, he claims, to require people to *believe* what they do not *understand*.

Sloss's case is not without substance. Henderson, his remote successor, quotes with approval Sloss's contention that while the tolerance and inclusiveness of the congregation at Castle Gate is well known, it is right to exclude from it those who by denying the true nature of Christ render impossible their participation in 'union with one Head'. He points to the all-but-entire transition to Unitarianism among the Congregational churches in Boston and throughout New England, and concludes: 'That Castle Gate was kept true to Evangelical Christianity at a most critical period was due in no small measure to the strenuous efforts of Mr Sloss.'[10] In his parodying reply to Taylor, Sloss sets the freedom of the church to exclude heretical members over against Taylor's claim for the freedom of the Christian to follow his reason. There must always be a tension, as William Temple once remarked, between the right of the individual to freedom and the right of the institution to have a determinate character. Taylor himself could be firm against Deism on the one hand and the Roman 'apostasy' on the other. Nevertheless one finds it hard to sympathize with the uncharitable and persecuting zeal that insisted on so probing a man's faith and sifting his expression of it. Even at the time, orthodox but moderate men like Doddridge and his friends thought the proceedings in Nottingham inappropriate.[11] This inquisitorial spirit is fostered by belief in a God who could create the human race with the deliberate intention of condemning the greater part to eternal torment, while saving only an arbitrarily elect few: and all for his own glory. The long story of heresy-hunting manifests again and again this strange conviction that deviation from strict orthodoxy will, at the Day of Judgement, bring down the wrath of God on the heretic and all who tolerate his error. Such a belief is accompanied by gross insensitivity to the plain teaching of the New Testament that lack of love, and failure to express it in practice, is the true object of divine condemnation.

These publications evidently circulated widely, interesting a much larger public than the local partisans in Nottingham. Taylor had powerfully espoused the cause, not just of Rawson, but of the right to free inquiry in religion, and the exercise of one's conscientious judgement, based upon Scripture and reason. These writings established his reputation as a radical champion of freedom of thought on theological questions, within the limit of the authority of Scripture;[12] but what was his own belief? It is misleading to call him 'Unitarian'. If labels are to be used, 'Arian' probably comes nearer the mark. He himself deplored such names, as tending to disunity among Christians and unnecessary strife over words. 'We are *Christians*, and only *Christians*,' he claimed. But he insisted that to be a Christian, it is not necessary to go beyond what is found in Scripture; and neither the term 'Trinity', nor the elaborate theological structures that have been evolved to explain it, can be found there. On the other hand, what is undoubtedly found there is language that indicates the pre-existence and supernatural nature of Christ, and he affirmed this, as did Arius long before; so if we must classify, 'Arian' is the least inappropriate label that has been affixed to him. It is, however, an anachronism: the thinking of eighteenth-century divines is by no means identical with that of the fourth-century Alexandrian presbyter. Taylor could express himself vehemently on occasion, and Harwood in his funeral sermon records that he said he hated 'Athanasianism' because it denies the unity of God. Yet he and Finch could share a pastorate; and while denouncing the intolerance that excommunicated Rawson, he was consistent in not wishing to exclude trinitarians. As he said in his sermon in the Octagon, 'We deny communion to none of our fellow-Protestants; we refuse communion, upon the same catholic foundation, with none of them.'

6

An Hebrew Concordance

The next twenty years saw the publication of a series of works which made John Taylor well known, and both admired and execrated. But underpinning them all was a study in which he was pre-eminent, that of the Bible in its original tongues, and especially the Hebrew Scriptures. It is therefore fitting to take note first of his greatest work of all, though it was not published until 1754, after his other major publications had already gained great acclaim.

Since the Scriptures of the Old and New Testaments are the foundation documents of the Christian religion, they have always been closely studied, but with the decline of literacy in the so-called Dark and Middle Ages, they came to be regarded as the preserve of the clergy. In Western Europe they were read in the Vulgate Latin translation. The Reformation both resulted from and stimulated renewed study of the Scriptures, by scholars in their original languages, and by a wider readership in vernacular translations. With the increasing emphasis, during the seventeenth century, on the Bible *alone* as the rule of faith, the study of its two languages, as the indispensable key to its true meaning, took pride of place in the curricula of the academies. The reading of each Testament in its own language, often even in the daily devotions, was at the heart of their studies. Proficiency in expounding the Scriptures, on the basis of a thorough understanding of the original, was the essential equipment of a minister in the Dissenting, and especially the Presbyterian, tradition.

John Taylor's early commitment to the study of Hebrew has already been noted. His great-grandson Richard Taylor records, 'I have a manuscript Hebrew grammar very neatly written by

him, and drawn up probably for his own use 100 years ago. It
appears on the last page that he finished it in 1712. He must have
been then 18.'[1] Thus early, then, he fell in love with the language,
and delighted in the study of it. We may be sure that throughout
the weary years at Kirkstead his familiarity with the Hebrew
Bible grew and deepened; but it was not until he was well settled
in Norwich that he embarked upon the compilation of his
Concordance. He tells us that this huge undertaking occupied
more than thirteen years, so he must have begun it about seven
years after his move there.

The lexicon available to students of Hebrew at that time was
that of Johann Buxtorf (1564–1629), completed by his son in
1639; but Taylor tells us it was very little used, because of the
difficulty of reading a work entirely in Hebrew. He saw the need
for a new work, brought up to date with original research, and
adapted to the use of English scholars. To this he must have
devoted long hours of close work over those thirteen or fourteen
years. He employed no amanuensis, and the sheer labour of the
research, writing, checking and eventual proof-reading, as well
as the level of scholarship required, is daunting even to imagine.
His letters to his friend Dr Benson between 1751 and 1754[2] are
predominantly concerned with this huge undertaking, the problems involved in its compilation, the troublesome negotiations
with booksellers, and the laborious collection of subscriptions.
They afford valuable insight into his methods of working, and
the unsatisfactory state in which he found Hebrew lexicography.
He takes note of other lexicographical works, and goes to great
pains to consult them, but finds them all wanting. There are
interesting *obiter dicta*, such as his judgement that 'The Greek is
often so very remote from the sense of the Hebrew that it serves
only to show how wild & extravagant a Translation the Septuagint is.' A discussion of that all-important root, *kaphar*
(Taylor's 'caphar'), a key word for the understanding of sacrifice,
and its bearing on the Atonement, occupies most of one letter.[3]
Taylor's references to his contacts with other scholars give a
pleasing impression of the mutual respect and support among
them, irrespective of denomination.

These letters clearly reveal the great labour it cost Taylor to get his Concordance published. There were in the eighteenth century no great publishing houses, with the resources to undertake such a venture at the risk of possible loss, for the sake of the honour and prestige it might bring. The publishers were booksellers, who had to weigh up the probabilities of gain or loss, and who haggled with the authors over the terms, as we see in these letters. By 1751 Taylor was ready to go into print; but the cost of producing such a book, requiring a fount of type for the Hebrew characters,[4] and giving meanings in Latin and English, with innumerable references to chapter and verse, was obviously far too great for a printer-bookseller to undertake as a speculative venture. Nor could Taylor himself take the risk of financing it. Back in 1744, he says he might have been prepared to do even that, to get his *Paraphrase* into print;[5] but the present venture was of a wholly different order of magnitude. It could only be done by subscription: a method that had been suggested for that earlier publication, but rejected as troublesome, and unpopular with the booksellers. It was now to prove both; but there was no other way.

So in 1751, Taylor printed for circulation to likely subscribers a pamphlet entitled: 'ADVERTISEMENT, *Offering to publick Notice and Encouragement an* Hebrew Concordance, *formed upon a new Plan, and so adapted to the English Bible as to render it easy and useful even to an English Reader*'. A specimen of the contents of the proposed publication was appended. The word chosen is that same root *kaphar*, and the opening paragraph of the *Advertisement* refers to Taylor's own publication on the doctrine of the atonement to introduce his argument for the necessity of lexical study for the right understanding of the scriptures:

> In examining the Scriptural Sense of *bearing Sin*, and of *Atonement*, in the Treatise upon the *Scripture Doctrine of the Atonement*, every attentive Reader will see the great Advantage I have gained by using, and could not otherwise have gained but by using, the *Hebrew* Concordance . . .

This little eleven-page document is itself of great interest. It sets out very clearly the reasons why it is important to understand the language of the originals, including that of the Old Testament. The Hebrew Concordance, he says,

> must be allowed to be the most authentic Interpreter of Scripture, not only of the Old, but also of the New Testament: seeing both are wrote, as to the main things, in the same Words and Phrases; those of the New Testament being but the Words and Phrases of the Old translated into *Greek*.

The Apostles, as St Paul informs us, wrote and spoke,

> *not in the words which man's wisdom teacheth*, not in philosophic Terms of human Invention, *but which the Holy Spirit teacheth* in the Writings of the Old Testament, the only Scriptures from which they took their Ideas and Arguments, *comparing spiritual things* under that Dispensation *with spiritual things* under the Gospel . . . to understand the Sense of the Spirit in the New, it is essentially necessary, that we understand it's Sense in the Old Testament. But the Sense of the Spirit cannot be understood, unless we understand the Language in which it is conveyed. For which purpose the Hebrew Concordance is the best Expositor. For there you have in one View presented all the Places in the sacred Code, where any word is used; and by carefully collating those Places, one may judge what Sense it will or will not bear.

His letter to Benson[6] well illustrates this principle. Again in reference to that very important root *kaphar*, he takes issue with an earlier interpreter, Schultens, who relies on what Arabs give him as the meaning of a related verb in Arabic, and translates it by *linire*, to smear; whereas he, Taylor, concludes the true interpretation is *tegere*, to cover. He remarks: '*Schultens* goes upon the *Arabic*; I upon common sense, considering & comparing the several Texts where the words are used.' He was right.

Of course, Taylor works from the view, at that date pretty well universal among Christian writers, that the Scriptures are the inspired and infallible Word of God. Moreover, modern scholars recognize other influences besides the Hebrew Scriptures on the language of the New Testament. But Taylor was quite right to emphasize the primacy of that connection, and to contend for the importance of his meticulous study of that language for the right understanding of both Testaments.

The *Advertisement* goes on to pay tribute to the work of Buxtorf, but notes that notwithstanding its great merits, it has been 'too much neglected, and too little, or not at all applyed to it's proper Purpose, the Explication of the holy Scriptures', because of its 'forbidding Aspect', being written entirely in Hebrew, save for a Latin translation of 'the Head Words', with Hebrew numerals for chapter and verse. 'To remove this great Inconvenience', Taylor says, he has undertaken a very thorough revision and recasting of the whole work, and 'thrown it into a Form quite new'. He describes in detail all the improvements and additions he has made, by which in truth it is clear that his Concordance is a new work, though based on Buxtorf's.[7] 'This Work', he tells us, 'hath fatigued my Industry for more than 13 Years: and having now at length, through the goodness of God, finished it, I am not willing to venture a Publication any other Way than by Subscription.' It will, he foresees, 'require a large Sum of Money to print it with that Care, Exactness, Beauty, and Distinctness, with which it ought, and, I am determined, it shall be done'. He therefore appeals for subscriptions, and for help in obtaining them.

So nothing remained, we might suppose, but to wait for the subscriptions to arrive. Far from it: for months, as his letters to Benson show, Taylor was indefatigable in soliciting subscriptions, gathering them in, and transmitting them to London. He is greatly indebted to his friend for his activity in the same endeavour. Most remarkable of all is the great pains that were taken to interest the bishops of England and Ireland. They each received a complimentary copy of that short work on *The Scripture Doctrine of the Atonement* to which the *Advertisement* refers.[8]

The appeal was splendidly successful, to Taylor's great relief. It must indeed have been a very anxious time for him as he waited to see what the response to his advertisement would be. When the subscriptions had accumulated to the point where the great undertaking was out of danger, we can well understand his pleasure in sharing the good news with a friend. Dr Salter, the rector of the parish in which he lived, tells that they met when out riding one morning, and Taylor greeted him with a beaming expression and exclaimed: 'I am certain, my good friend, you will heartily rejoice with me when I tell you that I now know to a certainty that I shall lose nothing by printing my Hebrew Concordance. '[9]

The list of subscribers is printed in the first volume, and includes all the archbishops and most of the bishops of England, Wales and Ireland. In recognition of this support, the work is dedicated to 'The Hierarchy'. He writes to his friend in April 1754, as the work nears publication: 'I have drawn up a kind of Dedication, which may be inserted, if you think it proper. The Archbishop of Canterbury I think should first see it, lest there should be anything in it which he dislikes.'[10] The impressive list of clerical and lay subscribers includes such notable Hebrew scholars as Benjamin Kennicott of Oxford, but also many clergy and laity whose three-guinea subscriptions attest the extent of a very creditable level of scholarship among them. There is one name that merits special mention: that of a young minister in Suffolk, as poorly paid as Taylor had been at Kirkstead, who yet managed, on £30 a year, to scrape together the three-guinea subscription. So much for the canard that the Dissenting clergy were ignorant and unlettered men.[11] No doubt many of the bishops and others also made good use of their purchase in diligent Bible study; but some may perhaps have made the acquisition because no respectable library should be without it. We may be sure that a poor minister who made real sacrifices to obtain the Concordance, did so to put it to diligent use. The young man was Joseph Priestley.

The first volume appeared in 1754, and the second a couple of years later, embellished with a handsome engraved portrait of the compiler. These two splendid folios, beautifully printed on good quality paper, abundantly fulfil Taylor's intention that his work should be produced with the 'Care, Exactness, Beauty, and Distinctness' befitting their high purpose and his dedicated labour. Their publication established their author's position in the very forefront of the leading Hebrew scholars of his day. The Concordance is also to all intents a lexicon, and represents the first authoritative work in this country on the exact meaning of Hebrew roots. It gave a great impetus to Hebrew studies. Scholars in both the English universities well knew its value; but just as they failed to honour that other great lexicographer, Samuel Johnson, they missed the opportunity to give due recognition to Taylor's achievement. No doubt the fact that he was a Dissenter was an obstacle. So it was the University of Glasgow that had the honour of confering on John Taylor its Doctorate of Divinity *honoris causa*.[12]

7

Scripture Doctrine

It is astonishing that alongside the enormous labour of compiling the Hebrew Concordance, not to mention his pastoral work among his congregation, Taylor found time to write other books that gained him acclaim in some quarters and obloquy and bitter hostility in others. Though hissed in the street as 'the arch-heretic', he did not originate the movement of thought which he so signally represented. Before considering his theological and expository books, it is relevant to notice the influences among both Dissenters and Anglicans which were at work in the formation of Taylor's mind, and then were so clearly perceptible in his controversial writings.

High tide for the dominance of strict Calvinism was marked on the continent by the decrees of the Synod of Dort in 1619, and in England by the Westminster Confession of 1643 and its related Longer and Shorter Catechisms of 1647–8. Even at the Synod itself, the triumph of Calvinism was perhaps a pyrrhic victory. It certainly did not carry the hearts and minds of all present. John Hales, who was there as an observer on behalf of the English Ambassador at the Hague, was won over by Episcopius' defence of the universal efficacy of the atonement, in his exposition of the text, 'God so loved the world', and records, 'I bade John Calvin good-night.' Balcanquall, a Scot attending the Synod among the British observers, reported to the ambassador that Bogerman, the strongly Calvinist president of the Synod, dismissed the defeated Arminians with

such a powdering speech as I doubt not but your Lordship hath heard with grief enough; I protest I am afflicted when I write of it. For if the Remonstrants should write, that the President pronounced a sentence which was not the sentence of the Synod, they should not lie.[1]

The grip of Calvinism on the Church of England began to be loosened in the years before the Civil War, under the influence of such Arminians as Andrewes and Laud. The Commonwealth re-established Calvinist dominance, but under the surface unease with that uncompromising system grew. The Anglican Jeremy Taylor's book *Unum Necessarium*, which includes a radical critique of the doctrine of original sin, appeared in 1655.[2] Baxter, for all his leadership of the Puritan participants in the Savoy Conference, was no strict Calvinist.

During the rest of the century after the Restoration, under the influence of Limborch in Holland, and his friend the philosopher Locke, a liberal spirit spread. Protestantism had been launched by the Reformers with a time-bomb embedded in it: the insistence that Scripture alone, and not tradition, is the rule of faith. Once the traditional interpretations of Scripture began to be subjected to critical scrutiny, it was inevitable that some of the doctrines held to be based on Scripture would be found to be less secure than orthodox theologians had deemed them. Moreover, when the interpretation of Scripture is disputed, the disputants have no resource save rational argument by which to sustain their respective views. Thus *reason* becomes an important determinant of belief; and if the very authority of Scripture itself is questioned, how can that authority be established but by reasoning? Baxter himself recognized this role for reason, though he remained confident, as did many, that the right use of reason, and the right interpretation of Scripture, established the orthodox position he held.

Within the Church of England, after its restoration along with the monarchy, the loosening of Calvinist orthodoxy continued. Alongside the High Church Arminian movement that had begun before the Civil War, there set in a reaction against confident dogmatism even among those more akin to the Puritans. Bishop Burnet describes the rise of 'a new set of men of a different stamp,

who had their education chiefly in Cambridge, under Dr. Whichcote, Cudworth, Wilkins, Worthington, and More'.[3] To those
who shared their tolerant outlook, the name of 'Latitude men'
was applied, and then lengthened to 'Latitudinarians'. From a
collection of *Moral and Religious Aphorisms* culled from Whichcote's manuscripts, first published in 1703, one may pick almost
at random typical expressions of their rational and eirenical
spirit, such as the following:

> We are not to submit our Understandings to the belief of those
> things, that are *contrary* to our Understanding. We must have
> a Reason, for that which we believe *above* our Reason.[4]

> Our Fallibility and the Shortness of our Knowledge should
> make us peaceable and gentle: because I *may* be Mistaken,
> I *must* not be dogmatical and confident, peremptory and
> imperious. I *will* not break the certain Laws of Charity, for a
> doubtful Doctrine or of uncertain Truth.[5]

Between men of this spirit in the established church and the
growing liberal wing of the Dissenters, friendly contact was
possible. Baxter, in the end, was among the ejected clergy, yet he
remained a friend of Tillotson, who became archbishop. John
Taylor himself found more understanding and acceptance
among 'Latitudinarian' bishops and clergy than from 'dogmati-
cal and confident, peremptory and imperious' Calvinist
Dissenters.

In this atmosphere, the study of the Bible was less and less
trammelled by confessional interpretation. Locke himself wrote
studies that handled the Scriptures with this new freedom. By the
beginning of the eighteenth century, books with titles proclaiming them as 'The Scripture-Doctrine' of this and that were
appearing. A very influential one was Clarke's *The Scripture-
Doctrine of the Trinity*, which we have encountered in Taylor's
theological pilgrimage. Such books put aside the dogmatic
approach that had controlled the interpretation of Scripture, and
sought to establish what the text actually says, and what it
means, without guidance from creeds or confessions of faith.

In this spirit John Taylor wrote his own first major work, published in 1740, with the title: *The Scripture-Doctrine of Original Sin Proposed to Free and Candid Examination*. Those two words, *Free* and *Candid*, are highly significant. His examination of the doctrine is to be founded on the Scriptures alone, to which he will come *free* of dogmatic blinkers and untrammelled by what he calls 'schemes', such as the Westminster Confession. Moreover it is to be *candid*, that is, open-minded, unprejudiced, guided by the light of reason. Proceeding in accordance with these two principles, Taylor demolished the doctrine of Original Sin as taught in the Westminster and other Reformed Confessions. This doctrine was widely believed to be fundamental to the evangelical scheme of salvation. It was the involvement of the whole human race in the sin of Adam that was supposed to have necessitated the incarnation and atoning death of the 'second Adam'. Naturally, therefore, such an attack provoked an outraged response. The book is by far the most important of Taylor's works excepting only the Hebrew Concordance; and for breadth of influence at the time, and continuing relevance to the discussion of an important subject, it must be held to outrank even that. An account of its contents and of the major attacks upon it will occupy later chapters. For the present, we leave it with the memorable words of an Irish Presbyterian preacher, who warned his congregation not to read it, 'For,' said he, 'it is a bad book, and an heretical book, and what is more, the book is unanswerable!'[6] After such warnings, it is not surprising that it passed through three editions in its author's lifetime, and a fourth posthumously in 1767, and was probably the most widely read of all his writings.

Another of Taylor's works to bear the 'Scripture-Doctrine' label was his short treatise (only 136 pages) published in 1751, *The Scripture-Doctrine of the Atonement Examined First in Relation to Jewish Sacrifices: and then, to the Sacrifice of our blessed Lord and Saviour JESUS CHRIST*. The highly laudatory memorial sermon preached by E. Harwood following Taylor's death in 1761 lists his published works for the most part with unstinted praise; but of this on the atonement the preacher is quite scathing. In it, he says, 'it must be confessed he failed most egregiously. His reasoning was neither clear nor satisfactory.'[7] The grounds for such a harsh judgement are not obvious from Harwood's brief paragraph. He suggests the alleged failure was 'owing perhaps to the doctrine being in itself *almost* unintelligible, and *hardly* capable of being rationally explained'. Any brief mental review of the wide range of the theories that have been propounded engenders some sympathy with that despairing conclusion. Most widely held in this country in the mid-eighteenth century were variants of the theory of penal substitution: that is, that Christ suffered the punishment due for the sins of the world, and thus appeased the wrath of God, satisfied the demands of justice, and made it possible for sinners to be forgiven. This may be expressed by saying that the sin of humankind was *imputed* to Christ, and conversely his righteousness is *imputed* to the sinners. Fierce controversy had raged for a century and more over the question whether Christ's sacrifice sufficed for the sins of the whole world, or only for those of the elect.

Taylor himself was very far from thinking he had failed. His letters to Benson show that when he was soliciting subscriptions for his great Hebrew Concordance, he presented bound copies of this work, first to all the English bishops, then to the Irish.[8] The choice of this particular book for this purpose was deliberate and very appropriate. His *Advertisement* for the Hebrew Concordance begins, as we have seen,[9] with the well-founded claim:

> In examining the Scriptural Sense of *bearing Sin,* and of *Atonement,* in the Treatise upon the *Scripture-Doctrine of Atonement,* every attentive Reader will see the great Advantage I have gained by using, and could not otherwise have gained but by using, the *Hebrew Concordance.*

Taylor's approach is remarkably modern. Since his day, much detailed study has been expended on the sacrificial system in the Old Testament, and on the possible similarities and differences with ethnic religions; but his painstaking examination of the

significance of the Jewish sacrifices led him to see some things
that have since become abundantly clear. The three chapters
Taylor devotes to the ancient system lead him to the conclusion
that

> it seems sufficiently to account for the Efficacy of piacular
> Sacrifices, that, *in the Sight of God, and with Regard to his
> Acceptance*, the Priest made Atonement for Sin, by sacrificing
> a Beast, only as that was a Sign and Testimony of the Sacri-
> ficer's pure and upright Heart, or of that pious Disposition,
> which the religious Shedding of Blood, and other Sacrificial
> Rites suggested to him.

The notion of penal substitution leads to a complete misunderstanding of sacrifice. The sacrificial animal was not being
punished for the sins of the sacrificer; whatever the significance
of the ritual was, it was not that. So Taylor proceeds in his next
chapter: 'Upon the whole, 'tis abundantly evident, no PROOF
can be drawn from Scripture, that *bearing Sin* includes the
Notion of transferring of Guilt from the Nocent to the Innocent.'
'Vicarious Punishment', he asserts,

> seems to be a Contradiction in Terms. For as there cannot be
> a vicarious Guilt, or as no one can be guilty in the stead of
> another; so there cannot be a vicarious Punishment, or no one
> can be punished instead of another. Because Punishment in its
> very Nature connotes Guilt in the Subject which bears it.

This is a point on which Taylor is very clear: we shall meet it
again in his treatise on Original Sin. Punishment implies guilt;
and as no man can be guilty of the sin of another, so no man can
be punished for the sin of another. If he is, what is inflicted is not
true punishment, but unjust maltreatment. In the present context, he therefore concludes:

> Nor will the notion of *Christ's dying in our stead, paying an
> Equivalent*, or *Suffering a Vicarious Punishment*, bear the test

of Scripture or Reason . . . Law and Justice can never admit of one Man's dying in the Stead of another; or of his suffering the Punishment which in Law and Justice is due to the Offender only. And if the Lawgiver should insist upon vicarious Punishment, or require the Innocent to die, or accept the voluntary Death of the Innocent, by way of Commutation for the death of the Nocent, this seems more inconsistent with Righteousness and Justice, and more remote from all the Ends of moral Government, than simply to pardon the Nocent without any Consideration at all. For it seems more contrary to Justice and Equity both to acquit the Nocent and punish the Innocent, than only to acquit the Nocent and suffer him to go unpunished.

There can be no thought that Jesus

by his Sufferings . . . satisfied Justice, or the Law of God: Justice can only be satisfied by the Penalty; but the pardoning Grace of the Lawgiver is not obstructed by any Demands of Law and Justice. For he can set them aside.

This line of argument may seem to do away with all need for an atonement, but Taylor does not come to that conclusion. On the contrary, he maintains

that the Sacrifice of *Christ*, was truly, and properly, in the highest Degree, and far beyond any other, *PIACULAR* and *EXPIATORY*, to make Atonement for, or to *take away Sin*. Not only to give us an Example; not only to assure us of Remission; or to procure our Lord a Commission to publish the Forgiveness of Sin; but moreover to obtain that Forgiveness, by doing what God in his Wisdom and Goodness judged fit and expedient to be done to the Forgiveness of Sin; and without which he did not think it fit or expedient to grant the Forgiveness of Sin.

So whereas 'In *private* Cases, where only the Offended and

Offender are concerned, Offences may well be forgiven simply, immediately, and unconditionally', God, 'as a *Magistrate*, or the *Governor* of the Universe', must 'consider the *public* Good', and therefore 'ought to guard, qualify, and circumstance his Pardon in such Manner, as not to propagate, but, if possible, to extirpate a Spirit of Disorder and Rebellion, and to spread a loyal, well affected Temper throughout the whole Community'. In the previous chapter, he has dealt with 'Mistakes about the Efficacy of Christ's Death', and has said categorically that

> The design of it could not be to make God merciful; or to dispose him to spare and pardon us, when, as some suppose, so great was his Wrath, that had not Christ interposed, he would have destroyed us. This is directly contrary to the most plain and certain Notions of the Divine Goodness, and to the whole Current of Revelation.

So in chapter X he explains 'Wherein the Virtue and Efficacy of Christ's Death consists'. 'Our Lord's Death', he says, 'took its value not from *Pain*, or *Suffering*, *Imputation* or *Punishment*; but from *Obedience* and *Goodness*.' There are, he argues, many instances in the Old Testament of God's 'bestowing Pardon, and sundry Blessings upon others' out of regard for 'the Virtue, Piety and Prayers of good Men'. 'How much more must the perfect Righteousness, or Obedience and Goodness of the Son of God be a Reason for remitting the Sins of Mankind?'

Many will agree with Mr Harwood that this is not wholly successful, but though this short treatise may not be regarded as an adequate treatment of its great subject, it hardly merits his dismissive comment. Underneath the eighteenth-century diction and typography, some very modern insights may be discerned. Moreover here as in all his writings, where the meaning of Greek or Hebrew is in question Taylor is magisterial. For example, in the course of an examination of the preposition ὑπερ (for, on behalf of, for the sake of, instead of), which is so important in texts about the atonement, he makes the very valid point that these are often highly figurative. Thus on Isaiah 53:6 he comments: 'But who knows not that our Redemption is imaged by various figurative Expressions? As healed by his Stripes; washed from our Sins in his Blood; he was made Sin for us: which, if understood literally and strictly, would supply very strange Doctrines.' It is not difficult to think of some very strange, not to say repulsive, doctrines which have resulted from just such literalism. Whatever may be thought of his own exposition of the atonement, he did a great service by clearing away misconceptions embodied in those then current.

Because Taylor deviated from the traditional orthodox doctrine of the Trinity, and was undoubtedly one of those who moved the Presbyterian congregations significantly in the direction of the Unitarianism that so many of them ultimately embraced, he is too readily dismissed as a 'heretic' whose teachings are best ignored or denounced. The truth is, he was a meticulous and very enlightened student of the Scriptures, whose search for 'Scripture Doctrine' often led him to conclusions that no longer seem egregious.

8

Broke in the Lock

Taylor's next major work was *A Paraphrase with Notes on the Epistle to the Romans To which is prefix'd A Key to the Apostolic Writings, or an Essay to explain the Gospel Scheme, and the Principal Words and Phrases the Apostles have used in describing it* ... MDCCXLV. It achieved an effect and influence comparable with his treatise on Original Sin. A dedication of several unnumbered pages in large print, 'To the Society of Christians in the City of Norwich', merits extensive quotation for its clear statement of Taylor's principles as a Christian minister and expositor:

> We may not indulge our own Conceits in matters of Revelation. Every Point, advanced as Christian Doctrine, ought to be found in Scripture, and explained by Scripture ... And it is the Design of this Essay, setting aside all human Schemes, and my own Imagination, to give you the true Scheme of Christianity, collected immediately from that pure Fountain ... that your Faith, Hope, and Joy may stand, not upon the wisdom of Man, but upon the firm and immoveable Foundation of the Word of God ...
>
> And yet ... I dare not pretend to be free from all Mistakes. The Apostles were inspired and infallible Writers, but we are none of us inspired or infallible Interpreters ... Nor is it necessary we should ... For while we every one of us sincerely endeavour to find the Truth, and to be governed by it ... we do all that is in our Power, and all that God requires of us; nor can we be destitute of that Faith, which is necessary to Salvation. So far as we *truly* follow the Scriptures, we are infal-

libly sure we are in the Right: and so far as we *honestly* and *sincerely* endeavour to follow them, we are infallibly sure of God's Acceptance. But none of us have Dominion over the Faith of our Fellow-Christians and Servants; nor must any one pretend to set up for Master in *Christ's* School. *Christ* alone is our Master and Lord; and we ought not, as indeed, justly, we cannot, substitute any supposed infallible Guide in his Place.

After this it is no surprise to come to a vehement condemnation of 'Popery', laced, as was usual in those days, with references to the books of Daniel and Revelation, 'The Mother of Harlots', and the like. But this is followed by a passage which is important, in view of the not infrequent slur that Taylor was almost a Deist, if not even 'a leading Deist'. Nothing could be further from the truth, as the following paragraph shows:

But you are not without Danger from another Quarter. Some, and not a few, in our Land, with unnatural Eagerness and Pleasure, set themselves openly to disparage and disprove the *Christian* Revelation. But where shall we find eternal Life, but in that Revelation? Will it be said, that the Light of Nature discovers it? But doth it discover Immortality, or Eternal Life? By no means . . . Is it not evident that the best Virtue any Man performs, needs the Relief of Grace and Mercy? And where is that Grace and Mercy revealed, but in the Gospel?

Four of Taylor's letters to Benson,[1] those written between April 1743 and February 1744, are largely concerned with the *Key* and the *Paraphrase*. They exhibit Taylor's anxiety to be correct in his interpretation of Scripture. He hopes 'Dr Hunt'[2] will note in writing 'any Thing he judges faulty or doubtful', and urges Benson, 'let nothing escape your Censure', for, says he, 'I have great reason to be Diffident of my own Judgment'. He makes it clear that in his view, the *Key* is by way of an Introduction to the all-important *Paraphrase and Notes* on the Epistle to the Romans. It is on this that he has expended by far the greater care and diligence. The other, he says, 'did not cost me near the Labour and Time that I have spent upon the

Paraphrase'. Again, in the later letter, 25 May 1743, he urges Benson to point out anything he finds 'false, faulty, obscure, defective, inaccurate, redundant', and adds: 'I never reviewed the Key to the Apostolic writings since it was done, and therefore am uncertain how much it stands in need of Correction, in some places I am sure it doth; but the Paraphrase and notes, I have gone over several Times, and have I think almost done my best.'

The first part, the 'Key to the Apostolic Writings', begins with four chapters devoted to the calling of Israel, in and through their ancestor Abraham, to be the vehicle of God's revelation to the world. To them are applied such terms as *Chosen, Elect, Delivered, Saved, Bought, Purchased, Redeemed*, etc. They are called *the Family of God*, and a *Nation, People, Holy City*, etc. But this is 'not prejudicial to the rest of Mankind . . . God is the GOD and FATHER of all; and his extraordinary blessings to some are not intended to diminish his Regards to others . . .' Taylor proceeds, in Chapters V and following: 'The Jewish Peculiarity was to receive its Perfection from the Gospel Dispensation under the Son of God.' All those words predicated of Israel are now applied to the whole body of Christians, who are *Chosen, Elect . . . Family . . .* etc. 'As *Christians* are, by the Will of God, set apart, and appropriated in a special Manner to his Honour, Service, and Obedience, and furnished with extraordinary Means and Motives to Holiness, so they are said to be SANCTIFIED.'

Chapter VII makes the important point

> that all the Privileges and Blessings of the Gospel, even the whole of our Redemption and Salvation, are the effect of God's pure, free, and original *Love* and *Grace*; to which he was inclined of his own Motion, without any other motive besides his own Goodwill, (that is, without being persuaded, induced, or prevailed with to grant it by any other Being or Person) in mere Kindness and Goodwill to a sinful and perishing World.

The next chapter is of central importance. Ten pages are devoted to close reasoning, on the theme that 'all the forementioned *Love, Grace*, and *Mercy* is dispensed, or conveyed to us, in, by, and through the Son of God, JESUS Christ our Lord.' In this context, the blood and death of Christ are of central importance: but how? As we have seen, Taylor totally rejects theories of penal substitution; but he must, in fidelity to Scripture, do justice to the language of sacrifice applied to the cross. 'His *Blood* and *Death* is indeed to us an *Assurance* of Pardon: But it is also considered as an *Offering* and *Sacrifice* to God, . . . highly pleasing to him, to *put away* our *Sin*, and to *obtain eternal Redemption*.'

How is this to be understood? Taylor's answer is that 'The *Blood of Christ* is the perfect *OBEDIENCE* and *GOODNESS* of Christ.' Considered 'as a mere corporeal Substance', his blood has no special significance. Nor has it value simply as denoting death and suffering, 'as if mere Death or Suffering were in itself of such a Nature, as to be pleasing and acceptable to God'. 'His *Blood* is the same as his *Offering himself without Spot to God*.' It thus signifies his perfect obedience and goodness. It is this righteousness, goodness and obedience which are in the highest degree pleasing to God, and thus constitute 'a very just Foundation of the Divine Grace, and the most proper Expedient to communicate it'. 'And that the Removal of Evils, or the Donation of Benefits in favour of some, should have respect to some signal Instance of Righteousness and Obedience performed by another, must be acknowledged a very just and proper Method of promoting the Moral Good.'

Always foremost among Taylor's concerns is the promotion of right conduct and the building of character through the acquisition of habits of obedience and benevolence. Convinced as he is that God is perfectly good, and therefore can only will the well-being of his creatures, he dismisses all theories of the atonement that imply a need for suffering and death in order to satisfy some abstract demand for justice, or that juggle with notions of transferring guilt and righteousness between the Saviour and the saved. The sole reason for the sacrifice of Christ, in his view, must be to effect forgiveness in such a way as to promote virtue, and not encourage laxity. Our redemption, he says,

is of the *Moral* kind; and therefore is most properly effected by
Moral means, *Goodness* and *Obedience*; both with respect to
God and ourselves. With respect to God . . . who delights in
doing Good, and in multiplying Goodness and Beneficence
among his Creatures . . . With respect to Us . . . for thus we are
taught the absolute Necessity and infinite Importance of
Obedience, and ingaged to it, in the most effectual Manner,
being Redeemed by Goodness and Love, we have the most perfect Example of Goodness and Love, and the most powerful
Inducement to exercise them toward others.

The gospel, then, is 'a Scheme for restoring and promoting
true Religion and Virtue'. The next three chapters demonstrate
this, first from 'our Saviour's Discourses and Parables', then
from the rest of the New Testament. Next, in Chapter XII,
another very important chapter, he draws 'Conclusions and
Inferences'. Taylor contends that 'Election, Adoption, Vocation,
Salvation, Justification, Sanctification, Regeneration' etc. are
'*ANTECEDENT Blessings* that "do, in a sense, belong at
present to all *Christians*, even those who for their Wickedness,
shall perish eternally". They are *FREELY* given us of God, I
Cor.ii.12.' This must be so, he maintains, since the first step in
the Christian life is faith; all are called to receive in faith this free
gift of God, therefore it must be antecedent to the faith which is
to receive it. If it were not so, 'some, indeed all, would be unsure
whether they were included' in these blessings. This leads to

a just Idea, what it is to *PREACH Christ*, or the *Gospel*. 'Tis
not telling People they are all *naturally corrupt*, under God's
Wrath and Curse from the Womb, and in a state of Damnation, till they come under the Influences of a supposed effica-
ceous, irresistible Grace, which yet works in a sovereign Way,
arbitrarily and unaccountably. 'Tis not teaching, that only a
small, uncertain Number among *Christians*, are arbitrarily
redeemed, elected, called, adopted, born again or *regenerated*;
and that all the rest are by a sovereign, absolute, and eternal
Decree passed by, or reprobated ∴ . . . The Apostles were abso-

lute Strangers to these Doctrines. The whole Scheme, and Method of the Doctrine they preached to *Gentile Christians* is comprehended in that single Sentence, Eph.v.8 *Ye were* SOMETIMES [in your *Heathen* state] *Darkness*, but now [in your *Christian* state] *are ye Light in the Lord; walk as Children of the Light*.

Taylor thus stands in diametrical opposition to the Calvinist orthodoxy which, by its insistence upon the absolute sovereignty of God, is driven to maintain that who shall be saved and who damned is determined by his inscrutable will, expressed in the decrees of election and reprobation. Taylor holds that the privileges of the gospel are there for all Christians, to be received by faith, and expressed in a virtuous life. They are forfeited by failure to live up to them. It is no surprise to find him asserting in Chapter XIII, in sharp opposition to the prevailing orthodoxy, that 'Virtuous Heathens shall be eternally saved'. He appeals to Matthew 25, where '*ALL NATIONS*' come to judgement, and the Lord 'will receive all the Righteous that are found among them to *eternal Life*, and condemn all the wicked to *everlasting Punishment*'. This is very different indeed from the use made of this passage among the alleged 'proof texts' for the doctrine of Original Sin, as we shall see; and Taylor's exposition, it can hardly be denied, is the one that does justice to the plain meaning of the text.

The remaining four chapters of the book are supremely important. In them, Taylor carefully examines the different Jewish reactions to the gospel, as recorded in the New Testament: outright rejection and opposition, by the Sadducees on the score of the resurrection, and by the Pharisees over the Law; and varying degrees of acceptance. Comparing the Epistles to the Romans and to the Galatians, Taylor concludes that the former is directed against those Jews who totally rejected the gospel, though with some notice of believing Jews in chapters 13—14; while the latter is against those believing Jews who sought to impose the Jewish Law on Gentile Christians.

The long chapter XVI deploys Taylor's unrivalled knowledge

of the biblical languages, and of the Septuagint as well as the Hebrew Bible, in the analysis of the meaning of justification. He points out that the derivatives of the root *ts-d-q*, usually translated into Greek by δικαιω and its cognates, and in English by such words as *justify, justification, justice* or *righteousness*, with their very forensic ring, are also sometimes represented by derivatives of έλεos, *mercy*.

> And when those words which we translate *Righteousness*, are applied to God, they frequently signify that *Goodness, Kindness, Benignity, Mercy, Favour*, by which he saves and delivers from *any* Enemy, Danger, Evil, or Suffering. And hence they are used to signify the *SALVATION* and *DELIVERANCE* itself, which the Goodness and Favour of God vouchsafes.

No less than five pages of texts follow, illustrating and confirming this point. Taylor concludes: 'The sense of Δικαιοσυνη, *Righteousness*, Justification, being so far settled, it will be easy to determine how it is to be understood in the Epistle to the Romans.'

Taylor finds two 'Justifications' in the New Testament: the one, at the beginning of the Christian life, when we are received into the Kingdom of God by his free mercy and forgiveness; the other at its end, when we are justified by our deeds done in the body. According to Taylor, 'The Apostle argues about the *first*, and not the *final* Justification, in the Epistle to the Romans.' The *Dikaiosuné, Righteousness*, of God here means his *deliverance*, totally free and unmerited, 'by grace', of the *entire* human race, both Jews and Gentiles, from the condemnation and destruction to which the universal sin and corruption, of Jews as well as Gentiles, rendered them justly liable. This deliverance is as free and unconditional as his choice and election of Israel in Abraham was in the first place. By acceptance of this free justification in faith, both Gentiles and Jews are received into the Kingdom of God. They have no need for anxiety about their 'election', and so forth; that is *antecedent* to faith, and is the ground of it. But then, faith must issue in obedience: and the second, or final justification, at the Last Day and the final Judgement, depends on works. 'Thus St. *James* and *Paul* are truly and perfectly reconciled.' This reconciliation, however, is effected in a way that really makes the 'first Justification' something that can be taken for granted by cradle Christians. They are virtually born into it, and this is sealed by their baptism as infants. Henceforth, their concern must be to live good lives, and so attain to the 'second Justification', by Works. Such a view of the 'first Justification' is incompatible with evangelical preaching of 'Justification by Faith' as the heart of the conversion experience.

Even so enlightened a fellow-Dissenter as Doddridge allowed himself the wry joke that this 'Key' is perhaps 'broke in the lock'.[3] Nevertheless, Taylor must be allowed to have made some very valid points; and his God is, dare we say, much more Christian than the Calvinists'. We have here yet another instance of the contrasting experience of the 'once-born' and the 'twice-born' types of Christian. Only a blinkered sectarianism will deny that each has both its insights and its blind spots. There is a lot to be learnt from Taylor.

This long and detailed work is described on the title page as 'prefix'd' to what is therefore the main part of the book, the 'Paraphrase with notes on the Epistle to the Romans'. No doubt it was this, even more than the 'Key', which many readers found most valuable. It does not lend itself to summary, nor is it easy to convey an impression of it save by examining a specimen passage. The obvious choice is that notorious *crux interpretum*, Romans 5:12ff., which we shall meet again in connection with the doctrine of Original Sin. The text of the Epistle is printed in italics in a wide margin down the outer side of the page, verse by verse alongside the much longer paraphrase. The text used is mainly the Authorized Version, but with Taylor's variant translations here and there: for example, in verse 13, '*when there is no law*' becomes '*when law is not in being*'. In the inside margin are summary headings in small print. Between, in large, clear type, is the main column, the paraphrase itself. Sigilla are used to link sections of the verse with the relevant passage in the paraphrase. This is, of course, quite lengthy as compared with the original, but no more so than is necessary to serve its purpose. Square brackets enclose linking sentences bringing out connections of thought which are implicit, but not expressed, in Paul's tightly packed prose.

The large, handsome and closely printed volume found wide acceptance, not least among Anglicans. The celebrated Archdeacon Paley of Carlisle advised candidates for priests' orders to study it carefully. Pasted inside the cover of the copy in the library of Harris Manchester College is a manuscript letter to Taylor's grandson expressing high commendation, from the Revd Peter Hansell (1764–1841), Vicar of Worsted and Precentor of Norwich Cathedral. Hansell's senior by twenty years, Henry Bathurst (1744–1837), Bishop of Norwich from 1805, said that if he understood St Paul's Epistle to the Romans at all, it was thanks to Taylor's book.[4] But by their time, the Evangelical movement was changing the tone of the established church; and within their lifetime, the Tractarians were to begin to change it even more, and in a different direction. Among the Dissenters also the Evangelical revival had made an impact, but in Presbyterian congregations there had been rapid development towards the much more radical rationalism and Unitarianism of which Priestley was an extreme exponent. Divisions had widened. Bathurst is described as 'the only liberal bishop' on the bench in his day.[5]

Nevertheless, at the time of its publication and well into the next century, it was possible for many Church of England clergy and laity to find sustenance in Taylor's book. Writing in 1848, a century after its publication, his great-grandson notes: 'This work has received commendations from many accomplished theologians, such as Bishops Watson, Law and Hurd, Dr Edward Bentham, the King's Professor of Divinity at Oxford, Dr Paley, Dr Parr, Dr Adam Clarke, and others.'[6] This last name has a special interest, in view of Wesley's vehement opposition to Taylor's views, and the tendency of Methodist writers to follow their founder's lead. The young Adam Clarke was received into the body of itinerant preachers by Wesley himself toward the end of the great man's life. Clarke became a notable scholar, and wrote an erudite eight-volume Commentary on the whole Bible, in which, in his introduction to the Epistle to the Romans, he quotes extensively from Taylor's *Key*. He concludes: 'In the preceding pages I have borrowed largely from the work of Dr Taylor, in a full conviction that it is the best ever written upon this subject, that it is indispensably necessary to a proper understanding of the Apostolic writings; and that I could not hope to equal it by any production of my own . . .'[7] Such a testimony, from such a source, three-quarters of a century after the publication of the *Key*, attests the remarkable influence Taylor's book exerted, even in quarters where his views on the Trinity and the doctrine of Original Sin might have been expected to close minds against him.

Does Taylor do justice to Paul? How does his work look today? Certainly there is a great difference between Taylor's paraphrase and, let us say, Barth's famous commentary. There is now in some quarters a strong reaction against the Enlightenment, while Taylor breathes its atmosphere. On the other hand, all our contemporaries, even 'conservative evangelicals' (excepting the downright fundamentalists) must work on the hither side of the nineteenth-century revolution in biblical studies, while Taylor can still say with untroubled confidence that the Bible is the infallible Word of God. Every commentator on this Epistle reads it in the light of his own time, and through the spectacles of his own intellectual equipment, be it the Enlightenment, nineteenth-century liberalism, existentialism, postmodernism, or whatever will come next. Like all the others, Taylor contributes some insights, and some questionable interpretations. There is room for debate, for example, in the passage before us, over his understanding of the second occurrence of 'the many' in verse 15. Is it strictly parallel to 'the many' in the former half of the verse, where it undoubtedly means 'all mankind'? He takes it so, and accordingly paraphrases:

That the GRACE of God, and the Donation of Benefits grounded upon the *BENEVOLENCE* and *WORTHINESS* of one Man, that great and most excellent Personage JESUS

CHRIST; do ABOUND and overflow to the many, that is, to all Mankind, beyond the mere Reversing of the Consequences of *Adam's* sin . . . [etc.].

Adam Clarke happily follows him in this interpretation: strong Arminians both. For Calvinists, the benefits of Christ's work are confined to the elect; and they are not the only commentators for whom the second occurrence of the phrase has a more restricted meaning than the former. But Taylor has a strong case: if read according to the syntax and common usage, 'the many' should be co-extensive in both parts of the comparison. Here, as everywhere, Taylor finds the wider, indeed universal, offer of the grace of God. His tendency is to interpret Paul in a sense that he and his contemporaries would find reasonable. He certainly did great service in combating the legalistic, dogmatic Calvinist interpretation of Paul's least perspicuous arguments. Again and again he points in the direction of the more liberal Protestant theology of the next two centuries, and will share the disfavour into which that has currently fallen in some quarters. Some of its gains, however, are irreversible. Whether 'God is dead' or no, the God of the inscrutable decrees is certainly dead, and Taylor was the unacknowledged ally of his fellow-Arminian Wesley in bringing about his demise.

It is strange how Calvinism is back again

9

Dr Taylor's Poison

While these other works were appearing, and the great Hebrew Concordance was in gestation, that earlier treatise, *The Scripture Doctrine of Original Sin*, first published in 1740, went through two further editions, and gained very wide circulation. John Wesley records in his *Journal* his experience of its effect in various places. In north Lancashire he encounters 'disciples of Dr Taylor, laughing at Original Sin, and, consequently, at the whole frame of scriptural Christianity'. Preaching in the open air in Belfast on the theme, 'All have sinned, and come short of the glory of God', he finds that 'many . . . had no ears to hear, being faithful followers of Dr Taylor'. Several of his letters express his alarm. Writing in December 1758 to the young Augustus Montague Toplady (later to be one of his own most vitriolic theological attackers) he says:

> I verily believe no single person since Mahomet has given such a wound to Christianity as Dr Taylor. They are his books, chiefly that upon Original Sin, which have poisoned so many of the clergy, and indeed the fountains themselves – the Universities in England, Scotland, Holland, and Germany.[1]

The very capital of Calvinism, he is appalled to find, has not proved impervious to the heresy. The *Journal* of 1 April 1757 records: 'In returning to London I read a tract on *The Law of Nature*, wrote by a counsellor of Geneva. I am sorry to find Dr Taylor's poison spread to the Alps also! And even printed and published at Geneva, without any hindrance or animadversion!' This evidence of the penetration of Taylor's influence into continental Protestant circles is supported by the listing of his treatise in the catalogue of Schleiermacher's library. As for Scotland, once the firm base of Calvinism in Britain, the effect of Taylor's writings there was evident in the spread of the 'New Light', and of 'moderate' ministry. It finds frequent reference even in the works of Robert Burns.[2]

Another stronghold of Protestant orthodoxy was the New England colonies; but the Atlantic proved no barrier to the spread of Taylor's ideas. By 1757 the great evangelist and theologian Jonathan Edwards found it necessary to counter-attack with *The Great Christian Doctrine of Original Sin Defended*. In the Preface, he says:

> According to my observation, no one book has done so much towards rooting out of these Western parts of New England the principles and scheme of religion maintained by our pious and excellent forefathers . . . and alienating the minds of many from what I think are evidently some of the main doctrines of the Gospel, as that which Dr. *TAYLOR* has published against the Doctrine of Original Sin.

The doctrine Taylor attacked has suffered so much further battering since his day, and has been so much modified and restated in consequence, that it is very necessary to be clear what it then was. The phrase 'original sin' is now very loosely used as shorthand for the perceived tendency of human beings to do wrong, and to create social networks that predispose to wrongdoing. Used as the title for a detective novel,[3] for example, it occurs once or twice within the story, simply in reference to the fact that someone is manifesting in some extreme form the common human tendency to wickedness. Those modern theologians who refer to it at all usually reinterpret the traditional doctrine to describe, rather than to account for, the obvious tendency of individuals to behave selfishly and worse, and the solidarity of human societies in evil institutions and patterns of behaviour which are often deeply rooted in their history.[4] But the doctrine of Original Sin in its classic form, originating from Augustine, and espoused by the Reformers, is far more specific and dogmatic than that. It purports to *account for* this state of affairs as the result of, and divinely ordained punishment for, the sin of the ancestor of the entire human race, Adam, in the Garden of Eden. It teaches that all his descendants are involved in his sin and its guilt, and therefore are rightly condemned to eternal punishment in hell, regardless of their own behaviour. This dreadful doom, according to Augustine and those who strictly apply his doctrine, is justly pronounced even upon newborn babes before they themselves commit any sin at all; while in those who survive the first moments of life, the corruption of their nature will inevitably issue in personal sins. Any virtues they may seem to display, any good deeds they may manage to do, are all nevertheless sinful because they cannot escape the taint of their inborn sinfulness. This lamentable state of affairs is transmitted from generation to generation, not merely by the force of example, upbringing and social pressure, but by the very way we are conceived and born, which is infected with 'concupiscence', and cannot be carried out without sin. Sin is thus *inbred*, in our very nature, and is inescapable except by the intervention of divine grace.

That the foregoing summary is no caricature or exaggeration may easily be verified by reference to the various Reformation Confessions of Faith. Anyone who possesses a copy of the Book of Common Prayer will find the Thirty-Nine Articles appended to it, and should read Article IX and others. Somewhat less easily accessible is the statement of the doctrine set out in the Confession of Faith produced by the Westminster Assembly of 1643, and the Longer and Shorter Catechisms approved by Parliament in 1647–8. Under the Commonwealth, this was authoritative for both kingdoms; and when, at the Restoration, England reverted to the Anglican establishment, it remained the doctrinal standard of the Church of Scotland. It also held sway among Nonconformists in England. This was the statement of faith that Taylor had in his sights.

As usual, Taylor prefaces his work with the assurance that it is based on the careful study of the meaning of Scripture, without reference to human authority or tradition, and he urges his readers to exercise their own reason and judgement upon what he has written. The treatise that follows is in three parts. Part I deals with the most directly relevant texts bearing on the doctrine of the Fall and Original Sin; Part II examines other passages that have been adduced in support of it in the Westminster Confession and Catechisms; and Part III deals with objections and queries, and examines the relation of the doctrine to other themes of theology.

Part I is dated 'Norwich November 20, 1735', so Taylor began work on this subject a couple of years after his arrival there, and more than four years before he published it. He approaches his theme as though addressing an inquirer: 'You want to be satisfied about *Original Sin*; that is, you would know, How far we, the Posterity of *Adam*, are involved in the Consequences of his first Transgression.' There are, he finds, 'no more than Five Places in all the Bible where the Consequences of the first Sin are *certainly* spoken of'. These are: Genesis 2:17; Genesis 3:7–end; Romans 5:12–20; 1 Corinthians 15:21–22; 1 Timothy 2:14. These, therefore, he subjects to the most careful scrutiny, bringing his great erudition, and especially his expert knowledge of Hebrew, to bear on their elucidation.

This process strips away from the story in Genesis all the accretions with which later Jewish and Christian imagination had burdened it. If read without such preconceptions, it simply tells that Adam and Eve were created immortal and free from disease, living in a harmonious and happy world, but that because of their sin, they became subject to bodily death and to a life of toil and hardship, and Eve to pain in childbirth. These consequences are shared by all their posterity. But there is no mention of a corruption of human nature, making sin inevitable. Nor is there any 'curse' upon humanity. The only mention of a curse is first upon the serpent, then upon the earth, making its cultivation laborious. There is thus no basis for a doctrine of Original Sin here. Nor is there any in 1 Corinthians 15:21–22. Taylor contends that the obvious sense of this passage is, 'in Adam *all* inherit and suffer *bodily Death*; and this is the Death from which *all* "are made alive" by the Resurrection'. This paradox, that the general resurrection of *all* is wrought 'in Christ', he defends in a long footnote, directed against those who 'imagine that the Apostle, in this Chapter, speaks only of the Resurrection of the *Just*, or of the Saints'. The two occurrences of the word *all* are strictly parallel; so down to verse 22, he says, 'Thus the Aposle *argues*. But when he explains the Resurrection, and what would follow upon it, he confines his Reflection, as he naturally would, to the Case of those who are Christ's at his Coming (ver. 23 and ver. 25, &c).' Therefore, 'From this Place we cannot conclude that *any other Evil* or *Death* came upon Mankind, in consequence of *Adam's* first Transgression, besides that *Death* from which Mankind shall be delivered at the *Resurrection*, whatsoever *that Death be.*'

It is true that if the attention of the reader be concentrated upon this passage in isolation, and if it be read strictly according to the construction, the parallelism of the verse makes the two uses of 'all' co-extensive; but it may be contended that St Paul's use of the phrase 'in Christ' in other contexts would suggest that the second 'all' is restricted to 'all who are in Christ'. However that may be, though, Taylor makes a strong case for his contention that we are concerned in this passage with resurrection from literal, bodily death: the death incurred by Adam. These verses certainly offer no ground for a doctrine of Original Sin. So Taylor concludes:

> Thus far we seem to have advanced upon good and solid Grounds. And the Truths we have found are these. – That by *Adam's* Sin, he and his Posterity were subjected to Sorrow, and Labour, and to that Death, or Loss of Life, which might never have been followed with a Resurrection or Revival, had not God in *Christ* provided that Mankind should be made alive again at the last Day. *As in Adam all die, even so in Christ shall all be made alive.*

But 'Now we are come to the most difficult Place of Scripture, which speaks of this point'. It must be agreed that if the doctrine of Original Sin is found anywhere, it is found in Romans 5:12–19. Only if it is securely based here can other passages be held to teach it, since they only do so if they are read in the light (if light it be) of the Augustinian understanding of this paragraph. It is therefore crucially important for Taylor to show that it bears a quite different sense from that. To this task he devotes many pages, and to it he brings all his formidable knowledge of the Bible tongues. Two important instances well illustrate his use of it.

At the heart of the matter is the question in what sense all mankind are 'made sinners' 'by one man's disobedience'. The Augustinian understanding of the passage requires that all his descendants are 'made sinners' by Adam's disobedience, in the sense that they somehow participate in his sin, and their nature is corrupted by it. But Taylor points out that though St Paul writes in Greek, his thought forms are thoroughly Hebraic, and his language should be read in the light of the Hebrew behind the Greek of the Septuagint and the expressions in the Epistles. 'For the Hebrew word' he writes, 'which signifies *to be a Siner* [*sic*], in the Conjugation *Hiphil* signifies *to make one a Siner* by a judicial Sentence, or to *condemn*; and so it is often used . . .'. Several instances are listed, e.g. Exodus 22:9; Job 9:20; Psalm 37:33. 'For *Condemnation in Judgement, and making one a Siner*, by a Judicial Act, by an Act of Judgement, are the very same thing in the *Hebrew* language.' Thus in Romans 5:19, the meaning is not that all mankind were personally guilty of the original sin, or that their nature was corrupted by it, but simply that they were, by the divine judgement, made liable to its penalty, viz. death. Once again, we are dealing with a verse in which two parts are parallel; and fifteen pages later, Taylor makes the point: 'For as the word . . . in *Hiphil* signifieth *to be made a Siner*, by a judicial Act, as I have shown before; so also the word . . . *to be righteous, to be justified*, in the same Conjugation *Hiphil* signifieth *to be made righteous*, by a judicial Act, i.e. *to be acquitted, absolved*.' Again, several references are given, e.g. Deuteronomy 25:1; Isaiah 5:23, etc. Paradoxical as this may seem, Taylor's case, based on the language of the Old Testament, is very strong; and the parallelism of verse 19 is difficult to read in any other way, since it can hardly be maintained that those who are 'made righteous' (which is the same Greek word as 'justified'), were somehow present in Jesus, and participated in his obedience, in anything like the almost physical sense in which Augustine held mankind to have been present proleptically 'in Adam', and even 'in his loins', and so to have 'sinned in him'.

The most notorious linguistic conundrum in this passage concerns the meaning of the Greek phrase ἐφ' ᾧ in verse 12. It was the misleading translation of this into the Old Latin, and then the Vulgate, as *in quo*, that gave Augustine the proof text he needed for his doctrine that all mankind sinned in Adam, in some quasi-literal sense. To serve this purpose, he understood *in quo* to mean 'in whom'. This understanding of the phrase is all but universally abandoned by modern commentators, even by those inclined to retain some form of the doctrine of Original Sin. Commentaries offer half a dozen different possible renderings, some more compatible than others with some such doctrine; but the best attested is probably 'inasmuch as', 'in so far as'. Taylor's interpretation, in the present work, is supported by a footnote:

> Here the particle ω [which] refers according to the rules of Grammar, to θανατος [death], the next Substantive going before that it can agree with; and the Preposition επι, when construed with a Dative Case, as it is here, signifieth, among other things [to, unto] ... Accordingly what we render FOR THAT *all have sined*, should rather have been, UNTO WHICH [Death] *all have sined*. ... I know that εφ' ω sometimes seems to be used absolutely, without any Antecedent, and then it may be understood *conditionally*, as 2 Cor.v.4 ... But where there is an Antecedent expressed, or understood, it agrees with it, as Mark ii.4 'They let down the bed εφ' ω wherein ...' etc.

So the phrase that Augustine took to mean 'in whom (viz. Adam) all sinned', Taylor interprets 'unto which death (the mortality incurred by Adam) all sinned', i.e., were made sinners, in the sense that they suffered the penalty incurred by Adam's sin, though not themselves guilty of it. No doubt this interpretation is, like the whole passage under discussion, open to dispute; but it has at least the merit of being backed by acute linguistic analy-

WESLEY'S ARCH-HERETIC

G. T. Eddy, *Dr Taylor of Norwich: Wesley's Arch-heretic* (London: Epworth Press, 2003. £16.99. pp. 265. ISBN 0-7162-0568-8).

This book is to be welcomed as doing belated justice to Dr John Taylor, an outstanding figure among eighteenth-century Nonconformist scholars. It is especially fitting that it should come from a Methodist, since it is mainly biographers of John Wesley who have denigrated Taylor, assuming, rather than demonstrating, that Wesley was the victor in their dispute over the doctrine of Original Sin.

Between 1733 and 1757 Taylor served the Presbyterian congregation in Norwich which

A POOR SHOWING

The text known as *The Showing of Love*, or *Revelations of Divine Love*, written by the female anchorite Julian of Norwich at the turn of the fourteenth and fifteenth centuries, has become something of a spiritual classic in recent decades. It is certainly a work which merits attention, and gives key insights into late medieval English spirituality. Julia Bolton Holloway adds to the modern versions with *Showing of Love* (London: Darton, Longman & Todd, 2003. £9.95. pp. xxxiv + 133. ISBN 0-232-52503-X). Unfortunately, it is not one of the better versions.

moved into its prestigious Octagon Chapel just one year before he left for Warrington. A diligent and faithful pastor, he nevertheless found time to pursue his biblical and theological studies which led to several important publications. His *Hebrew Concordance*, the fruit of thirteen years' work, 'to all intents a lexicon', represented 'the first authoritative work in this country on the exact meaning of Hebrew roots' and earned him a doctorate *honoris causa* from the University of Glasgow.

But it was his *Scripture Doctrine of Original Sin, Proposed to Free and Candid Examination* (1740) which made him most widely known and in due course exposed him to obloquy. Here was a doctrine which, to the orthodox mind, was pivotal to the whole of Christian theology and which one questioned at one's peril. A third edition appeared in 1750 and it was only after that two prominent evangelicals on opposite sides of the Atlantic, Jonathan Edwards and John Wesley, saw fit to enter the lists.

Geoffrey Eddy deals judiciously with the controversy, and in just enough detail to enable us to arrive at our own verdict. Sadly, the final chapter of Taylor's life, spent as a tutor at Warrington Academy, is far from worthy of a man of ability and integrity.

JOHN A. VICKERS
Emsworth, Hants

at Westminster Chapel to show the centrality of thanksgiving in Christian discipleship. Written from a Reformist/Calvinist background he combines biblical insights with contemporary comments to ask: are we really thankful?

In an age characterized by complaint and self-pity he finds people more ready to criticize than praise. He believes the primary Christian response must always be one of thanksgiving. In spite of the popular belief that some are born with a grateful nature, thanking, he says, is an art to be learned. Constantly we need to remember to thank God, even through setbacks and difficulties. The humdrum and negative experiences of life can be turned to praise. For the Christian, thanksgiving is duty, obligation and privilege. The author claims thanksgiving always brings reward. He says: 'God can't stand praise.' He means, God always rewards gratitude with blessing. At low points of self-doubt and sadness the daily discipline of thanksgiving can transform the worst into unexpected joy. Kendall calls for a grateful nation and cites the American Day of Thanksgiving as a national response to God's blessing by the first settlers. By contrast he believes the tragedy of September 11 2001, a 'wake-up call to all the nations of the world in advance of final judgment.

We take so much for granted. We fail to recognize the service of those about us. He counsels: count your blessings – show your gratitude to God. He examines sis, and the further merit of making tolerable sense of a notoriously difficult passage. At the very least, Taylor has succeeded in showing that this crucial paragraph is very far from establishing the doctrine of Original Sin on so secure a foundation that the many other texts cited in support of it may now be read in its light; and as he shows, if read without such support, none of them requires such an interpretation. He concludes:

> It appeareth therefore, for anything that I can see, that the true Answer to this Question – *How far are we involved in the Consequences of* Adam's *Sin?* is this, *We are thereby, or thereupon*, subjected to temporal *Sorrow, Labour, and Death.* These things can be a *punishment* only to Adam and Eve; to their descendants, they are a discipline, which may well prove to be beneficial. Punishment implies guilt, and the race descended from Adam and Eve cannot be guilty of transgressions they did not commit.[5]

Having disposed of the five passages which have some explicit reference to Adam's sin, Taylor turns in Part II to the far more numerous texts 'which have by Divines been applied in Support of the common Scheme of Original Sin', that is, those so used by the Westminster Assembly. Some of these are very far-fetched indeed, and would never have been read in the required sense but for the powerful grip of the Augustinian scheme on the minds of the theologians. One of the most egregious of such misapplications is the citation of Matthew 25:41 in support of the contention that the whole human race is justly condemned to eternal hell by Adam's sin. This calls forth one of Taylor's finest expressions of outrage:

> Behold the Force of Prejudice, and the great Evil of blind Resignation to Schemes! Is it possible anyone can mistake this Scripture? Is there any apparent Difficulty in it? And yet it stands here applied to a Purpose quite different from its plain and obvious Sense. In vain hath JESUS brought the Doctrine of Life from Heaven, and lodged it in his Word, if men through Carelessness, or something worse, will thus wrest and pervert

what he hath taught . . . I hope, my Friend, that you have all along observed the Difference between Truth and Error; but here the Darkness and Day appear in their Extremes. The glorious LORD of Life teacheth in these Texts above quoted, that want of Love, Compassion, and Benevolence, toward our Fellow-Creatures, will exclude us from the Kingdom of Heaven . . . But lo! Men met together, in solemn Assembly, to settle religious Truths, have pointed out these Texts to prove, that Christ will or may justly, condemn us all to Tortures of Body and Mind in Hell-fire, without Intermission, to all Eternity, only for One Sin, committed Thousands of Years before we had a Being, without taking into Account any of our own personal Iniquities. This is perfectly astonishing. Surely the heavenly Rule of our Faith shall not always be thus trampled upon.

Many of the texts thus cited scarcely merit attention, and are dismissed with a sentence. Acts 17:26, for example, 'and hath made of one blood all nations of men' etc., is cited to prove that Adam was 'a public person'. Taylor comments, 'For my own part, I see nothing in the text that intimateth any such thing.' Romans 3:23 and Ephesians 2:1–3 receive similarly terse dismissal. 'Nothing is here said, or intimated, concerning *Adam*, or any ill effects of his sin upon us.' Taylor's judgement anticipates that of many modern commentators. One or two texts, however, call for fuller treatment, and among these the foremost is Psalm 51:5, 'Behold, I was shapen in iniquity: and in sin did my mother conceive me.' This is one of Augustine's five principal proof texts for his doctrine, and the one that supplied the basis for his disastrous teaching about marital relations. Taylor's handling of it exhibits his intimate knowledge of the Hebrew Scriptures, but also his use of it on this occasion in support of a rather far-fetched argument. His aim is to show that in this context the verb translated 'conceive' should be translated 'nursed', or 'warmed'. 'To CONCEPTION,' he says, 'it is nowhere applied but in Gen. xxx.38,39,41, – xxxi.10. But the sense it hath there will by no means suit the place under consideration.' It is somewhat amusing that he finds it necessary to use Latin from this point, '*ut castibus auris parcerem*' – 'that I may spare chaste ears'. In the story of Jacob's sheep, the verb is applied to the mating 'heat' of animals; but it is unthinkable, he contends, that David would apply it in such a sense to his mother. In such a context, it must mean 'to warm', and hence 'to nurse'. This is an exegetical tour de force if ever there was one; and in the great Hebrew Concordance, fourteen years later, it seems to be forgotten. Under the root *r-h-m*, Psalm 51:5 is cited for the meaning 'conceive'. Much more convincing than this display of ingenuity is the robust common sense with which Taylor dismisses any suggestion of Original Sin in this text: 'Which hath no Reference to the original Formation of his Constitution; but is a Periphrasis of his being *a Siner from the Womb*; and is as much as to say, in plain Language, *I am a great Siner*? I have contracted strong Habits of Sin.'

Taylor is not directly concerned with Augustine, whom he does not mention, but with the texts cited in the Westminster Confession and Catechisms. These include those on which Augustine relied, of course, and it is of interest to notice Taylor's treatment of those five. Three have now been noted. Two remain. One is John 3:6, 'That which is born of the flesh is flesh' etc. Only if one brings to its understanding a preconception based elsewhere does this suggest Original Sin. Once again, Taylor's good sense is revealed in his comment that it means no more than that we are born with 'the parts and powers of a man'. The other is Job 14:4,5, 'Who can bring a clean thing out of an unclean? Not one.' Along with Psalm 51:5, this is used to prove that '*Original Sin is conveyed from our first parents to their posterity, by natural generation, so that all that proceed from them in that way, are conceived and born in sin.*' It is characteristic of this use of 'proof texts' that they are plucked out of various parts of the Bible with no regard for their context. Taylor, like a modern commentator, often finds that in their setting they look quite different. Thus he points out that 'Job is here speaking of the common Weakness and Frailty of our Nature, not with regard to Sin, but to the Shortness and Afflictions of

Life', as in the preceding three verses. He makes the telling point that if the text is taken to refer to Original Sin, it does not support the case, since Job pleads his weakness as a reason why God should *not* bring him into judgement.

Again and again, an unprejudiced reader must share Taylor's astonishment at the extent to which the grip of the traditional doctrine on the minds of the Westminster divines could lead them to cite in its support texts which, when read in their natural and obvious sense, have the very opposite bearing. A good instance is James 1:14, 15, 'Every man is tempted when he is drawn away of his own lust, and enticed', etc. 'How, I pray,' says Taylor,

> doth it appear from this Place, that all Transgressions and Wickedness proceedeth from our nature's being corrupted, &c, By Adam's one Sin? Certainly the Apostle neither affirm-eth nor intimateth any such thing, but chargeth the Wicked-ness of Man upon its proper Cause, namely, their being drawn away and enticed by their own Lust.

He then puts his finger on one of the weakest points in the whole scheme of attributing all sins to the effect of a corruption of our nature by the one sin of Adam:

> If you say, *that Lust proceeds from* Original Sin, I ask, Whence then proceeded the Lust of our first Parents? For *Eve* saw that the forbidden Fruit was pleasant to the Eye, and to be desired to make one wise, and accordingly she indulged her irregular Desires, and did eat. What was the Cause of *her* lust, *her* irregular Desire, or Inclination? Shall we feign an *Original Sin,* a prior Corruption of Nature for her, as we have done for ourselves?

If, prior to the fall, those two archetypal human beings were free from all corruption of their nature, yet could succumb to the first temptation that came their way, there is no need of a universal corruption of human nature to explain the lapses of all their descendants!

To a modern reader, the strangest aspect of the Calvinist

theology Taylor attacked is the conception of the character of God to which it leads. Theologians who believed in a God of love and mercy could nevertheless, without any apparent sense of contradiction, hold that for his own glory he created human beings whom he *predestined* to be sinners and to be condemned to eternal hell. Some even concluded that the fall itself must have been predestined. Most modern Christians will surely agree with Taylor in finding this preposterous, and indeed blasphemous. He comments on the Proposition: *The Fall brought unto Mankind God's Displeasure and Curse, so as we are justly liable to all Punishments in this World, and that which is to come . . .* etc.: 'And pray, consider seriously what a God must he be, who can be displeased with, and curse his innocent Creatures, before they have a Being. *Is this thy God, O Christian?*'

More instances of his trenchant attack could be given, but these are enough to give a fair impression of the strength of his case, and the skill of its presentation. We may leave Part II with a good specimen of his eloquent indignation. Still commenting on the above Proposition, he writes:

> The whole of this Proposition, excepting temporal Evils, and Mortality (which yet are no Punishment upon us for *Adam's* Sin) certainly hath no Foundation in Scripture. I have no Inclination to expose it in all its frightful Consequences. How highly injurious it is to Divine Justice anyone may see. But give me leave to commiserate with the mistaken Many, with whom such Points as these pass for Articles of the Christian Faith. Their Eyes are covered with a thick Cloud of Error, and the All-Perfect Goodness of God, which should be their Joy and Life, is thereby intercepted from their View, or appeareth quite deformed; and they sit astonished in the gloomy Cave of SUPERSTITION, haunted with causeless Fear, Terror, and Despair, and resounding with the horrible Murmur of Blasphemy.

In Part III, 'some Objections and Queries are answered, and the Connection of the Doctrine of *Original Sin*, with other parts of Religion, particularly REDEMPTION and REGENERA-

TION is considered.' This indicates a very wide field, in which
Taylor deploys his arguments. At their heart is the fundamental
principle, that there can be no *sin*, properly so called, except by
personal choice, will and responsibility; therefore we cannot be
sinners by birth and inheritance. He appeals to Ezekiel's prophecy to this effect. There is indeed much sin and corruption in the
world, but this is due to the aggregation of individual choices,
not to an inescapable corruption derived from Adam. *Redemption*, therefore, is deliverance, not from an imagined Original
Sin, but from *actual* sin and its penalties. It is in his treatment of
regeneration that a very wide difference opens between Taylor
and his orthodox, and especially his evangelical, opponents.
Taylor holds that regeneration is indeed necessary: but it is a
voluntary process: a matter of acquiring habits of virtue and
holiness. If it were not so, he argues, how could it be required of
us, as it is in the text, 'Ye *must* be born again'?

Taylor identifies and deals with seven 'Objections' to his
thesis. These comprise the well-known contentions of the proponents of the doctrine of Original Sin: that we all have a 'moral
taint', derived from Adam; that all mankind were 'in his loins'
when he sinned, and sinned with him; and that there is 'a law in
our members' which 'warreth against the law in our minds', and
so forth. This last point, derived from Romans chapter 7, leads
Taylor to paraphrase that passage. He contends that it cannot be
taken as the experience of a regenerate man, but represents the
experience of a Jew under the Law, which St Paul tactfully
expresses in the first person.

No longer constrained to the study of particular texts, this
third Part of the Treatise is more free-ranging in its examination
of the ramifications of the doctrine. One of the more absurd of its
developments was the growth of increasingly fantastic notions of
the spiritual, mental and physical perfection of Adam before the
fall. This began among the rabbis and pseudepigraphists, but
was carried to ridiculous lengths by Christian writers. Adam
was not only imagined to be of transcendent beauty, and even
gigantic stature, but was believed to enjoy unbroken communion
with God, and to be possessed of all knowledge and wisdom, and

of intellectual powers far beyond those of any of his descendants. This fantasy was memorably expressed by Robert South in the single sentence from his sermons that has earned him a place in *The Oxford Dictionary of Quotations*: 'An Aristotle was but the rubbish of an Adam, and Athens but the rudiments of Paradise.' To the question, 'How far is our present state the same with that of Adam in Paradise?' Taylor replies with cool good sense:

> As to our mental Capacities, for anything I can find in Scripture, they are the same as *Adam's*, saving so far as God sees fit to set any Man above or below *his* Standard. Possibly the Force and Acutness of Understanding, was much greater in our *Sir Isaac Newton*, than in *Adam*. And there are many in the World probably much below *Adam* in rational Endowments.

This was greeted with scorn by his orthodox critics; but even more unacceptable to them was his contention that Adam could not have been endowed with the sublime spiritual qualities attributed to him, since in rational created beings, these are the fruit of responsible choice and disciplined development. In contrast to the weird unreality of the flights of fancy of which South's is typical, Taylor is the model of sound common sense when he contends that Adam as created could only have had the *potential* for wisdom, knowledge, virtue and holiness, not their fruition.

In this third Part, there is some exploration of the bearing of the doctrine upon the practical and devotional life of ordinary Christians. Himself a father, Taylor is very much concerned with the upbringing of children. On becoming a grandfather, he wrote a letter to his daughter, published in 1752 as *The Value of a Child*. Its tone is anticipated by the following passage in the present treatise:

> WHICH notions are most likely to operate best upon Parents' Minds, and most proper to be instilled into a Child? That it is born a Child of Wrath, that it comes into the World under God's Curse, that its Being, as soon as given, is in the worst

and most deplorable State of Corruption? Or that it is born under the Smiles of Heaven, endowed with noble Capacities, and formed in Love for the Glory of God and its own Happiness, if his Goodness is not despised and neglected?

This must be read against the background of contemporary notions of nurture and education, well illustrated by Isaac Watts' *Divine Songs* (1715), 'attempted in easy language for the use of children'. They contain not only such well-known lines as 'Let dogs delight to bark and bite', but gems like:

'Tis dangerous to provoke a God!
　　His power and vengeance none can tell!
One stroke of his almighty rod
　　Shall send young sinners quick to hell.

Their author showed early evidence of his later skill in pious versification with the lines, written at the age of seven:

I am a vile polluted lump of earth,
So I've continued ever since my birth.

Nowhere, perhaps, does Taylor appear more ahead of his time.

A curious echo of the kind of devout talk thought appropriate in Calvinist circles at the time is conveyed by the following passage:

To hear some Christians talk, one would imagine they thought it their Duty, and a Mark of all Sincerity and Goodness, to be always complaining of corrupt and desperately wicked Hearts, and consequently that they ought to have, and in fact should always have, such Hearts to complain of. But let no Man deceive himself. A wicked and corrupt Heart is too dangerous a thing to be trifled with. I would not here be thought to discourage the humble Sentiments every Man should have of himself, under our present Infirmities; but we may greatly wrong ourselves by a *false Humility*; and whoever carefully peruseth the New Testament will find, that however we are obliged to repent of Sin, a Spirit of bewailing and complaining is not the Spirit of the Gospel; neither is it any rule of true Religion, or any Mark of Sincerity, to have a corrupt Heart, or to be always complaining of such a Heart.

Enough has been said, and extracted from this remarkable book, to exhibit its author's case against the doctrine of Original Sin as it was held and taught at the time. Not only did his formidable biblical scholarship enable him to undermine its alleged foundation in Scripture; his recognition of the need for good sense in religion, and of the role of reason in the formation of doctrine, enabled him to see clearly, and express trenchantly, the downright absurdity of it. As he says, by this doctrine, 'We are made Siners we know not how, and therefore must be made sorry for, and repent of, we know not what.' He takes leave of his readers with a confident appeal to their own judgement. For him, as for them, 'The Word of God is infallible', and is 'the Rule of Faith'; but every reader must judge for himself whether it has been rightly understood:

And if any one undertaketh to give you a better Account of things, hear him willingly; but give him no Dominion over your Understanding or Conscience. Judge for yourself; weigh coolly and impartially what he advances. And if he convinceth you by Scripture Evidence, that I have taken anything wrong, you are bound in Conscience and Duty to receive the Truth he discovers, and to reject my Error; but in the Spirit of Christian Love and Peace. And in so doing, you will approve yourself to God, and please every honest Man; and among the rest,

Your Friend and Servant,

JOHN TAYLOR

In what spirit his opponents took up this challenge we shall now see.

The Frowns of God

Such a forthright attack upon what had so long been held to be a fundamental Christian doctrine was bound to provoke a vigorous response. Champions of orthodoxy soon came forward to prove the Irish preacher wrong when he said the book was unanswerable; but seventeen years were to pass before the evidence of Taylor's pervasive influence provoked the two most significant responses. In 1757, John Wesley in England and Jonathan Edwards in New England both published treatises upholding the traditional doctrine, and answering Taylor in detail. Wesley's works continue to be republished and studied, and his reply to Taylor is therefore the one most readily available to a modern reader. It is now the fate even of Taylor's book to be introduced to more readers through Wesley's attack upon it than by direct encounter; and with one important exception, his other critics are most likely to be read in the long extracts from their works that Wesley incorporated into his own. The exception is Jonathan Edwards. Neither Wesley nor Taylor alludes to his treatise.

First in the field was *A Vindication of the Scripture-Doctrine of Original Sin from Mr Taylor's free and candid Examination of it*, dated MDCCXL,[1] the very year of Taylor's own publication. No author is named on the title-page, but it was the work of David Jennings, 1691–1762, a very close contemporary of Taylor. He was the son of John Jennings, scholar of Christchurch, Oxford, one of the ministers ejected in 1662. Educated at Kibworth Grammar School and Moorfields Academy, he combined the role of pastor of the Independent congregation at Wapping New Stairs with that of divinity tutor to young men preparing for the ministry, and was awarded the degree of DD by Aberdeen University. Though in the Salters' Hall debate of 1719 he had sided with the non-subscribers, he was himself a strict Calvinist, and reacted strongly to heterodoxy among his students. Despite his teaching, the majority of these eventually went with the current towards Arianism. He clearly felt he was defending a threatened fortress, and saw Taylor's book as a deadly danger.

There is nothing very original in this restatement of the orthodox Calvinist doctrine. It is written in a good, clear style, and the tone is on the whole civil, though somewhat sarcastic and triumphal, in the manner of the theological controversies of the time. Jennings is quite sure the old teaching is right, and restates it with the well-worn proofs. 'From all which,' he says, 'were I to borrow a little of our Author's modest Language, I might say, *'it certainly, clearly and infallibly appears*, that *Adam* stood in the relation of a foederal Head to all his Posterity; and it is, therefore, no improper Language to say, *that they all sinned in him, and fell with him in his first Transgression.'*

He scores some shrewd points. For example, Taylor has argued that if we are born corrupt, and cannot help but do wrong, then this can be no sin, because it is not voluntary. Jennings retorts:

> If a corrupt Biass makes Sin to be necessary, and, consequently, to be no Sin, then the more any Man is inclined to Sin, the less Sin he can commit: and, as the corrupt Biass of his Heart grows stronger, his actual sinning becomes more necessary; and so the Man, instead of growing more wicked, grows more innocent.

He pours scorn on Taylor's tour de force over 'shapen' and 'conceived' in Psalm 51:5, but like all the defenders of the Augustinian doctrine, makes the hyperbole of a penitent sinner into an intolerable doctrinal statement. In the same confident spirit he deals with Romans 5:12ff. attacking Taylor's most vulnerable point, his interpretation of the statement that 'all sinned', and of course defending the orthodox understanding of this key passage. He concludes:

> Thus we have gone through this difficult Place of Scripture, as Mr Taylor calls it; and I persuade myself, if we be allowed to take the Words and Phrases, which the Apostle here uses, in the most obvious and natural Sense, we can have no great Difficulty to understand it, even without the Help of our Author's Paraphrase. And here I would ask, supposing the Apostle, or, rather, the Spirit of God, did really intend to teach us the Doctrine of the Imputation of the Guilt of *Adam's* first Sin to all his Posterity, and of both the first and second *Adam's* foederal Relations and Transactions, what plainer, stronger, and more expressive Words and Phrases could he have used to convey those Ideas to us, than those which are made use of in this Chapter?

Such complete confidence in the invulnerability of the orthodox interpretation of this vitally important passage is characteristic of the defenders of Original Sin. A modern reader who consults the commentaries will rather come to the opposite conclusion: if God really intended to establish so important and paradoxical a doctrine as this of Original Sin, he could hardly have done so more obscurely and uncertainly.

Among Taylor's strongest lines of attack upon the received doctrine was his insistence that one cannot be justly punished for the sin of another; and that therefore, though mankind may suffer the consequences of Adam's sin, these can be no punishment upon us, but only upon him. Nor can later generations share his guilt. Jennings is sure that they can, and that they are therefore justly punished. He reiterates the standard contention that all mankind are involved in the sin of Adam as their 'foederal head', and appeals to the usual string of Old Testament stories of punishment entailed upon succeeding generations: Noah's curse of Ham; the fate of 'not only the wives and sons, but also the little children of *Corah*, *Dathan*, and *Abiram*'; Achan's whole family; and the descendants of Gehazi. 'Will he be bold to say,' he asks, 'that in these Cases, the Judge of all the Earth did not do right?' Taylor's principle that 'the Word of God is infallible' lays him open to this line of attack; but a modern reader is likely to feel that his repudiation of this crude primitive belief is a laudable inconsistency. We meet here a line of reasoning that all the defenders of Original Sin fall back upon, circular though it is. When challenged over the manifest injustice of imputed sin and the involvement of all his posterity in Adam's punishment, they appeal to a number of Old Testament stories. This is how God does behave, they say, therefore it is just: God is 'the Judge of all the earth', and is therefore just by definition: therefore what he does is just, even when by any rational test it is not.

The gross imperfection of human justice is also overlooked in the supporting argument Jennings and others employ:

> In the next Page, our Author proves . . . that Original Sin as it is Guilt imputed, is no Object of Redemption; because imputed Guilt is only imaginary Guilt – for I am not guilty of a Sin I never committed . . . I would only now ask again, when Poverty and Distress come upon the Posterity of a Traitor, for his treasonable Act, is it only imaginary Guilt that lies upon them, and for which they suffer? And when the King, by a gracious Act of Pardon, restores the Estate and Honours to the Children, is it supposed the Children never had the Guilt of Treason imputed to them?

It is difficult to think of a worse argument than this. Obviously many innocent people suffer the consequences of others' wrongdoing; but it is monstrous to maintain that the fact that they suffer proves that they are punished, and the fact that they are punished proves that they are guilty! To such straits, however, are the defenders of this doctrine reduced.

Writing to Benson in April 1743,[2] Taylor expresses disappointment that his rejoinder to Jennings has received no answer, for, says he, 'I . . . had laid a Scheme in my Head for bringing them into some order in the Debate, and of obliging them to a Review of every Scriptural Argument. But I suppose they'll save me that Trouble.' When it came to the appeal to Scripture, Taylor felt himself to be in a very strong position. As he remarks in the same paragraph, 'We have great need to look well to our Hearts, and to use much Caution and Attention in Reading the Scriptures, for our Forefathers used too little.'

All the foregoing arguments and more are deployed at much greater and more tedious length by James Hervey, 1714–58. His huge three-volume work, *Dialogues between Theron and Aspasio*, appeared in 1755.[3] At daunting length – over 1300 pages in aggregate – Aspasio labours to convince Theron, who raises difficulties against the orthodox Calvinist theology. It is astonishing that this ponderous work ever found readers, but it is said to have been 'once popular'. The style is stilted and formal, and the argumentation, to a modern reader, tedious in the extreme. Perhaps the dialogue form made it readable to some, but surely no two human beings ever really conversed like this.

Hervey's book is not cast in the form of a reply to Taylor's, but it is clearly directed against his teaching, and its spreading influence. It quotes Article IX, and Milton's *Paradise Lost*: 'Adam's crime Makes guilty all his sons', and 'In me All Posterity stands curs'd', and continues:

> For my own part, I must confess, That if the Transmission of the original Depravity be granted, I know not how the Imputation of *Adam's* destructive Apostacy can be denied. If We had no concern in the one, how could We be justly punished with the other? I say *punished*. For to lose the primitive Integrity of our Nature, and inherit a depraved Disposition, is at once a most deplorable Calamity, and a most terrible Punishment. Corruption transmitted, and Guilt imputed, seem to be Doctrines *indissolubly* connected. . . .

– and so on, for many pages. In Volume II, Hervey quotes at length from a work by a Puritan divine, John Howe, 1630–1705, *The Good Man the Living Temple of God*, in a passage which Wesley reproduces in his excerpts from Hervey. Then, at

Theron's request, Aspasio retells the story of the fall, with all the usual embellishments about Adam's bliss in paradise, his exalted state, and the dire consequences of his sin, and so forth. He finds deep significance in the difference between verse 1 and verse 3 of Genesis 5, in that Adam

> *begat a Son in his own, not in the DIVINE, likeness . . . After his own Image*, Moses adds: as contradistinguished to the Image of GOD, mentioned in the preceding verse. Which Expressions are evidently intended to denote the Difference between the State, in which *Adam* was created, and *Seth* was begotten.

To Theron's question how all this affects Adam's children, Aspasio responds with a stout assertion of the transmission of corruption through natural generation, as distinct from the mere influence of example and upbringing.

Once again, there is nothing new in all this. The work is chiefly noteworthy for the elaborate, not to say wearisome, thoroughness of the exposition of the traditional scheme. Hervey was not by nature a controversialist, but a rather gentle and unassuming clergyman, who entered into the Calvinist controversy out of a sense of duty. He had already gained some acclaim for his verse work, *Meditations among the Tombs*. As a young man at Oxford he had come under the influence of John Wesley, and was a member of the circle nicknamed 'The Holy Club'. They remained on friendly terms until Wesley, though in general sympathy with the argument of *Theron and Aspasio*, offered some critical comments, whereupon Hervey took umbrage, and the breach was never healed.[4] Nevertheless, Wesley made considerable use of Hervey's work in his own attack on Taylor.

Until Wesley and Edwards entered the lists, the most formidable riposte to Taylor was Isaac Watts' *The Ruin and Recovery of Mankind*.[5] Watts' fame will endure as the writer of many of our finest hymns. He was eulogized by the great Dr Johnson, who insisted on including Watts in his series of *Lives of the Poets*. As we have seen, he was also the author of some hymns for children that we may be thankful are now hardly likely to be sung. Though brought up in the accepted Calvinist conviction that he was born 'a vile polluted lump of earth', he can hardly be regarded as a bigoted Calvinist. In the Salters' Hall controversy he took the side of the non-subscribers, who declined to require acceptance of any human formulation of doctrine beyond Scripture itself as a test of fitness for ministry. Moreover in his later years he agonized over the question whether God be One or Three, thereby inviting the suspicion that he himself was unsound as regards the Trinity. But on the fall and original sin he is very firmly traditional and orthodox. He opens his case with the argument that seemed so irrefutable before the revolutionary changes in the understanding of man's nature and the origin of the world that were to occur in the next two centuries:

> Man is a creature made up of an animal body and a rational mind, so united as to act in a mutual correspondence, according to certain laws appointed by his Creator. Now, suppose the blessed God, who is perfect in wisdom and power, in justice and goodness, were to form such a new creature, with what qualifications may we conceive such a creature would be endowed, by a Being of such goodness, justice, and wisdom?

Such an opening leads naturally to pages of unrestricted idealization of Adam himself, and the paradise in which he was placed. Since his Creator is perfect, the creature must have been perfect in every way: physically and mentally, but also morally and spiritually. 'A rational creature thus made must be not only innocent, as a tree, but must be formed holy . . . he must have . . . a supreme love to his Creator, a zeal to serve him, and a tender fear of offending him.' Nevertheless, he is in 'a state of probation', in which he has 'a power to choose either evil or good', and yet 'a full sufficiency of power to preserve himself in love and obedience to his Creator, and to guard himself against every temptation'. Obviously, 'the habitation in which a God of infinite goodness would place such an innocent and holy creature', must itself have been free from every kind of evil, 'a garden of pleasure', in which Adam and Eve were made 'lords . . . of all the creatures, animal and vegetable, that were round about them'. But:

> Now, if we may judge from the wisdom, justice, and goodness of God, that these are the qualifications with which such a new-made creature would be endued, these the circumstances in which he would be situated; then, by a careful survey of what mankind is now, we may easily judge whether man is now such a creature as the great and blessed God made him at first. And this is the subject of the present inquiry.

It is unnecessary, and would be wearisome, to wade through all the rest of Watts' long book, or to quote extensively from it. As a result of Adam's sin, human nature is ruined, and the whole creation is transformed. It still retains traces of the goodness and wisdom of God, but these are now intermingled with features expressive of his wrath and his punitive intentions. In page after page of purple prose, he expatiates upon the ruin both of human nature and of the whole creation. Even the map of the world is evidence of it! We can only surmise what Watts supposes it might have looked like before the fall: were the continents perfect geometrical forms? Or was there only one perfect circle, something like the *Mappa Mundi*? Whereas now:

> Is not the present shape of our earth, in its divisions of seas and shores, rude and irregular, abrupt and horrid? Survey a map of the world, and say, does the form of it strike our eyes with any natural beauty and harmony? Rather does it not strongly bear on our sight the ideas of ruin and confusion? Travel over the countries of this globe, or visit several parts of this island, – what various appearances of a ruined world! What vast, broken mountains hang over the heads of travellers! What stupendous cliffs and promontories rise, – high and hideous to behold! What dreadful precipices . . . What huge caverns, deep and wide, big enough to bury whole cities! When I survey such

scenes as these, I cannot but say within myself, 'Surely this earth, in these rude and broken appearances, this unsettled and dangerous state, was designed as a dwelling for some unhappy inhabitants, who did or would transgress the laws of their Maker, and merit desolation from his hand. And he hath here stored up his magazines of divine artillery against the day of punishment.

The animal creation, of course, affords similar evidence of ruin due to the fall. 'If man had not sinned,' Watts asks, 'would there have been in the world any such creatures as bears and tigers, wolves and lions', and 'would innocent children' have been allowed to become their prey? 'If man were not fallen, would there have been so many tribes of the serpent kind, armed with deadly venom?'

It may seem strange that in a different frame of mind, and writing for a different purpose, Watts could say,

> Nature with open volume stands
>   To spread her maker's praise abroad;
> And every labour of his hands
>   Shows something worthy of a God.

But this doctrine of Original Sin does indeed allow the theologian to have it both ways: what we find agreeable in nature is evidence of God's goodness and beneficence; its harsh and threatening features are his punishment for our sin in Adam, and therefore also 'worthy of a God'.

Needless to say, when Watts turns to the human condition, all is gloom and despondency. The universality of sin and misery is proof that human nature is fallen. Children manifest this evil inheritance from their very earliest days. 'Even from their first capacity of acting as moral creatures, how are they led away to practise falsehood and injury to their play-fellows, perhaps with cruelty or revenge!' But this cannot be traced to 'custom, education, or example; for many of these things appear in children before they can take any notice of ill examples, or are capable of imitating them'. All this, and much more, is proof that 'mankind have a corrupt nature in them'.

Not much amusement is to be found in ploughing through all this, so we must be thankful for the occasional light relief. We may be pardoned for so regarding Watts' claim to refute one of Taylor's arguments against this notion of a 'corrupt nature'. Taylor has maintained that in order to account for the universality of human sin, it is not necessary, and is indeed absurd, to trace every sin of later generations to a corruption of their nature brought about by the one sin of their ancestor. If one man who did not have a corrupt nature, namely Adam, could nevertheless sin, so can every other man, without any need to postulate a corrupt nature, an 'original sin', to account for it. The universal sin of the race is the sum of all the individuals' wrong choices. Watts believes he can refute this mathematically:

> It has been said, indeed, that 'if the first man fell into sin, though he was innocent and perfect, then among a million of men, every one might sin, though he was as innocent and perfect as Adam.'
>
> I answer, There is a bare possibilty of the event; but the improbability of it is in the proportion of a million to one.
>
> And I prove it thus: If a million of creatures were made in an equal probability to stand or fall; and if all the numbers, from one to one million inclusively, were set in a rank, it is a million to one that just any single proposed number of all these should fall by sin. Now, the total sum is one of these numbers, that is, the last of them; consequently, it is a million to one against the supposition that the whole number of men should fall.

To ponder this alleged refutation may perhaps be a useful occupation for a sleepless night; even less profitable is it to pursue further Watts' confident exposition of the familiar theme sufficiently indicated in the title of his work.

A remarkable feature of all the defences of the doctrine against Taylor's critique is the extent to which, despite their scorn of

Taylor for relying upon reason, they themselves feel able to build long chains of a priori reasoning about what God could do or could not have done, and to reach huge conclusions from the slenderest of premises. This is well illustrated in some tracts by Samuel Hebden,[6] parish priest of Wrentham, Suffolk, which were rescued from oblivion by John Wesley, who taxes Taylor with failing to answer them although they had been alluded to by Watts. One of these is based on Ecclesiastes 7:29, 'Lo, this only have I found, that God made man upright, but they have sought out many inventions.' This is one of those many texts cited in support of the doctrine of Original Sin, which a glance at any modern translation shows to have no such significance. The Jerusalem Bible, for instance, has: 'This, however, you must know: I find that God made man simple; man's complex problems are of his own devising.' For Hebden, however, as for many others, the meaning is much more sinister:

> When, therefore, Solomon says, God 'made man upright,' the plain, undeniable meaning is, God at first formed man righteous or holy; although 'they have sought out many inventions.' *They*, – this refers to Adam, which is both a singular and a plural noun: They, our first parents, and with them their posterity, have sought out many inventions; many contrivances, to offend God, and injure themselves. These 'many inventions' are opposed to the uprightness, the simplicity of heart and integrity, with which our first parents, and mankind in them, were originally made by God.

Once again we meet the contention that God could only have created man perfect in every way. Taylor's very reasonable claim that a newly created being could not be holy or righteous in any moral sense, since to be so requires personal responsibility, moral choice, and the formation of habits of virtue, is met with a chain of logical reasoning using such dilemmas as 'Either man was created with principles of love and obedience, or he was created an enemy to God.' What one misses continually in these orthodox theologians is a touch of empiricism, a breath of reality! Hebden concludes:

If man was not holy at first, he could not fall from a state of holiness; and, consequently, the first transgression exposed him and his posterity to nothing but temporal death. But, on the other hand, if man was made upright, it follows, (1) That man, when he fell, lost his original righteousness, and therewith his title to God's favour, and to communion with God. (2) That he thereby incurred not only temporal but spiritual death. And (3) That all his posterity are born with such a nature, not as man had at first, but as he contracted by his fall.

'QED' as you might say. Those few lines give us a good, succinct statement of the doctrine of Original Sin. But what a flimsy structure, what a house of cards, has been erected, with the aid of logic, on a single misunderstood text!

More formidable than all these was the book published in New England in 1757 by Jonathan Edwards, one of the ablest of the Calvinist theologians of the time, entitled, *The Great Christian Doctrine of Original Sin Defended*.[7] Unhappily, the author died of smallpox just before his book appeared, though he tells us in his preface that he had himself prepared it for the press. That preface is dated Stockbridge, 26 May 1757. Stockbridge was the scene of the ministry from which he was called, just before his death, to be President of the College of New Jersey; so the book had been written in the midst of his pastoral labours. His tribute to the devastating effect of Taylor's book in that once staunchly Calvinist colony has already been noted. Edwards further tells us that its influence had been spreading for some fifteen years; and though he has heard that there has been a reply by Dr Jennings, he has not seen it, and therefore has felt it incumbent upon him to undertake the task of answering Taylor, and of reaffirming what he regards as this cardinal doctrine. Only after his own work was ready for printing, he tells us, has he come across another reply to Taylor, by one Revd Mr Niles, and he hopes the two works will supplement each other.

Alongside Dr Taylor, Edwards also answers a Dr Turnbull, who has written on the subject to similar effect, but it is Taylor's work that is principally in his sights throughout the book. He shows himself familiar not only with Taylor's book on Original Sin, but also with his *Key to the Scriptures and Paraphrase of the Epistle to the Romans*, of which he makes a good deal of use. He is an acute logician and a formidable debater, and scores some palpable hits. From time to time, he is able to use Taylor's own statements against him, and to exhibit some inconsistencies, whether within the one book, or between passages in the two.

Edwards marshals all the familiar statements and scripture 'proofs' with considerable skill. In Part I, he establishes 'from Facts and Events', as well as from 'the Testimonies of holy Scripture', 'That all Mankind in all Ages, without Fail in any one Instance, *run into that moral Evil*, which is in effect their own utter and eternal *Perdition*, in a total Privation of God's Favour, and suffering his Vengeance and Wrath.' This clearly indicates a universal tendency in man's nature; the soul is in 'a corrupt and fallen state', and so forth. It is familiar ground; and though it is obvious that such a universal negative can never be proved, either empirically or a priori, it is, unhappily, only too plausible, in view of the atrocities humanity has proved capable of throughout history, not least in the twentieth century. Edwards makes the point that man is even worse than the animals: wolf does not destroy wolf, nor viper poison viper. Nevertheless, it is obvious that what we have here is special pleading for an already established dogma, not what Taylor would recognize as a 'free and candid' inquiry.

This is the strongest of the defences of the doctrine noticed so far. It is unlikely that Taylor ever read it. He certainly never replied to it, even to the extent of the kind of notes he left on Wesley's treatise. Modern readers are unlikely to think it worth while to plough through the book, based as it is upon a cosmology and a view of Scripture neither of which can any longer be the basis for argument. Like all the other disputants, Edwards uses Scripture quite uncritically, as though every part is of equal authority. Thus he quotes the words of Eliphaz in Job 4:7, 'Who ever perished, being innocent?' to establish his point, quite missing the intention of the writer to question, not to assert, what

Job's neighbours so confidently maintain. Yahweh's own verdict on their traditional piety in 42:7 he completely overlooks. To establish the meaning of 'flesh' in John 3:6, against Taylor's contention that it simply means our human nature apart from the work of the Holy Spirit, Edwards embarks on a long analysis of *Paul's* use of the word, which he simply assumes must also be the meaning for John. Like most of his contemporaries, he did not question that the 'inspired writers' functioned as amanuenses of the Holy Spirit. All the usual 'proof-texts' appear, interpreted to support the doctrine of Original Sin in a sense to which most of them are now recognized to be irrelevant.

Anyone who may wish to form an impression at first hand of the book, without putting himself to the task of ploughing through the whole, would do well to read the score of pages that form Chapter II of Part I. The thesis of this chapter is that 'Universal Mortality *proves Original Sin, particularly the* Death of Infants, *with its various circumstances.*' Here we encounter an argument we shall meet again in Wesley's book: that if there is punishment, there must be guilt, and since all die, all must be guilty. The unexpressed major premise is, of course, that God is by definition perfectly wise and good, and therefore just. It follows that 'The universal reign of *death*, over persons of all ages indiscriminately, with the awful circumstances and attendants of death, proves that men come sinful into the world.' All sorts of calamities are spoken of in Scripture as divine judgements on the wickedness of men. But death is the greatest of all calamities; therefore:

> If those particular and comparatively trivial calamities . . . are clear evidences of God's great anger; certainly this universal vast destruction, by which the whole world in all generations, is swallowed up, as by a flood, that nothing can resist, must be a most glaring manifestation of God's anger for the sinfulness of mankind.

Edwards is now in full flow, and heaps on the horror. Death, he says, is often 'attended by that awful appearance, that gloomy and terrible aspect, that naturally suggests to our minds God's awful displeasure . . . These gloomy and striking manifestations of God's hatred of sin attending death, are equivalent to awful frowns of God attending the strokes of his hand', and may be likened to the frowns of a 'wise and just' father engaged in beating his child. The reader may well recall that Edwards' most famous sermon was entitled *Sinners in the Hands of an Angry God*.

This may seem repugnant enough, but much worse is to come. In that century, and long after, mortality was highest in the earliest years, or even days, of life – a circumstance which one might have expected to cast doubt on the direct linking of death with God's displeasure at sin. Not so! 'We may well argue from these things, that infants are not looked upon by God as sinless, but that they are by nature children of wrath, seeing this terrible evil comes so heavily on mankind in infancy.' The Old Testament is dredged again for stories of God's wholesale acts of slaughter, in which infants must obviously have been involved. One such is the destruction of Sodom. God, we are assured, would have spared that city if even ten good men could be found in it. But obviously there must have been at least so many infants who had not yet themselves sinned; therefore, since God did not spare the city, the infants were not innocent, but guilty of original sin! This argument seems to overlook the implication that if all infants are involved in original sin, God's bargain with Abraham was a sham, since *no* righteous person, of any age, could ever have been found anywhere.

Again, Edwards contends, there must obviously have been newborn babes among the firstborn of the Egyptians, who were slain by God's own angel; therefore they cannot have been regarded as free from sin. There must have been many such babes involved in the sack of Jerusalem by Nebuchadnezzar, and again by Titus. In the punishment of Jerusalem prophesied by Ezekiel, chapter 9, verse 6, little children are expressly mentioned among those not to be spared; therefore clearly God does not regard them as innocent.

But now comes what is surely the most appalling passage, not only in this book, but in any of the defences of this frightful doctrine. We have seen that for Edwards, the horrors and agonies that sometimes accompany death are seen as evidence of God's extreme displeasure with sinful man. Now it is obvious that the death of infants is no less liable to such terrible accompaniments; so the death agonies of babes are 'the frowns of God'! But that is not all. Consider this:

> Especially may death be looked upon as the most extreme of all temporal sufferings, when attended with such dreadful circumstances and extreme pains, as those with which Providence sometimes brings it upon infants: as on the children that were offered up to Moloch, and some other idols, who were tormented to death in burning brass.

The plain meaning of this paragraph is that the extreme sufferings of infants as they die, including the torments of those who, *in the providence of God*, are sacrificed by their parents to Moloch, represent 'the frowns of God' as he visits his wrath upon sinful mankind. It is difficult to imagine a more repulsive exhibition than this of the horrible corollaries of the doctrine of Original Sin which could apparently be accepted without a qualm by its advocates.

Of course, some of them did have qualms. Augustine himself was troubled by the implication of his ferocious doctrine for unbaptized infants.[8] Any theologian in whose breast dogma has not totally extinguished common humanity must feel uneasy with the thought that newborn babes, who have committed no personal sin whatever, are condemned to eternal torment in hell because they are born sinners 'in Adam'. Much later in his book, Edwards records the suggestions of 'two divines, of no inconsiderable note among the Dissenters of England', who accept the doctrine of Original Sin, but offer modifications that would avoid supposing infants to be fully involved in the dreadful doom of the unredeemed. One of them suggests that God may perhaps attribute a lesser degree of Adam's sin to infants, and impose on them only the penalty of annihilation. The other 'thinks there is truly an imputation of Adam's sin, so that infants cannot be looked upon as *innocent* creatures; yet seems to think it is *not agreeable to the perfections of God*, to make the state of infants in another world *worse* than a state of *non-existence*'. But our author is of sterner stuff. He will have no truck with such pusillanimity. It is all or nothing with him. Adults or infants, there can be no half measures. All inherit original sin and guilt from Adam, and all, that is, 'by far the greater part of mankind', are destined for eternal damnation. Though he does not say it in so many words, the clear implication is that those luckless babes that were thrown into one fiery furnace went straight into another, from which there could be no deliverance for all eternity. In face of such a 'defence' of the doctrine, what need is there to attack it? As Taylor says, 'How highly injurious it is to divine justice, anyone may see.' We may say of Jonathan Edwards what Julian of Eclanum said of Augustine: he makes God 'a persecutor of babes, who throws tiny infants into the eternal fire'.[9]

It is very difficult to understand Edwards who in other respects can sometimes be enlightened.

Worse than Open Deism

Jonathan Edwards' counter-attack was launched from a firmly Calvinist position; but in John Wesley, Taylor's views provoked a critic who was, like him, an Arminian.[1] Indeed, his stout championship of that position against the predestinarians brought him into sharp controversy with such determined Calvinists as A. M. Toplady, and even his fellow evangelist George Whitefield. The monthly publication Wesley founded in 1778, and himself edited, was entitled *The Arminian Magazine*. There is therefore something of a paradox here; and indeed one cannot but feel that twenty years earlier, in the vehemence of his opposition to Taylor on the subject of Original Sin, Wesley in middle life veered a long way in the direction of the Calvinism he fundamentally opposed. But whereas 'that melancholy system', as he himself called it, is logically consistent, however repugnant, in his reply to Taylor on Original Sin he is driven to make concessions in the Arminian direction which sit uncomfortably with the main argument of his treatise.

It may seem strange that he waited so long before writing his reply to Taylor's book; and even more astonishing that until he did so, he seems to have overlooked the existence of the earlier replies we have noticed. Just when did he himself first read Taylor's book? In the Preface to his own, in 1757, he writes: 'A Few Years ago a Friend put into my Hands Mr Taylor's "Doctrine of Original Sin"; which I read carefully over and partly transcribed: and have many times since diligently considered.' But how many years is 'a few'? His first mention of it in the *Journal* gives us no clue; it simply records his horrified experi-

The Arminianism of the Heart

ence of its effect upon those whom he was seeking to awaken to
their need of Christ: *You bet!*

(Sunday 18 August 1748) We came to Shackerley . . . before
five in the evening. Abundance of people were gathered before
six, many of whom were disciples of Dr Taylor, laughing at
Original Sin, and consequently at the whole frame of scriptural Christianity. Oh what a providence is it which hath
brought us here also, among these silver-tongued Antichrists!
Surely a few, at least, will recover out of the snare, and know
Jesus Christ as their wisdom and righteousness!

So much for the Catholic spirit!!

Despite the sharpness of this condemnation, for several years he
does not appear to have been sufficiently alarmed to do more
than make occasional references to the threat, in the *Journal* and
in his correspondence. There was evidently a strong and pervasive influence at Shackerley (near Bolton, Lancashire), for it is
when he visits the place again three years later, in August 1751,
that he first mentions his intention to answer Taylor:

Wed. 10. – I rode to Shackerley. Being now in the very midst
of Mr. Taylor's disciples, I enlarged much more than I am
accustomed to do on the doctrine of Original Sin; and determined, if God should give me a few years' life, publicly to
answer his new gospel.

But another five years went by before he settled to the task. In the
meantime, he became more and more aware of the spreading
influence of Taylor's views, in Ireland, in the universities, and
even on the continent of Europe. He does not mention New
England, where, however, as we have seen, Jonathan Edwards
was as perturbed as Wesley, and was also moved to write his
trenchant counter-attack. In the autumn of 1756, Wesley at last
took time off from his tireless evangelistic and pastoral labours
and retired to Lewisham to do battle against what he saw as a
deadly threat to the heart of the gospel.
The resulting book, *The Doctrine of Original Sin According to
Scripture, Reason, and Experience*, is certainly one of Wesley's

major works. In its first edition of 1757 it runs to 522 pages, plus one of Errata, and seven of Preface; but many of those pages are taken up with extracts or abridgements of the work of others. It is one of the curious features of the book that in his Preface, which evidently was written first, Wesley asserts that he has only undertaken the task because no better qualified or more leisured writer has done so; yet a very considerable part of his book is filled with long extracts from others' work, especially that of Watts. To the words in his Preface, 'But since none else will', he adds a footnote: 'Since writing of this, I have seen several Tracts, which I shall have Occasion to take Notice of hereafter. There are likewise many excellent Remarks on this Subject, in Mr. *Hervey's Dialogues*.'

Wesley's followers became very numerous, especially in the rapidly expanding United States, and Methodist Churches now form one of the largest Protestant denominations worldwide. One consequence of this is that his voluminous writings have been collected and republished from time to time. They are accessible in nineteenth-century editions, and are now in process of republication in a much larger Bicentennial Edition. Taylor's book, though there is at least one nineteenth-century edition, will not be so readily accessible. Unitarianism, towards which his views on the person of Christ proved to be a half-way stage, also became a widespread but smaller family, not least in the United States; and we have Jonathan Edwards' testimony to the importance of Taylor's influence in the loosening of Calvinist orthodoxy in New England that undoubtedly prepared the way for that development. But Taylor has not had the significance for them, or for any large body of Christians, that Wesley has for Methodists. Consequently his fate is to be remembered chiefly as the author of a book Wesley answered, and to be read, if at all, in the quotations of his opponent. He deserves better than this.

Such of Wesley's followers as have written on the subject have tended, upon the whole, to accept uncritically his own assumption that he had decisively defeated his adversary, and triumphantly upheld the doctrine of Original Sin. In a recent brief study of Wesley's relation to 'the Age of Reason', for example, the late

one gets
a little
fond of
Tyerman!

Dr A. Skevington Wood quotes Luke Tyerman's judgement, in his important nineteenth-century *Life and Times of John Wesley* (1870): 'Is it too much to say that Wesley's book is the ablest refutation of the Socinian errors regarding original sin to be found in the English language? Throughout, he treats Taylor with the utmost respect, but, at the same time, utterly demolishes his system.' Wood comments, 'We may perhaps detect more than a touch of Methodist *pietas* in such an assessment', but he himself claims that Wesley was 'undoubtedly successful' in refuting 'the unscriptural and illogical theory propounded by John Taylor'. Wesley himself, in his Preface, brands Taylor's teaching as 'worse than open Deism'.[3] With the republication of Wesley's book, in so far as it is read, will Dr Taylor be seen once again as the dreadful 'Socinian' and 'Pelagian' heretic for whose 'poison' Wesley successfully provided the antidote?

Wesley opens his case with a survey of the story of the human race from earliest times and in every part of the world, which affords a very interesting insight into the information, and misinformation, accessible to a well-educated and well-read Englishman in the mid-eighteenth century. It is, however, dominated by his aim, which is to sustain the thesis that 'the flood of miseries which covers the face of the earth – is a demonstrative proof of the overflowing of ungodliness in every nation under heaven.'[4] Moreover there is an underlying assumption that this lamentable state of affairs represents a fall from some primeval perfection in which mankind was endowed with almost godlike intelligence and wisdom. Thus the humble achievements of primitive races are not seen as the first steps in progress towards civilization and greater enlightenment, but as pitiful smatterings painfully and very imperfectly recovered amid the sad ruins of lost arts. The great civilization of China, therefore, is not admired for its achievements, but condemned for its 'great want of common sense', shown not only in the barbarous custom of foot-binding, but in having an 'alphabet of 30,000 characters'. Wesley is on firmer ground when he exhibits the terrible cruelties that disfigure human history, as in Caesar's treatment of Vercingetorix, 'tortured to death'. He quotes the passages in Swift's *Voyage to*

Brobdingnag and *Voyage to the Country of the Houyhnhnms* in which Gulliver's magnanimous hearers are horrified by his bragging accounts of European politics and wars, and his evident pride in the carnage and destruction made possible by new engines of warfare. Wesley draws on his own first-hand knowledge of the native Indians of North America to explode any notion of 'the noble savage', so admired by later romantics. Visits to Ireland, too, gave him direct acquaintance with the miserable condition of the peasants there, which he describes as furnishing evidence of the ruin of our fallen race.

The dreadful events of the twentieth century, which have shattered the nineteenth's optimistic dreams of perpetual progress, may seem to justify a wholesale condemnation of the human race after the fashion of Wesley. The horrors of the First World War, the Holocaust, Stalin's 'Gulag Archipelago', the regime of the Khmer Rouge, and many more, would furnish him with even more frightful evidence for his case. But as Dr E. H. Sugden says, in his introduction to Wesley's sermon on Original Sin,

> His account of the natural condition of mankind is felt to be unreal. This is more obvious still in the first part of the treatise on Original Sin, in which all the vices of humanity are combined in a lurid picture without the admission of a single redeeming feature . . . The whole thing gives the impression of an advocate, who piles up and exaggerates everything that can be said for his side of the case, and ignores all the facts that are against him.[5]

One-sided, then, Wesley's description of the human condition undoubtedly is; nevertheless, the universal presence of sin, and the unspeakable depths of horror into which it can plunge individuals, families and whole societies, constitutes a problem for theology, to account for it, and for religion, to remedy it. John Wesley and John Taylor offer contrasting responses to the problem in both its aspects. It is obviously impossible to follow Wesley step by step in his attempted refutation of Taylor. A fair sample of the argument may be obtained if we select passages to illustrate their conflicting views as to the *origin* and *transmission* of man's tendency to sin, and the *remedy* for it.

The *origin* of the universality of sin, Wesley holds, along with Augustine, the Reformers and the Westminster divines, lies in the fall of humankind as recorded in the first three chapters of Genesis. These he takes as literal truth. Having established, in Part I, 'the overflowing of ungodliness in every nation under heaven', he proceeds: 'The fact then being undeniable, I would ask, How is it to be accounted for?' So opens Part II, which is the heart of his treatise. He sees only two possible explanations. One is that proposed by Taylor, namely 'bad education', by which he clearly means all the familial and social influences which bear upon a child's development. But, asks Wesley, 'How came wise and good men (for such they must have been before bad education commenced) not to train up their children in wisdom and goodness; in the way wherein they had been brought up themselves?' We meet here at the very outset the uncriticized assumption about what *'must have been'* that bedevils the whole doctrine of Original Sin, and Wesley's case for it. To its advocates it is obvious that since God is perfect, his creation *must have been* originally perfect, and human beings, made 'in the image' of God, *must have been* all but godlike in their intellect, wisdom, moral character and unbroken communion with God, as well as in their physique and paradisal setting. Wesley later expresses this very forcibly; addressing Taylor, he says:

> It is you who believe . . . our nature to be in the same state, moral and intellectual, as it originally was! Highly injurious indeed is this supposition to the God of our nature. Did he originally give us such a nature as this? so like that of a wild ass's colt; so stupid, so stubborn, so intractable; so prone to evil, averse to good? Did his hands form and fashion us thus? no wiser or better than men at present are? If I believed this, – that men were originally what they are now, – if you could once convince me of this, I could not go so far as to be a Deist; I must either be a Manichee or an Atheist. I must either believe there was an evil God, or that there was no God at all.[6]

Having disposed of the explanation in terms of 'bad education' to his own satisfaction, Wesley turns confidently to 'the oracles of God'. Like all the other opponents of Taylor, he is quite sure that in the early chapters of Genesis, and the other scripture passages that bear upon it, the orthodox doctrine of Original Sin is established beyond cavil. He proceeds to answer Taylor point by point, almost paragraph by paragraph, with a thoroughness the others do not match, and which it is impossible to reproduce in detail. Taylor did not publish an answer to Wesley; a fact which the latter took, mistakenly we may think, as a sign of conceded victory. It is more likely that by 1757 Taylor was far too preoccupied with other matters, as we shall see. But he did leave a number of manuscript notes which he may have intended to prepare for publication when he should find the time. These were published posthumously in 1767 as an appendix to the fourth edition of his own treatise. They certainly indicate no capitulation, but on the contrary are often very shrewd and effective. Whether or not Wesley was aware of them, he did not offer any response.[7]

Despite the growing scepticism of the 'Age of Reason', the eighteenth century was the last in which it was still possible for well-educated Europeans to be completely untroubled in their acceptance of the Bible as the inspired and therefore inerrant 'Word of God'. This was common ground between Wesley and Taylor. The difference between them, therefore, lay in the interpretation. We have seen how Taylor handled the stories in Genesis 2 and 3, and the passages of Scripture he recognized as referring to them. Wesley contends vigorously for the traditional exposition, and challenges Taylor's at every step. Thus where Taylor sees only physical mortality as the penalty of Adam's sin, Wesley argues for a 'spiritual life' which is lost by the fall. Where Taylor reads no more into the story than is manifestly there, Wesley follows the custom of seeing all sorts of deeper meanings, and summons the aid of Hervey's *Theron and Aspasio* to find many other dire consequences of Adam's sin in the story. He introduces a long quotation with the words, 'This is all you discern in the Mosaic account as the consequence of our first

parents' sin, before God judged them. Mr Hervey discerns something more':

> Adam . . . possessed a divine life, consisting, according to the
> Apostle, 'in knowledge, in righteousness, and true holiness.'
> This, which was the distinguishing glory of his nature, in the
> day that he ate the forbidden fruit, was extinct.
>
> His understanding, originally enlightened with wisdom,
> was clouded with ignorance. His heart, once warmed with
> heavenly love, became alienated from God his maker. His
> passions and appetites, rational and regular before, shook off
> the government of order and reason. In a word, the whole
> moral frame was unhinged, disjointed, broken.[8]

And so on. As Taylor tartly comments, 'Rather, Mr. HERVEY
imagines something more.'[9] Hervey, and Wesley, and all the
other advocates of the doctrine of Original Sin, claim to be
expounding the story in Genesis 2 and 3, when in reality, they are
reading into it ramifications elaborated by generations of rabbis,
pseudepigraphists and Christian theologians who between them
built up a tradition that culminated in the full-blown doctrine
promulgated by Augustine.

Into what absurdities this 'exposition' of the Genesis story can
run is well illustrated by the wresting of a simple element in the
myth, the naming of the animals by the first man, to provide
evidence of his godlike intelligence. This is taken to mean that he
anticipated, and exceeded, the achievements of all later scientific
study of species! The vast wisdom and knowledge that *must have
been* innate in this godlike creature were lost by his fall, and all
our modern knowledge and scientific theorizing represents the
painful effort of intellects beclouded by that fall, to recover a
little of the sublime knowledge Adam was endowed with by his
Creator. Taylor, as we have seen, speculates that Adam was
probably of about the average we see in our contemporaries as
regards mental capacity: and that whereas a Sir Isaac Newton
may be well above him in that respect, others may fall below
him. This Wesley dismisses with contempt: 'He that can believe

this, let him believe it.' He himself, as we have noted, quotes with approval Hervey's fanciful attribution to Adam, not only of intelligence, but of knowledge far exceeding anything that Newton attained, or that anyone else now possesses.[10]

Wesley is sure that the only satisfactory explanation of our sinful and miserable condition is found in this story:

> It remains then, all that has been advanced to the contrary notwithstanding, that the only true and rational way of accounting for the general wickedness of mankind, in all ages and nations, is pointed out in those words: In Adam all die. In and through their first parent, all his posterity died in a spiritual sense; and they remain wholly 'Dead in trespasses and sins,' till the second Adam makes them alive. By this 'one man sin entered into the world, and passed upon all men:' and through the infection which they derive from him, all men are and ever were, by nature, entirely 'alienated from the life of God; without hope, without God in the world'.[11]

This, of course, simply restates the Augustinian thesis, and bristles with begged questions and unexplained statements. How are we all 'in Adam'? What is meant by saying that sin 'passed upon' all men? What precisely is meant by the metaphor of 'infection'? And what is this 'nature' which we inherit, yet which makes us all sinners, alienated from God? In modern terms, is it genetic, a matter of DNA, or what? So we come to the question of the *transmission* of this alleged original sin.

Now that commentators are free to read the Genesis story as an aetiological myth or a non-historical folk tale, it is possible to find much spiritual truth in it. It can be seen as a parable or metaphor for the solidarity of the human race in sinful patterns of behaviour, and for the 'sociality and intergenerational transmission of evil'. The very names of Adam and Eve point in this direction. But so long as the story was read as a literal, factual account of a real pair who were the ancestors of us all, and whose one sin had such catastrophic effects, it raised enormous prob-

lems. At the heart of these is the question how the sin of one pair
can be imputed, and indeed transmitted, to all their posterity, so
that for it they are 'justly condemned to all punishments, in this
world and that which is to come'; and moreover are so corrupted
in their very nature that they cannot help but commit actual sin
in everything they do.

It is to Augustine of Hippo that Western theology owes the
answer to this problem which ever since his day has cast a
shadow on human life, wherever this doctrine has been taken
seriously. Sin, he believed, is transmitted from generation to
generation through the very act of begetting and birth. This
teaching is embodied in the Reformation Confessions. As the
Church of England's Article IX so graphically puts it:

> Original Sin . . . is the fault and corruption of the Nature of
> every man, that naturally is ingendered of the offspring of
> *Adam* . . . And this infection of nature doth remain, yea in
> them that are regenerated; whereby the lust of the flesh, called
> in the Greek, *phronema sarkos* . . . is not subject to the Law of
> God. And although there is no condemnation for them that
> believe and are baptized, yet the Apostle doth confess, that
> concupiscence and lust hath of itself the nature of sin.

In other words, the sexual impulse is unavoidably to some extent
sinful, even in believing and baptized Christian couples, and
inescapably transmits original sin to their offspring. This chilling
information is conveyed to young parents presenting their child
for baptism in the opening address in the baptismal service in the
Book of Common Prayer: 'Dearly beloved, forasmuch as all men
are conceived and born in sin . . .'. Good Anglican that he was,
Wesley stands by this teaching. It raises, however, an obvious
problem: since every human soul is created by God, how can it be
created actually sinful? Does not this make God the author of
sin?

Solutions to this problem have been offered along two different lines. One is *traducianism*: the theory that the soul is generated from the parents along with the body. This fits neatly into

the doctrine of Original Sin, and was adopted by Augustine. But the view that came to be more generally held is *creationism:* the belief that each individual soul is directly created by God, and implanted in the body generated by the parents. It is unthinkable that God would create a sinful soul; therefore the transmission of sin must be through the body, by which the soul is contaminated with sin from the moment it enters there. To what further problems this leads is obvious; it is of the nature of this doctrine of Original Sin that every solution it seems to provide for one problem raises further and even more intractable ones. But we are not for the moment concerned with those; only with Wesley's answer to Taylor. There is one very important passage which encapsulates much of the difference between them. Wesley quotes, and then responds to, Taylor's expostulation against the conception of God to which the doctrine of his opponents inevitably leads:

'What a God must he be, who can curse his innocent creatures before they have a being? Is this thy God, O Christian?' Bold enough! So Lord B——, 'Is Moses's God your God?' He is mine, although he said, 'Cursed be Canaan,' including his posterity before they had a being; and although he now permits millions to come into a world which everywhere bears the marks of his displeasure. And he permits human souls to exist in bodies which are (how we know not, but the fact we know) 'conceived and born in sin;' by reason whereof, all men coming into the world are 'children of wrath.' But he has provided a Saviour for them all; and this fully acquits both his justice and mercy.[12]

The expression, 'he permits human souls to exist in bodies', is not absolutely clear, but it seems to lean in the creationist, rather than the traducianist, direction. What is clear, though, is that Wesley endorses the grim doctrine that the body is the seat of original sin, which is transmitted in the natural process of generation. Of central importance in support of this is Psalm 51:6, 'In sin did my mother conceive me'; so it is no surprise that Wesley goes to some length to controvert Taylor's exposition.

Jacob's bizarre experiment in genetics is again subjected to solemn scrutiny, to establish the meaning of the word translated 'conceive' in Psalm 51, as against Taylor's plea for 'warm' or 'nurse'. Wesley is right as to the meaning of the verb. But he throws in one piece of information of the sort that very occasionally lightens the toil of wading through all this outdated wisdom:

> And when is it that females of any kind mark their young? Not in that act, but some time after, when the foetus is either forming or actually formed. Throw a plum or a pear at a woman before conception, and it will not mark the foetus at all; but it will, if thrown while she is conceiving, or after she has conceived; as we see in a thousand instances.[13]

This remarkable observation is only incidental to the argument about the meaning of a word, however. It is not suggested that 'the female marks her young' with original sin; that comes down the male line, and is passed on in the very act of generation, as Article IX and the Westminster Catechism say. And clearly, its seat is the body, by which the soul is contaminated when God 'permits' it to reside there. Like all the other defenders of this mischievous doctrine, Wesley reads it into the Psalmist's tormented cry of personal guilt, failing to recognize the hyberbole. Taylor is right to maintain that the Psalmist (whom he and his opponents all take to be David, in bitter penitence for his sin with Bathsheba) is not thinking at all about the sin of Adam, or asserting that his parents transmitted original sin to him, but accusing *himself* of being a great sinner, even from the first moment of his existence. The exaggeration is an understandable expression of deep remorse, which becomes intolerable when it is taken in the Augustinian sense.

It will be noted that Wesley, like all the others, can give no adequate answer to Taylor's question, in the passage quoted above, 'What a God must he be, who can curse his innocent creatures before they have a being? Is this thy God, O Christian?' His only reply, at this point, is, 'He is mine, although he said,

"Cursed be Canaan," including his posterity before they had a being', and his assurance that 'he has provided a Saviour for them all'. But the question cannot be so lightly brushed aside, and elsewhere Wesley attempts to deal with the problem of reconciling the doctrine of Original Sin with belief in a God of justice, let alone of love. That doctrine, let us remind ourselves, requires belief that God condemns all generations of mankind to inherit a sinful nature, which makes it impossible for them not to sin; and he condemns them to eternal torment in hell, not only on account of their own actual sins, but on account of the sin of Adam, into which they are conscripted from conception, with no volition on their own part. With chilling logical consistency, Augustine and those who have followed his lead conclude that babes who die before they have any opportunity for personal sin, are nevertheless lost souls by reason of original sin. Wesley, to his credit, shrinks from this. His Arminianism peeps out when he says: 'That all men are liable to these' (viz. 'all punishments in this world, and that which is to come') 'for Adam's sin alone, I do not assert; but they are so, for their own outward and inward sins, which, through their own fault, spring from the infection of their nature.' Again, 'I believe none ever did, or ever will, die eternally, merely for the sin of our first father.'[14] On this Taylor tersely notes: 'This is denying one principal Article of Original Sin. See Assembly's Catechism.'[15] Well, thank God for that much; but it runs counter to the tenor of Wesley's whole case, and is hardly consistent with his contention that newborn children are not innocent in the sight of God, but 'children of wrath', whose all-too-obvious participation in the mortality we all suffer on account of Adam's transgression proves this. The fate of unbaptized babes who die before they commit actual sin, he does not here discuss. But he is quite clear that if they survive even briefly, original sin quickly lands them in actual sin. All the tantrums and wilfulnesses of tiny children – 'frowardness' is his word – are seen as proof of that.

To anyone who approaches the subject not strongly indoctrinated in its favour, but in the spirit of 'free and candid' inquiry, the doctrine of Original Sin must appear to impugn God's justice. 'How highly injurious it is to Divine Justice anyone may see,' as Taylor says. Wesley, like Augustine before him, is sensitive to this, and attempts to meet the difficulty. It seems on the face of it unjust to visit the one sin of one man, Adam, in so dire a fashion upon the entire human race descended from him.[16] Wesley, as we have seen, shrinks from this to the extent of saying they do not suffer eternal death for Adam's sin alone, but 'for their own inward and outward sins, which, through their own fault, spring from the infection of their nature'. We pass over, for the moment, the question whether something that springs from a prior infection of our nature can be our own fault. What is more important is to note that this 'infection' of human nature is itself part of the penalty of Adam's sin. In other words, God punishes all mankind for Adam's sin by allowing them to be born with a sinful nature, and condemns them to hell for committing actual sins that spring from this infection.

The first strand to draw out from this tangled skein is the notion of punishment. Nowhere does justice or injustice manifest itself more clearly than in the adjustment of punishment to guilt. But on the face of it, the punishment of remote generations for the sin of their ancestor appears very unjust. Wesley, however, like Taylor's other opponents, appeals to several Old Testament instances in which the sins of the fathers *were* visited upon the children: the descendants of Ham; the posterity of Canaan; the families of Dathan and Abiram; and the descendants of Gehazi. Writing when they did, and both arguing from the position that Scripture is the infallible Word of God, it was not open to either Wesley or Taylor to recognize that these stories emanate from a stage of human thinking that has been outgrown, and that ill accords with the New Testament. Taylor argues, however, that though these families suffered on account of the sin of their progenitors, such suffering cannot be regarded as *punishment* except in so far as it falls on the actual perpetrator of the crime. For his descendants, it is suffering, but not punishment. To regard it as punishment is to confuse the two, to 'confound suffering with punishment'. Not so, Wesley maintains. Taylor has conceded 'that the posterity of Ham and

Gehazi, and the children of Dathan and Abiram, suffered for the sins of their parents'. 'It is enough,' says Wesley:

> You need allow no more. All the world will see, if they suffered for them, then they were punished for them. Yet we do not 'confound punishment with suffering, as if to suffer, and to be punished, were the same thing.' Punishment is not barely suffering, but suffering for sin: to suffer, and to be punished, are not the same thing; but to suffer for sin, and to be punished, are precisely the same.[17]

It is strange that such an acute logician as Wesley should have failed to notice the ambiguity of that little word, 'for'. A child born syphilitic, or with AIDS, may be said by some to suffer for the sexual misbehaviour of a parent; but it is monstrous to say the child is justly punished for that sin. Taylor's posthumous note on the above passage is: 'To *suffer* in Consequence of another Man's Sin, in which I had no hand, directly or indirectly, and to be *punished* for it, cannot be precisely the same.'[18] He is obviously right.

Those who maintain that the sufferings of mankind are a *punishment* for the sin of Adam must, of course, hold that such punishment is just. Taylor argues that it could not be just, therefore it is not a punishment, but merely suffering. Wesley maintains that it is a punishment, that God inflicts it, and that therefore it is just. What God does must be just. This position, however, proves to be tenable only if the word 'just' is emptied of all meaning when applied to God; and this Wesley in effect acknowledges. Taylor has argued that language about justice must have the same meaning, whether applied to ourselves or to God; and if we perceive some thing to be unjust, it must also be so in the eyes of God. Now for all mankind to be 'brought under God's displeasure for Adam's sin', strikes us at once as unjust. Taylor argues:

> And therefore, unless our understanding and perception of truth be false, it must be unjust. But understanding must be the

same in all beings, so far as they do understand. Therefore, if we understand it to be unjust, God understands it to be so too.

Not so, says Wesley. The ways of God are so far beyond our understanding that we can draw no such conclusion:

> 'How mankind could be brought under God's displeasure for Adam's sin, we cannot understand.' I allow it. I cannot understand, that is, clearly or fully comprehend, the deep of the divine judgment therein . . . it is quite beyond my understanding. It is a depth which I cannot fathom . . . 'Therefore, if we understand (apprehend) it is unjust, God understands it is so too.' Nay, verily, 'As the heavens are higher than the earth, so are his thoughts higher than our thoughts.'[19]

On that footing, further discussion becomes impossible. It is true, of course, that our human perception of justice is very imperfect and variable, and it behoves us to be very cautious in reasoning from it to conclusions about the justice of God. But if our human language has no meaning when applied to God, and if the clearest deliverances of our moral judgement can be brushed aside by an appeal to the inscrutability of God's mind, 'free and candid examination' of this or any other doctrine is futile. The appeal to the inscrutability of God silences all further argument.

Nowhere does the Augustinian doctrine run into greater difficulties than over the question of God's alleged treatment of children. It was, indeed, in the widespread practice of paedo-baptism that Augustine found some support for his doctrine: since baptism is 'for the remission of sins', newborn infants must have some sin to remit, and this can only be original sin! This belief has dire implications. It led to the dreadful superstition that failure to get the child baptized meant the difference between heaven and hell in the event of infant death.[20] Wesley does not here address the problem of the fate of 'unchrisom babes'; but we may note thankfully that, though he clung to belief in baptismal regeneration, his concession that no one suffers for Adam's sin *alone* is incompatible with Augustine's terrible teaching. It is also inconsistent with his own determined defence of what is, after all, the basis of that teaching: the belief that children are born under the wrath of God, with a nature that is inherently corrupt and wicked.

Taylor, a married man with a happy family life, has an altogether sunnier view of childhood. As we have seen,[21] he greeted the birth of a grandchild with a very positive short essay on *The Value of a Child*, and in his treatise on *Original Sin* he maintains that the 'notions are most proper to be instilled into a child' are *not* 'that it is born a child of wrath' and 'comes into the world under God's curse', but that 'it is born under the smiles of Heaven'. Wesley has that passage in mind when he writes:

> This doctrine . . . is the 'most proper' of all others 'to be instilled into a child:' That it is by nature a 'child of wrath,' under the guilt and under the power of sin; that it can be saved from wrath only by the merits, and sufferings, and love of the Son of God; that it can be delivered from the power of sin only by the inspiration of his Holy Spirit; but that by his grace it may be renewed in the image of God, perfected in love, and made meet for glory.[22]

Perhaps it is natural that in a treatise on Original Sin, it is the former, grimmer, negative part of this statement that finds fuller expression.[23] Like Jonathan Edwards, Wesley holds that the fact that infants suffer disease and death is clear proof that they are under the wrath of God by reason of original sin: 'God does not look upon infants as innocent, but as involved in the guilt of Adam's sin; otherwise death, the punishment denounced against that sin, could not be inflicted upon them.'[24] Small wonder that by the twentieth century, his followers had 'quietly abandoned' the doctrine.

That very first reference to Taylor's influence at Shackerley in Wesley's *Journal* reveals the reason for his determined defence of the doctrine of Original Sin. There and elsewhere, wherever he encountered that influence, it made people impervious to the

appeal of the gospel he preached. He found them 'laughing at
Original Sin, and consequently at the whole frame of scriptural
Christianity'. He appeared to them to be offering a *remedy* for a
condition in which they no longer believed themselves to be.
Differing as Wesley and Taylor did as to the *origin* and *transmission*
of sin, of course they differed widely in their understanding
of its *remedy*. Here Taylor is thoroughly Pelagian. Since, in his
view, there is no 'pravity' of human nature derived from Adam,
no original sin, but sin is the result of each individual's wrong
decision, when it was and is quite within his power to make a
right one, the remedy lies in an exertion of the human will. In his
Third Part, Taylor treats of several topics related to the subject of
sin, among them redemption and regeneration, or the new birth.
Redemption is not related to some fancied original sin, but is
concerned with our actual sins. Regeneration is a voluntary
process, 'the gaining those habits of virtue which make us children of God'. It must be a voluntary process, otherwise it could
not be required of us, as it is in the injunction 'Ye *must* be born
again'. Wesley will have none of this. Quoting Taylor, '"Upon
the whole, regeneration, or gaining habits of holiness, takes in no
part of the doctrine of Original Sin"', he rejoins:

> But regeneration is not 'gaining habits of holiness;' it is quite a
> different thing. It is not a natural, but a supernatural, change,
> and is just as different from the gradual 'gaining habits,' as a
> child's being born into the world is from his growing up into a
> man.[25]

Underlying all this is the question of the operation of the *grace of
God*. According to high Calvinism, human nature is so utterly
corrupt by reason of original sin that it can make no move at all
towards salvation, but is totally dependent upon God's free
grace. 'Free will' has been lost by the fall; human beings no
longer have freedom to do good, only to do evil, until and unless
God, by an act of totally undeserved favour, enables them.
Therefore those who are saved, are saved by God's unconditional grace. Carried to its logical conclusion, this means that

individual person have no part in the matter: if God has chosen to save them, they will be saved; if not, they will be damned, and that justly, because of their wickedness. God's choice is sovereign, therefore his grace is irresistible. It follows that those whom God selects for salvation are *predestined* to be saved. Whether the rest are *predestined* to be damned, or only omitted from the positive predestination to salvation, has been a subject of debate in Calvinist theology; but it is a distinction without a difference. Those predestined to be saved will be saved, do what they may; and those not so predestined will be damned, do what they will.

Wesley, at this point no less Arminian than Taylor, rejected much of this 'melancholy system'. He wrote and preached vigorously against the dreadful doctrine of predestination, proclaiming that Christ died for all, and the offer of salvation is open to all. The grace of God is available to all who will accept it. His brother's hymns set people singing this universal gospel:

> Thy *undistinguishing* regard
>> Was cast o'er Adam's fallen race;
> For *all* thou hast in Christ prepared
>> Sufficient, sovereign, saving grace.

or rather
Neo-Calvinism.

This splendid, liberating message did perhaps more than anything to dispel the dark cloud of Calvinism. But it carries an implication that Wesley, in his controversy with Taylor, struggled hard to avoid: that we must *respond*, if we are to be saved. If the offer is open to all, yet not all are saved, it must follow that those who are not saved are excluded *by their own choice*. If there is no element whatever of human volition in the matter, grace is irresistible, and we are back to God's arbitrary donation to some, and not others, of the grace that enables them to respond – in other words, to predestination. Anxious as he is to avoid this, Wesley is no less anxious to preclude any human contribution to the work of salvation. Taylor's frank Pelagianism really means we are saved by our own efforts, with a little help from the Holy Spirit. Wesley's strong resistance to this has him teetering on the brink of the Calvinist doctrine of irresistible grace, but at the crucial point he denies it. In the following passage he quotes and answers Taylor:

'However, I allow the Spirit of God assists our endeavours; but this does not suppose any natural pravity of our minds' . . . How very slender a part in sanctification will you allow to the Spirit of God! You seem very fearful of doing him too much honour, of taking from man the glory due to his name!

. . . Accordingly you say, 'His aids are so far from supposing the previous inaptitude of our minds' (to the being born again), 'that our previous desire of the Spirit's assistance is the condition of our receiving it.' But who gave us that desire? Is it not God 'that worketh in us to will,' to desire, as well as 'to do?' His grace does accompany and follow our desires: but does it not also prevent, go before, them? After this we may ask and seek farther assistance; and if we do, not otherwise, it is given.[26]

It is that last sentence, with its 'we may', and 'if we do', that draws back from treating grace as irresistible. Wesley is right to emphasize the divine initiative, and to insist that the first stirrings of spiritual life within us are themselves due to the Holy Spirit. God seeks us before we seek him. Nevertheless, there has to be a human response. If 'God worketh in us' in such a way that we are totally passive, the whole drama is a puppet show: grace is irresistible, and we follow our predestined lines to salvation or damnation.

If we imagine a scale extending between extreme Calvinism at one end, and extreme Pelagianism at the other: in other words, between the total exclusion of human effort on the one hand and total reliance upon it on the other, these two Arminians stand toward opposite ends, but short of them. Neither takes the absolute extreme position. Taylor says we must do our best to acquire 'habits of holiness', and if we do, 'the Spirit of God assists our endeavours'. Wesley retorts that it is the grace of God that initiates our desire for him, but that only if we respond is further grace given. Far apart though these statements may be, they both approximate more closely to the median position sometimes called 'Semi-pelagian' than to the respective extremes. Their differing emphases illustrate yet again contrasting types of spirituality that can both find some support in the New Testament. These two protagonists offer one more instance of the ever recurrent contrast between the 'once born' and 'twice born' types of spiritual experience. Their respective understandings of the gospel also reflect their very different spheres of ministry. Taylor's was that of the highly respected pastor of a settled, respectable congregation of 'worthy citizens' whom he sought to persuade to endeavour after 'habits of holiness'; Wesley's, that of the evangelist among the 'outcasts of men', whom such exhortations could only drive to despair, and whom only the grace of God could save.

Of isn't published yet.

Handsome though the new edition of Wesley's book may be, it may be doubted whether it will be widely read. Only dedicated researchers in the history of Methodist doctrine are likely to wade through its hundreds of pages of detailed argument, and the long excerpts from other writers. The fact is, though Wesley makes many good points, he had espoused a cause, in this particular controversy, that was doomed to fail. The doctrine of Original Sin, in the form in which it is stated in the Westminster Catechism and the Thirty-Nine Articles, has simply ceased to be credible. The Darwinian revolution in our understanding of the origin of the human species has destroyed many of the assumptions common to both these treatises. So too has the vast change in our understanding of the Bible.

Though these changes profoundly affect both authors' theses, it is to the doctrine that Wesley was defending that they are fatal. Far from being the triumph that some of his followers have thought it, his book espouses a lost cause. Moreover, the doctrine is not, as he supposed, fundamental to 'the whole scheme of scriptural Christianity'. It cannot be, for it is not found in the Greek Fathers, nor, in its fully developed form, in the West before Augustine. Whatever may be the explanation of the universality of human sinfulness, and need of salvation, it cannot be this. The essentials of Wesley's own gospel do not in fact depend upon it, and they have survived its demise. Taylor's book, despite his outdated view of Scripture, and what many will think his inadequate understanding of the problem of sin and the means of salvation, must be recognized as a prophetic and liberating challenge to the tyranny of this unscriptural and irrational doctrine.

12

A Place of Variance and Contradiction

Boswell cunningly manoeuvred a meeting between Samuel Johnson and John Wilkes, and the great moralist was surprised to find himself quite charmed by the profligate radical. Wesley and Taylor would surely have found more in common than that unlikely pair, but unhappily there was no Boswell to cajole them, and they never did meet. Even had such a meeting ever taken place, it is unlikely that they would have reached agreement, any more than did Johnson and Wilkes; yet perhaps one may hope that Wesley would have warmed a little to the benign personality and manifest Christian character of his adversary. Sharply defined differences that are easy to sustain in a war of books or pamphlets sometimes soften and blur a little when antagonists come face to face. As it was, they missed each other by only a matter of weeks when Wesley was in Norwich in November 1757. He had published his treatise against Taylor's doctrine that very summer. On Wednesday, the 23rd, he was shown round the beautiful Octagon that Taylor had opened the previous year, and records his visit in the *Journal* with a characteristic sting in the tail:

I was shown Dr Taylor's new meeting-house, perhaps the most elegant one in Europe. It is eight-square, built of the finest brick, with sixteen sash-windows below, as many above, and eight sky-lights in the dome, which, indeed, are purely ornamental. The inside is finished in the highest taste, and is as clean as any nobleman's saloon. The communion table is fine mahogany; the very latches of the pew-doors are polished brass. How can it be thought that the old, coarse gospel should find admission here?

Many years were to pass before he himself opened a building in City Road, London, with its mahogany communion table and pulpit, where 'the old, coarse gospel' could be preached in surroundings of some elegance; but in 1757 there was certainly a marked contrast with such a Methodist meeting place as the New Room in Bristol. Who showed the celebrated visitor around 'Dr Taylor's new meeting-house'? Not Dr Taylor, for he had left Norwich only the previous month, in response to a call to a very different sphere, where his life was to end in personal tragedy.

Ever since the 'Cavalier Parliament' had passed its hostile and repressive legislation against Dissenters, contrary to the pledges Charles II had given at Breda, one of the greatest disadvantages they suffered had been in the sphere of education. The universities of Oxford and Cambridge required conformity to the established church, and no doubt many waverers submitted, with greater or lesser inward reservations; but many highly principled families now found it impossible to complete their children's education in the established schools and colleges without compromising their conscience. Many of the ministers ejected under the Act of Uniformity were graduates of the universities, among them some distinguished scholars, such as Dr Samuel Annesley, the maternal grandfather of the Wesley family. His daughter, and her husband Samuel Wesley, son of another ejected minister, had conscientiously examined the points at issue, and had returned to the established church; so there was no difficulty, save cost, in their children's access to school and university. Those ministers and lay folk who in conscience could not conform, were faced with the acute problem of educating their sons to the standard they desired.

Despite all the restrictions, even on the establishment of private schools, which had to be licensed by the diocesan bishop, ministers here and there took pupils into their own homes, and from such initiatives sprang the 'Dissenting Academies'. Under what difficulties these sometimes operated we have seen in the case of Thomas Hill in the reign of Queen Anne.[1] Under the Hanoverians, toleration quietly grew, and in every part of the kingdom there were small centres of Dissenting education, one of the most celebrated being that of Philip Doddridge at Northampton. Many, like his, achieved a remarkably high standard. Their curricula were more liberal than those of the establishment, and the testing was more rigorous, at a time when examinations in the two universities were sometimes absurdly perfunctory. They received a good deal of support and encouragement from the Scottish universities, to which some of their alumni proceeded, and which from time to time recognized the scholarship of Dissenting pedagogues by the award of a degree.

By the mid-eighteenth century, however, the day of these domestic, informal academies was passing. Those at Kendal and Findern closed in mid-century, and even that of the great Dr Doddridge closed in Northampton on his death, though an attempt was made to continue its tradition at Daventry. Some Dissenters were beginning to feel the need for a more carefully planned and structured alternative to the public schools and universities. Not only did they wish to ensure a supply of scholarly, well-trained ministers for their congregations; they also desired an education adequate for their sons who were destined for secular careers in business or the professions. It was in response to this widely felt need that a more ambitious project than had hitherto been attempted was conceived at Warrington in Cheshire.

Warrington differed in many ways from the earlier academies. It was not the private enterprise of an individual minister, but a corporate institution managed by lay trustees, though led by a minister, John Seddon. Secular subjects appropriate for students destined for lay life took greater prominence, though divinity still had precedence. Something of the old domesticity persisted, but a collegiate atmosphere began to predominate, as the buildings took the form of a quadrangle, meals were taken in hall, and daily prayers were conducted for the whole tutorial and student body together. It has been described as 'the first redbrick university'.[2]

This was to prove a pattern into which Dr Taylor did not easily fit; he belonged to the old order. In a strangely nostalgic reference[3] to the advantages of the rural seclusion of his little boarding school at Kirkstead, he shows that what he envisages is a much more enclosed, almost domestic, establishment, though on a large scale. We shall see that his attempts to maintain something of this pattern in his own enclave at Warrington became a cause of dissension between him and his colleagues.

Pasted into the Minute Book of the Trustees of Warrington Academy are two printed appeals that were obviously circulated to likely supporters, setting out the reasons and aims of the enterprise, and soliciting annual subscriptions. This dependence on subscriptions, rather than solid endowments, was to prove a source of weakness. The response, however, was good, and the constituent meeting of the Trustees was convened on 20 June 1757. A prestigious figurehead was found in Lord Willoughby of Parham; far more important was the appointment of 'the Revd Mr John Seddon of Warrington as Secretary'. John Seddon was the minister of the Dissenting congregation in Warrington. He had been the prime mover in the whole enterprise, and it was only fitting that he should be put in this executive position; but perhaps inevitably it encouraged in him a disposition to assume a control which others might find excessive.

The Trustees were certainly not dilatory. At this, their very first meeting, they were ready to act at once, with a view to opening in the autumn, and they proceeded forthwith to the appointment of staff. They envisaged an establishment of four tutors, but decided for the present to limit themselves to three. Even that number seems generous when we note that they were sure of an enrolment of only four pupils! They clearly expected that the reputation of the scholars they hoped to appoint would quickly attract more. For what was in those days considered the premier position, that of tutor in divinity, they were confident of securing the service of no less a luminary than Dr John Taylor. They resolved: 'That the Revd Dr John Taylor of Norwich be chosen Tutor in Divinity; that a letter of invitation be immediately sent him; and at the same Time another to the Gentlemen of Norwich acquainting them with this application, and requesting the Favour of their Concurrence therein'. They also resolved to invite 'Mr Holt of Kirkdale near Liverpool' to teach 'Natural Philosophy and the Mathematicks'; and 'Mr Samuel Dyer of London' for 'Languages and polite Literature'. Mr Dyer, however, declined the invitation, and it was later resolved to manage for the time being with only two tutors: which, since the initial enrolment shrank by 25 per cent, still leaves the very favourable staff to student ratio of 2:3! The work was to be divided between the two, and since the teaching of moral philosophy later became a sore point with Dr Taylor, we note the resolution: 'That during the Infancy of the Design, he be desired to undertake the province of Moral Philosophy till a particular Tutor is appointed for that service'.

Soon after that June meeting, then, Dr Taylor would receive the letter of which a copy is appended to the minutes of the meeting. It was not unexpected. Seddon indicates that he has been much in communication with Taylor about the project, and says: 'the Society has had its attention turned upon you, ever since this design was first formed; it was a great measure through the Authority of your Name, and the Hopes of engaging you in the Scheme, that subscriptions have been collected with so much success.' The whole letter is couched in the most respectful, not to say reverential, terms, and it is clear that Seddon and the other movers attached very great importance to securing so eminent a scholar to head the staff. What they do *not* suggest, however, is that he will be the Principal, or will exercise any direction over the other tutors. Seddon really seems to have intended to reserve the key role to himself, as Secretary of the Trustees. It will become apparent that it is doubtful whether Taylor fully understood this.

That Taylor already knew he was to be invited to join the academic staff of the Academy is clear from his letter of June 1757 to his close friend Dr Benson.[4] It clearly indicates that he was expecting to teach divinity there, and that he knew Samuel Dyer was to be invited to teach moral philosophy; but it does not mention receiving Seddon's letter, which indeed is hardly likely to have reached him so soon after the decisive meeting of the Trustees on 20 June. His letter shows that Taylor still thought the location of the new academy was open to debate, and he has a strong view on the question, quite opposed to siting it in Warrington. He believes that a rural setting is preferable, under one roof, where the students can be gathered and shepherded '*in uno claustro*', and shielded from the lures of 'alehouses, Taverns, Gaming, Girls, idle Company, Frolics, Vice'. A vacant country house, Hoghton Tower, the property of a family 'in the Dissenting interest', could, he believes, be made available and would be far better than Warrington or Ormskirk, where

> an Academy, in any Degree numerous, will probably in no long time be infected with Vice, perhaps in several Shapes, nor will it be in the Power of the most vigilant Tutors to prevent it, so the Academy will be as bad for the Town as the Town for the Academy, & both very troublesome and discouraging to conscientious Tutors.

He also asserts his opposition to Francis Hutcheson's system of moral philosophy, which, as we shall see, became a *casus belli* between him and Seddon. It is truly astonishing that he could be expressing such radical criticisms of the scheme at the very time when the letter inviting him to take a leading part in it was already on its way. This clearly reveals the inadequacy of the preparatory discussions between himself on the one hand, and Seddon, the Trustees, and the cluster of ministers and lay supporters around Warrington on the other. In fact, this letter makes the difference of outlook between them obvious enough to call in question the wisdom both of the invitation and its acceptance; but we read it with the hindsight that came to them too late.

The Trustees certainly went to considerable lengths to anticipate any difficulties Taylor might feel about the financial and domestic terms of the appointment. They recognized that at his age, it might not seem prudent to leave the security of his position in Norwich for a venture which, after all, might fail: a group therefore undertook to assure his income to him for life, 'independent of any unfavourable Accidents, which may possibly attend the Academy'. They also took account of the fact that divinity students would be a minority, and that therefore their tutor would be at a financial disadvantage, since in addition to the stipend of £100, each tutor was to receive two guineas per annum from each student attending his classes. They therefore promised to 'reduce things of this kind', so as to ensure 'equality'. They undertook to reimburse him for the heavy cost of removal from Norwich to Warrington. Two houses, they assured him, were available for consideration: a larger one, which would be suitable if he would consent to take in students with his family, or a smaller one if he did not wish this. It must all have appeared attractive enough, and by October he was in Warrington, in time for the projected commencement of the new Academy, with its three pupils and two tutors.

The Minutes of the Trustees from that first meeting onwards convey the impression of a scheme not sufficiently carefully worked out, and too hastily embarked upon before quite basic requirements had been met. Premises are still being negotiated for when the Academy is already in operation. It is by no means clear where the tutors were housed on arrival, and before long Taylor and his household are apparently sharing accommodation with college activities. In the first letter dated from Warrington to Dr Benson, two years after his arrival, he writes of having met with 'ill usage' from the very beginning, and of having been 'forced' to move house 'much against [his] will'.[5] He and poor Mrs Taylor must have rued their move from Norwich almost from the day they arrived.

Nevertheless he applied himself to his new task with characteristic thoroughness. Two more students brought the enrolment to five during that first year, and thereafter the numbers grew into double figures. Probably the student body became a little less submissive as it grew more numerous and more diverse. Divinity students preparing for ministry would always be a minority, but others would receive some tuition from Dr Taylor. Ostensibly, he meant to be the reverse of authoritarian in his teaching. His opening address to his students at the beginning of their course has often been quoted as a model of that open-minded and rational approach to religious belief which was challenging the old orthodoxy, and which ultimately led to the wholly undogmatic 'Faith and Freedom' of modern Unitarianism. We must remember, though, that for Taylor, the Scriptures were still authoritative, indeed infallible:

> I solemnly charge you that in all your religious inquiries, you carefully, impartially, and conscientiously attend to evidence, as it lies in the holy scriptures. That you keep your mind always open to evidence; that you labour to banish from your breast all prejudice, prepossession, and party zeal; that you study to live in peace and love with all your fellow Christians; and that you steadily assert for yourself, and freely allow to others, the inalienable rights of judgement and conscience.[6]

Long after Warrington Academy had ceased, and its successor, Manchester College, had moved to York, Wellbeloved, one of the tutors there, continued to refer his students to this statement.

Unhappily, Taylor does not seem to have been able consistently to adhere to his own principles. His students found him 'dictatorial and impatient of contradiction'. This is hardly surprising when we reflect on the enormous gulf between his learning and their first fledgling efforts. It is, perhaps, a little unwise to encourage beginners to think that their reasonings will be as just and well-founded as those of an expert who has devoted a lifetime to intensive study of the subject. Humility and readiness to learn before forming a judgement become the novice in any field. But it is easy to pick up, from the reminiscences and hints that have survived, a clear impression that the appointment had not, after all, been a wise one. Dr Taylor was already over sixty. For years, his contact with young people had been in the very different setting of pastoral relations in a congregation where he was respected and loved. Returning to the classroom, he was using the teaching methods of an earlier day. Some of the pupils were only what today would be senior schoolboys, not all very seriously disposed to study. He gave them a hard time, and some of the youths perhaps reciprocated.

I know the feeling!

Even divinity students preparing for the ministry must have found the course very demanding. The Revd William Turner gives the following account of the rigorous grounding in linguistic study which Taylor made the foundation of his teaching of divinity. It is drawn from the papers of the Revd Thomas Astley of Chesterfield, who had been one of Taylor's pupils:

> . . . in addition to the ordinary mode of grammatical instruction, he drew up for them, and caused them to copy and get by heart, a sort of sacred vocabulary, containing copious and elaborate lists of the various Hebrew denominations of persons, things, relations, qualities, &c.; distinguishing the various synonyms, with their different shades of meaning, and often supplying the corresponding Greek terms in the Septuagint and New Testament.
>
> He afterwards gave them a course of lectures on the idiomatic phraseology of the Hebrew Scriptures, at the same time pointing out the influence which these idioms frequently have upon the Greek of the New Testament, and the necessity of being acquainted with and constantly attending to them, in order to attain a just idea of the exact sense of many passages in the New Testament writers. The rules and observations contained in those lectures were illustrated by a vast number of quotations from both parts of the sacred volume, as well as by many from Greek and Latin classics.[7]

It is hardly surprising that the students were sometimes 'restive'; but one can only admire both the liberal spirit and the profound scholarship Taylor regarded as essential equipment for the ministry, and sought to awaken in those preparing for it.

Despite all his frustrations and miseries at Warrington, the story of these years is by no means a record of failure. Although his major works were behind him, some further publications belong to this period. One is the 'Scheme of Scripture Divinity' which he drew up for his classes in that subject, and printed privately for their use – an anticipation of the modern practice of providing students with pages of prefabricated notes. These were published posthumously, and were apparently useful not only to ministers in his own tradition; we find the document republished by the very liberal bishop Watson of Llandaff,[8] who says they were 'much sought after' by the clergy.

Another product of these years is of greater interest, arising as it does, not from the daily requirements of the curriculum, but in response to a challenge which aroused deep feelings in the old man. Once more, as long before in defence of Joseph Rawson, he is moved to write and publish in a cause about which he has strong convictions. As early as 1750 and 1751, in Lancashire, there had been stirrings of interest in making provision for 'a proper variety of public devotional offices' for Dissenting congregations, and in 1752 a committee had been formed to frame proposals. Leading Dissenting ministers were sounded, among them both John Seddon and John Taylor. Taylor declined to be involved, but Seddon was an enthusiastic participant in the scheme. There was controversy, of course, over such an innovation. Its advocates pointed to the needs of some adherents of the established church in Liverpool who were finding themselves attracted to the liberal theology and freedom of thought they encountered among some Dissenters, but not to the non-liturgical form of their worship. Some introduction of liturgical forms, it was alleged, might help them to feel more at home among their new-found spiritual kin. This aroused all Taylor's Puritan instincts, and he wrote a vigorous reassertion – defence is too weak a word – of the tradition of free prayer by the minister. He did not live to see it published: it was finished only just before his death, and the preface is dated 25 February; but it added posthumously to his reputation. Even his Calvinist opponents could welcome this book, and express gratified surprise that the great scholar still had 'so much of the old Puritan in him'.[9]

The book is entitled '*The Scripture Account of PRAYER in an Address to the Dissenters in Lancashire Occasioned by a new Liturgy some Ministers, of that County, are composing for the use of a Congregation of Liverpool . . .*'. Though it is a defence of free prayer as against prescribed forms, Taylor is careful to emphasize 'That by *free* or *extempore* Prayer is not be understood any crude, unpremeditated effusion in an entire dependence upon some supposed sudden extraordinary motion or suggestion of the Spirit of God'. The minister is to be thoroughly disciplined by the study of Scripture and the practice of constant prayer and devotion. In support of his case, Taylor appeals to the practice of the first three centuries in the church, and shows familiarity with the Fathers, quoting Justin Martyr, Tertullian and Origen. A typical passage will give the feeling of this earnest little treatise:

> Natural plainness and simplicity in divine Worship is most suitable to the Gospel; which simplicity if we destroy by adding to it the paint and patches of bold and wanton fancies, we destroy its purity, power, and truest beauty. That way of worship is most pleasing to God, not that we imagine, but which he chooses. And, my Countrymen, may you not more stedfastly believe, that your own scripture-way is more acceptable? And is it not much safer for you to adhere to what you know Revelation will vindicate? And surely you may bear with some improper expressions, or even incongruities of speech, (if it should so happen,) if the Prayer be affectionate, and hath such Oratory as the great God is pleased to listen to, the Oratory of a warm and sincere heart. Some in St *Augustin's* days ridiculed the coarse and uncouth language, which some of the Bishops and Ministers then used in Prayer. 'But, saith he, let them know, there is no voice besides the affection of the soul, that reaches the ear of God; and they will not jeer, if perchance they observe that some of the Bishops and Ministers of the Church do call upon God with barbarisms or solecisms,' that is, with odd and improper ways of speaking. 'For,' according to *Chrysostom*, 'God seeketh not the eloquence of the tongue, nor the elegant composition of words, but the flower and vigor of the soul.'[10]

One of Taylor's arguments is of some interest for its reference to the success the Methodist movement was enjoying. Advocates of the proposed liturgy had suggested that it would make

Dissenting worship more acceptable to Anglicans who were not entirely happy with their own, and would make it easier for them to 'come over'. Taylor retorts:

> But if this Letter Writer wants to make Proselytes, it is plain, in the case of the Methodists, that free Prayer is the more successful way. If their Preachers (though professed Churchmen) had read their Prayers, they would have made no great impressions; but in the use of free Prayer they have drawn considerable numbers out of the Church, and settled them in Congregations all over the land. For one Churchman this Author will bring over to the Dissenters by his Liturgy, the Methodists, I will venture to say, have brought over a hundred, if not a thousand, in the use of free Prayer[11]

It would have been unwelcome to John Wesley, and would have appalled his brother Charles, to hear that they were taking people out of the church and settling them in separate Methodist congregations; but whatever their intention might be, this clear-sighted observer describes what was in fact happening.

He concludes his appeal on a rather touching personal note. Though a native of Lancashire, he has ministered so long elsewhere, he says, that he comes back there 'in the capacity of a stranger', to participate in the training of young men for the ministry: 'And now I have consecrated my ripest, the declining years, to the service of true Religion among you . . . I most heartily wish that the Gospel may shine among you in all its heavenly Splendor.'[12] The slightly plaintive tone of this appeal, written so shortly before his death, reflects the situation in which he found himself at Warrington, where he and Seddon were on opposite sides in this controversy. Without doubt, this difference was a major cause of friction between them.

John Seddon continued to be deeply involved in the scheme, and was chiefly responsible for the eventual publication of the liturgy, which appeared after Taylor's death;[13] but he declined an invitation to the Octagon Chapel in Liverpool, where it was introduced and used, and we are told he himself continued to use extempore prayer in his own ministry. The scheme produced no lasting effect, but is an early manifestation of the desire for more formally ordered worship that emerged more strongly in later years, and produced eventually the splendid *Free Church Book of Common Prayer* of 1929, and the service books now published by the Free Churches. But Taylor's book is worth its place in the library of Puritan spirituality as an admirable apologia for the use of disciplined extempore prayer in public worship.

It speaks volumes for Taylor's dedication that he accomplished so much when his personal situation was very far from happy and comfortable. His discomfort cannot be attributed entirely to the treatment he received. It is hard to disagree with the judgement that Taylor's appointment as divinity tutor 'was an unfortunate choice; he belonged to a generation which was passing, and the students were restive'.[14] It would hardly be surprising if in his unhappiness he became somewhat crotchety and difficult in these last years. His physical condition would certainly be a factor in any such development. The rheumatism that was the legacy of those cold, damp winters at Kirkstead had now taken a strong hold, compelling him to use a crutch. Such pain is very wearing in the daytime, and doubly wearisome in the nights of broken sleep. Elizabeth was also in poor health. But much more must be put down to the insensitivity with which he was treated, and to the indignities which he suffered. Towards the end of his life, he wrote a letter to a friend which paints a very gloomy picture of these last, sad years:

Before I came hither, and in order to induce me to engage in the academy, the principal gentlemen at Manchester, in their several letters to me said everything encouraging, promising or intimating that my life should be as easy, comfortable, and happy as ever. I was also assured that my joining in the design was the very foundation of the whole fabric. I believed them; I came in hope of being more extensively useful, not doubting but I should enjoy the remnant of my life in tranquility and peace. But alas, sir, I am sorry to tell you, I have found quite the reverse. My condition ever since I came to Warrington, has been very uneasy, and I may say, wretched. Under which, had I not been habituated to hope and trust in God, I must have sunk. It is not possible I should continue here, either on my own account, or that of the academy; for what good can be done in a place of variance and contradiction? Under that reasonable and friendly usage I had a right to expect, I should perform my work with alacrity and pleasure, and, by the blessing of God, with good success; but under such contumelious treatment, my spirits are sunk, my good designs and endeavours are discouraged, and my health affected and impaired.[15]

The tone of so despondent a letter accords well with the situation that followed the crucial meeting of the Trustees, when he must certainly have felt that his position had become impossible. He was in fact delivered from it by his sudden death, not long after that painful episode. But the letter clearly indicates that from the very beginning he had found himself in a situation very different from his expectation, and that it had declined from bad to worse. What were the roots of the trouble?

Conclusive evidence is wanting, and 'reading between the lines' is a hazardous undertaking; but those early minutes do suggest that too many matters had been left incomplete before the first tutors and pupils arrived. There is no clear indication how the Taylors were housed when they came from Norwich – a very big upheaval for an elderly couple not in good health. It is only in the minutes of the fourth meeting of the management committee, 9 March 1758, that it is resolved to pay the two tutors their first half-year's salary of £50 each, and also to reimburse Taylor for his removal expenses, as had been promised the previous year. If that is typical of the casual way the glowing promises of the invitation were kept, the Taylors must very soon have regretted that they had ever left Norwich.

Even more serious was the failure to make clear to Taylor beforehand precisely to what role he was being invited. The terms of the correspondence, as well as his own standing and scholarship, must have led him to expect to be treated with a good deal of deference, which he evidently felt he was not. As he says in his letter, he had been 'led to believe' that his presence and prestige were 'the very foundation' of the whole enterprise. But on arrival, he encountered John Seddon, a vigorous and forceful personality, without whose driving energy the whole project would never have been brought to fruition. The minutes of the Trustees and their committee convey a distinct impression of Seddon managing everything. As secretary of the Trustees, he seems to have exercised executive powers, perhaps rather dictatorially. Moreover, he took upon himself to give some tuition in fields of study which Taylor regarded as within his own responsibility. He was also appointed librarian, and seems not to have responded as readily as Taylor would have wished to his requests for the purchase of particular books for the use of his students. Underlying these apparently trivial irritations there was evidently a serious clash of personalities.

It is when we take a closer look at John Seddon that we begin to understand the depth of animosity that came to a head in the final event. His many undertakings indicate one of those able, active, organizing people without whom nothing much would ever get done, but who can be difficult colleagues for those who do not share all their convictions and enthusiasms. There were at least two important areas in which he and Taylor held sharply conflicting views: the use or non-use of forms of prayer in public and collegiate worship; and the basis for the teaching of moral philosophy.

As we have seen, Taylor was strongly opposed to the plan to produce a liturgy for Dissenters, in which Seddon was a prime mover. It was not until 1763 that he and others published *A Form of Prayer and a New Collection of Psalms for the use of a congregation of Protestant Dissenters in Liverpool*, but it is easy to imagine the tension between the two while the old man was still alive. It can be no coincidence that one of the matters of difficulty with Taylor, mentioned more than once in the Minute Book, is his reluctance to allow the pupils under his care to join in the common prayers, preferring to conduct devotions for them in the house they shared with him. It becomes clear that this reflects a difference between himself and Seddon, and possibly other colleagues, over the form and manner of the prayers, when we read in the Minutes of 14 December 1758:

> Determinated: That the Business of the Devotions of the Academy is a Public Concern, common to all the Tutors; That it should seem proper, and it is desired that the Tutors would All in their Turn frequently bear a part in conducting the Devotions of the Academy; and that the young gentlemen be always permitted to have a Written Prayer before them, to prevent the necessity of an Impromptu, and those Confusions, which must otherwise frequently and unavoidably occur.

This was obviously a severe and wounding defeat for Taylor, who seems to have fought a losing battle to hold those students within his household to his own practice. Seddon and others evidently did not find the good doctor's 'Impromptu' prayers as appropriate as he thought them. Perhaps their length made the students 'restive', and caused the 'confusions' which it was desired to prevent.

An even sharper subject of disagreement between the two was the teaching of moral philosophy. Taylor had a very strong interest in this, and took a well-defined position, for which he was well known. The system of Francis Hutcheson, professor at Glasgow, he strongly opposed. In that letter of 25 June 1757, to his friend Dr Benson, he says:

> I am much pleased that they have nominated Mr *Sam Dyer*, for moral Philosophy and polite Literature, as hoping that he is not in Mr *Hutcheson's* scheme of *Glasgow*, which would by no means suit my Divinity, nor be any proper foundation of it, but believing that he understands better principles. I hope he will accept the useful office. Pray my kindest respects to him, when you see him.

But as we have seen, Mr Dyer did not accept the invitation, and at first, owing to the decision to open the Academy with only two tutors, this subject was entrusted to Taylor. Later, when his poor health led him to suspend lectures in this field for a time, Seddon started to study it with some of Taylor's pupils. This should obviously not have happened without consultation with Taylor; but what made it totally unacceptable to him was that Seddon embraced the very doctrines that Taylor was known to abhor. Seddon, who had been educated at Caleb Rotheram's academy at Kendal, and then Glasgow University, is said to have been a 'favourite pupil of Francis Hutcheson and William Leechman'.[16] Leechman was an admiring friend to Taylor, and it was he who had moved the university to award him the Doctorate of Divinity on the score of his Hebrew scholarship; but Hutcheson was the moral philosopher to whose teaching Taylor was so strongly opposed.[17] This may sound like a storm in an academic teacup, but that would be a very superficial impression. For a modern parallel, compare C. S. Lewis's revulsion at the statement in a school textbook of English, that to say a spectacle is 'sublime' is not really to say anything about the scene we are surveying, but actually means only 'I have a sublime feeling as I look at it'.[18] Hutcheson's system was based on the view that we have a 'moral sense' by which we discern the difference between good and ill. To his critics, this seemed to make ethical judgement very subjective, almost a matter of feeling. Taylor was vehemently opposed to this, and followed Richard Price in maintaining that to say an action is right or wrong is not to make a statement about my feelings of approbation or disapprobation, but about what the action *is*. 'Good' and 'evil' are clear and distinct ideas, incapable of analysis, and intuitively discerned by the reason, like the self-evident axioms of the mathematician. From them, by the right use of reason, authoritative moral judgements may be deduced. Here was another area of sharp disagreement between the two men. Seddon would doubtless feel personally challenged by Taylor's publication of two short works on this subject, *An Examination of Dr Hutcheson's Scheme of Morality* (1759), and *A Sketch of Moral Philosophy* (1760).

Taylor and Seddon were of different generations, at a time of great change that is graphically described by H. L. Short:[19]

> By the middle of the eighteenth century, the English Presby-
> terians . . . were facing a new situation, and they themselves
> changed to meet it. It can be seen even in their faces. The
> portraits of the Presbyterian divines of the early part of the
> century show men of assured dignity, in formal wigs and
> clothes of elegant cut. But in the second half of the century the
> faces have become more individual and calculating, either
> with natural hair or with less pretentious wigs and much more
> sober dress. Formerly clients of the Whig magnates and not far
> from the seats of power, they have now become a segregated
> middle class.

The two men well illustrate that divide. Seddon was one of the
new men, and Warrington Academy was designed for this new
world. He and Taylor had evidently corresponded, but had they
ever met, before that fateful October of 1757? In a short note to
Dr Benson in April 1754, Taylor says, 'I purpose, when Mr
Bourn comes home, to go into Lancashire, where I have not been
for several years.'[20] Did he go? And even if he did, was the
scheme beginning to be formed at that date? And if it was, did he
meet Seddon and discuss it? It is unlikely; and it would seem that
almost from the moment they did meet, when it was too late,
these deep differences led to difficulty. There seems to have been
a mutual antipathy that made it impossible for these differences
to be overcome. Maybe an important factor in the tragedy was
the length and difficulty, in mid-eighteenth century, of the
journey from Norwich to Warrington. In modern times, there
would surely be many meetings between all parties before such
an important appointment would be offered and accepted. But
the negotiation with Taylor was probably all by correspondence,
and the long trek to Warrington was a one-way journey, undertaken only when the decision had been made.

The committee minutes of 9 March 1758 record the decision
to approach Mr John Aikin of Kibworth as a third tutor. Aikin
had been Philip Doddridge's first pupil at Kibworth, and after
further studies at Aberdeen University, had become his assistant
at Northampton. He then kept a school at Kibworth. He was a

man of 'a gracious and a liberal spirit'. We have a happy glimpse of the lighter side of student life in a Dissenting Academy from Philip Doddridge during his Kibworth days. He mentions students' amateur dramatics, for which costumes had been improvised from some of 'Miss Jennings' petticoats'! This same Miss Jennings became Mrs Aikin, and she and her husband brought with them to Warrington an appreciation of the value of such innocent recreation. There are signs that not only the doctrinal grimness, but also the repressive narrowness that sometimes disfigured the older Puritanism, was undergoing modification.[21]

The long letter of invitation to Aikin, copied in the minute book, shows how important the name and fame of Dr Taylor had been for the launch of the Academy, and were still thought to be for attracting students and staff:

> The Society had their eyes on Dr. Taylor from the beginning; he most cordially approved the Scheme, gave us encouragement to hope he would undertake the Province assigned him; and it was through the Authority of his Name that the Subscriptions were solicited with so much success.

We notice once again that there is no suggestion that Taylor will be the Principal, or exercise any leadership or direction over his colleagues. At subsequent meetings of the committee, it becomes necessary to make it clear that each tutor is quite autonomous within his own province. Among the three tutors, as in the Trinity, 'none is afore or after another'! But Taylor may be forgiven for having expected to be treated with greater deference, in view not only of the tone of his own letter of invitation, but of such a use of his name in writing to another prospective member of staff.

The Minutes of the meeting of the Committee of 14 December 1758, the same that appointed Seddon librarian, record the curious resolution 'that Dr Taylor be desired to remove his bed out of the library as soon as he conveniently can'. This apparently reasonable request must surely be seen as evidence of the inadequacy and discomfort in the arrangements for the Taylors' housing, which appears to have been in a building now to be used in part for other college purposes. Detailed regulations for the use of the library follow. All the tutors are to have keys, but Seddon is to be in attendance every Saturday morning to issue books to the students.

Another resolution deals with that troublesome matter of fees: 'In consideration of the Inequality of the Salary which according to the present appointment of the Fees will unavoidably take place among the Tutors, and particularly that the Tutor in Divinity will at all Times have the least', it is agreed 'to the full satisfaction of All the Tutors' to increase all their salaries to £120 per annum, and that for the future, the students' fees for lectures be paid to the Treasurer, to be received into the common fund'. Well, better late than never; but it will be noted that more than a year has passed before anything is done to fulfil the undertaking clearly made in that letter of invitation to Dr Taylor in the summer of 1757. Had he been humiliated by having to draw attention to the 'inequality', and remind the Committee of that promise? It seems quite possible; but in any case it is obvious that he had suffered for more than a year the indignity of being financially the least rewarded though by far the most eminent of the tutors, despite the firm promise made in the letter of invitation before he moved.

That egregious bed is not the only ominous hint, in the Minutes of that December meeting, of growing friction between Taylor and Seddon and the Committee. On the recommendation of two of his correspondents, Dr Taylor had brought before them the name of a Mr William Campbell as Tutor in moral philosophy, but the Committee directs him to reply that 'the present state of the fund would not permit' the appointment of a fourth tutor. That may well have been a prudent decision, but Taylor must have felt deeply humiliated. Moreover it is easy to see that Taylor's choice would be of someone who shared his views, and this would not be acceptable to Seddon. The financial consideration may have been genuine enough, but it was a handy means of thwarting an unwelcome proposal.

In his funeral sermon, Harwood assures us that Taylor 'always spoke . . . with the greatest respect of his *Fellow-Tutors*', and that there was 'always the greatest harmony' among them. This may be substantially true, and yet may not exclude the possibility that their understanding of their respective roles, in relation to each other, was perhaps not always identical. This seems to be suggested by two paragraphs in the Minutes recording directions 'that the Tutors should pursue the Duties and Business of their several Provinces perfectly distinct'; that in matters of common concern, 'the Power of the Tutors be perfectly equal, and their Votes Determined'; and that they be 'desired to meet together frequently', with Seddon in attendance, 'for friendly consultations on such particulars as shall appear to concern the General Good of the Academy; and the Useful and Honourable discharge of the Duties of their respective Stations'. Here also are those directions relating to the daily devotions, which were another problem between Taylor and his colleagues.

It is easy to see that the obsequious terms in which Taylor had been invited to his post had led him to expect that he would be, if not the Principal of the new Academy, nevertheless a very powerful voice in the shaping of the curriculum and the direction of the tutors; it is equally clear that neither Seddon nor the other tutors shared that understanding of his position. Such want of clarity in the initial arrangements was bound to lead to difficulty. When, subsequently, another tutor did take over the teaching of moral philosophy, this became a major source of friction. Taylor had been teaching it since the opening, but he now found that Hutchesons's system was to be followed. His abhorrence of this was widely known; he published his critique of it in 1759, along the line taken by Richard Price in his attack on Hutcheson's system the previous year. Taylor had evidently expected to decide the system to be followed, and was rather bluntly told that this was no longer his province. This represented a heavy defeat in a field in which he had expected to exert a determinative influence. It is easy to understand that he was deeply mortified.

The minutes that record the final acts in this tragedy make painful reading. In his frustration and misery, the old man had evidently poured out his troubles to some of his friends, perhaps in letters similar to the one we have seen. Inevitably, reports of this had come to some of the committee members, who were naturally concerned at the damage it was doing to the Academy. In the minutes of the management committee dated 10 January 1760, we find the following paragraph, scored in the margin for emphasis:

> Agreed that a letter be wrote to Dr. Taylor to acquaint him that the complaints he had made in various places of the uneasiness he is under in his present situation, have come to the knowledge of the Society, and which it is apprehended will be greatly to the detriment of the Academy – to desire that he would be very explicit in pointing out his complaints in a letter to some of the Gentlemen of the Committee – and that a meeting shall be appointed upon his return to enter upon the consideration of them: and that Mr Haywood and Mr Bentley do immediately prepare the same, and that it be signed by all the Trustees present.

The letter was written, and Taylor responded, but the meeting to resolve the matter was not held until 18 September 1760, eight weary months later. It is easy to imagine the petty irritations and miseries of that last year; and Taylor, who had been solicited in such flattering terms three years before, must have come to the fateful meeting with the gloomiest of expectations, and have left it utterly humiliated.

In the minutes of the meeting, 18 September 1760, Taylor's nine paragraphs of complaint are set out on the left hand side of the page, which is divided by a ruled line down the middle, with the Committee's response opposite each. While some of Taylor's points are trivial in themselves, and the Committee's responses may appear reasonable enough, the overwhelming impression is of the depth of Taylor's misery, and the unfeeling frostiness of the Committee's response, behind which we must surely detect Seddon's attitude. Both are well illustrated in the first item. Taylor writes:

I am greatly dissatisfied and disgusted that almost from the first of my coming, and all along I've been contradicted, counteracted & opposed in things relating to my repose or that were the result of my Judgment in the discharge of my Duty: Insomuch that my Life from first to last has been made very unhappy, my sleep broke, my spirits sunk, my mind disturbed, and rendered incapable of doing my Business with that Freedom and alacrity, Life & Vigour which the high importance of it requires.

Alongside this we read:

In Answer to the Doctor's first Article of Complaint we say that when the particulars to wch he refers were mention'd it appears to us that they were either such as had no relation to the Academy; or such as it was highly expedient that this Committee should interfere in. Of the first kind was his dissatisfaction about the price he paid to Mr Holt for his Board; and of the latter was the Desire of the Committee that he should remove his bed from the public Library: in one of these we have no concern: and in the other we think we need no Defence.

It is quite impossible to think that such trivial matters were all that Taylor had in mind when he wrote such a bitter complaint, and the tone of the answer reveals an insensitivity utterly unworthy of the occasion. This impression is not mitigated by the other eight complaints and responses, even where Taylor may seem querulous and the Committee formally in the right. It is all too obvious that behind the trivialities lies a huge unhappiness, for which Seddon and the board must take a large part of the responsibility.

This becomes clearest in Taylor's sixth article and the reply to it. These make manifest the personal incompatibility of the two men which is at the root of the particular ground of complaint, and also the difference of understanding of Taylor's right to exert influence over the curriculum. Taylor writes:

I am greatly dissatisfied that a Lecture in Moral Philosophy has been set up of late, and some of my Pupils drawn to attend it, in direct Repugnance to my Principles; and in support of such as I expressly declared against before I came into Lancashire. This must be judged to carry the face of a designed Opposition to me. This is to prepossess and prejudice my pupils against my Instructions. This Confirms all my other Complaints, evidently discovers the true Source of them, & points to the proper remedy. Other Articles I have been careful to Conceal, but this it was not in my power to Conceal. It spread over the Country while I was silent about it, and presently reached Bristol; and was known at London before I got thither. This with other Instances of the like Contumelious and Overbearing nature renders my present situation Odious (and) Intolerable.

Alongside this in the minutes is the following response:

The person here aimed at is Mr. Seddon, who at the request of some of the pupils that were ready for that Branch of Study, consented to read over with them Dr. Nettleton and some other Books, as they understood that the Dr., from the Ill state of his Health, did not intend to give any lectures in Moral Philosophy that session; And as this method taken by Mr Seddon appears to us to have been conducive to the Improvement of the Young Gentlemen, and not in the least intended in Opposition to the Doctor, tho' it was not undertaken by our particular Direction, we cannot help expressing our Approbation of it, and of doing this justice to Mr. Seddon to declare that on this Account and many others, he is entitled to the Cordial Thanks, of all the Friends of this design in wch we are engaged.

Perhaps that minute gave Seddon a certain smug satisfaction; but he must have realised that the whole episode revealed an animosity between himself and Taylor which made the latter's position untenable. It is remarkable that after such a snub, the

1. Dr John Taylor: print engraved for the Hebrew Concordance by
Jacob Houbraken in 1754 from a portrait of 1746.

2a. The Octagon Unitarian Chapel, Norwich, from a drawing by James Sillett, 1828.

2b. An interior view of the Octagon, from a sepia drawing by Maria Clark, c. 1870.

A

SPECIMEN

OF THE

Hebrew Concordance

Adapted to the

ENGLISH BIBLE.

Note; this Mark ¶ diftinguifhes the various Englifh Tranflations.

This Mark * fhews where the Verbs end, and the Nouns, or fome new Form of them, begin.

This Mark † fignifies *in the Hebrew*: as *Lev*. 6. 7. † 5. 26. read thus; in the Englifh Bible *Chap*. 6. 7. in the Hebrew *Chap*. 5. 26.

When any Verfe is repeated, as *Exod*. 25. 20, 20, the Meaning is, that the fame Hebrew Word, tranflated by the fame Englifh Word, is found twice in that Verfe.

כפר

כפר 886
hath feven Significations.

    I. *Picare*, *pice* *obtegere* : *Propitiatorium*.

Et picato וְכָפַרְתָּ   1

כפר

and fhalt pitch *Gen*. 6. 14,

Cum pice בַּכֹּפֶר   *   2
with pitch — 14.

Propitiato- כַּפֹּרֶת   *   3
rium

a, the Mercy-Seat *Exod*. 25

---

3. Specimen used by Taylor to solicit three-guinea subscriptions for his Hebrew Concordance.

My dearest Friend,   Norwich Apr. 16. 1754.

Glad am I, and thankful to God, you are so well recover'd
from your late Indisposition, wch gave me much uneasiness. I am
very loth to trouble you with any of my affairs. I wish you could
at Leisure look over the Preface. I have drawn up a kind of
Dedication, wch may be inserted, if you think it proper. The Arch -
bishop of Canterbury I think should first See it, left there should
be any thing in it which he dislikes. But Mr Waugh can
wait upon his Grace for that. But I would have you See it
first; and if you think it needless or improper it shall be
left out. I have here added a List of those who have
pay'd ye whole Subscription. Our Service to Mrs Benson.
I purpose, when Mr Bourn comes home, to go into Lanca -
shire, where I have not been for Several years. When
I return I should be glad to see you at Norwich & Mrs
Benson. If you have any Inclination to come, I will
make all ye Haste back again, that I can. I pray
God continue & establish your Health. I am,

                    my dear Friend, your
                    Sincerely affectionate

                                        John Taylor

The 2d Vol. will be, I apprehend, much larger than the
first, and I would gladly
prevail with Mr Waugh to
be a little more frugal of
ye Paper; & not make such
large Breaks.

4. Facsimile of letter 14, Appendix V, slightly reduced. Taylor's
medium careful hand, exhibiting his idiosyncratic formation of
the letter *e*. See p. 200.

great man did not immediately leave the place; but perhaps he
had no ready refuge. He was by now in such poor health that
such action would have been difficult. But the depth of his misery
was obvious. Harwood tells us:

> The last time I saw him, he bitterly lamented his unhappy situ-
> ation, and his being rendered, (all proper authority, as a Tutor,
> being taken from him) utterly incapable of being any longer
> useful; said his life was not an object of desire to him, when his
> public usefulness was no more, and repeated with great emo-
> tion some celebrated lines to this purpose out of *Sophocles*.[22]

The last of his letters to Dr Benson, dated 7 October 1760,[23]
expresses the same despair. He speaks of 'a thoughtless party,
who are meditating innovations prejudicial to the Dissenting
Interest, & the cause of religion', and prays for 'prudence,
patience and steddiness' to meet this worsening situation, but
adds:

> I cannot now have long to act upon the theatre of life. What I
> earnestly desire is that my conduct, situation and temper of
> mind may be such that the hope of a better world may grow
> stronger and brighter as I am drawing near to the end of this.

He had lost the will to live. His sudden death in his sleep, 5
March 1761, may have seemed to solve the problem; but P.
O'Brien, in his history of Warrington Academy, records the great
damage this dissension did to the infant enterprise. Rumours and
reports of such deep disaffection on the part of so distinguished
a tutor, whose name, as its promoters frankly acknowledged,
had been of great value in securing support for it, could not but
be extremely damaging. Many of Taylor's admirers were outraged by his treatment, and withdrew their support. O'Brien, a
Doctor of Medicine, comments on the action of the trustees:

> This was a tragic and savage wound, which in retrospect was
> quite avoidable. Seddon, the trustees and others, should have

realised that they were dealing with an elderly man in poor health, who was also concerned about his wife's ill-health. His own longstanding rheumatism was a painful and disabling condition, probably with many sleepless nights and other problems which come with age . . . Reasonable tact with a modicum of compassion would probably have assuaged the old man and made his final days a lot happier . . . Instead, he was made thoroughly miserable, and the memory of him in the years ahead was that of a sort of bogeyman who had soured relationships in a most damaging manner for the young Academy.[24]

There is obviously much truth in that judgement; but we have seen, with the help of his letters, that the roots of the trouble went too deep to be removed even had there been, as there certainly was not, a high degree of tact and Christian charity. Taylor and Seddon's Warrington Academy were simply mismatched.

On the manner of his death, Dr O'Brien comments, 'It is likely that the rheumatic disease had affected his heart, thus bringing on sudden failure and death in his sleep.' For his poor wife, Elizabeth, who was some five years his senior, this bereavement must have been the crowning sorrow upon their shared misery, and it is perhaps a mercy that she too was delivered by death a matter of weeks later, at the age of 71. They were both buried at Chowbent, where their married daughter had made her home, and were commemorated by a tablet in the Dissenting chapel there.

It is remarkable that the minutes of the fifth general meeting of the Trustees, held on 25 June 1761, include no mention whatever of the death of Dr Taylor, no tribute or expression of regret: simply a record of letters recommending 'Mr Aikin as successor to Dr Taylor', and resolutions appointing him 'to the Province of Tutor in Divinity'. They also record the appointment of Joseph Priestley 'of Namptwich' to succeed Aikin in charge of 'Languages and polite Learning'. So much for the great man who had been so eagerly recruited at the launch of their enterprise.

A rather sad story

13

That Great Man

So he was described, not by a friend, but by one of his vehement opponents, John Wesley. Though he was widely admired during his lifetime, it has been his fate, during the two-and-a-half centuries since his death, to be remembered chiefly by those who have held him in obloquy. That scurrilous pamphlet by 'Antisocinus', reprinted again and again for more than a hundred years, ensured him a place among the targets of the hate of the Protestant underworld; while on a more respectable level, his name has been chiefly remembered only as one whose teaching Wesley regarded as 'poison', and Jonathan Edwards held responsible for the religious decline of New England. Even studies of the history of the doctrine of Original Sin fail to mention his contribution to its demise. N. P. Williams, for instance, in his Bampton Lectures of 1924, *The Ideas of the Fall and Original Sin*, takes note of the contribution of Jeremy Taylor a century earlier, but never mentions John Taylor, despite the great stir his book made in its day, and the cogency of its arguments.

The reason for this general neglect is probably that Dr Taylor was so vigorously attacked and branded a heretic by his orthodox opponents that it is mainly in that character that he is remembered. It is an unhappy feature of the history of theology that if a writer is thus classified, what he says is suspect, even when it is obviously good sense; while the views of an acknowledged 'Father' such as Augustine, or a revered Calvinist theologian like Jonathan Edwards, are treated with respect, even when they stray into pernicious nonsense. Thus, though Jeremy Taylor criticized the doctrine of Original Sin as taught in his day, and was even suspected of heresy on that account, he became a bishop, and a highly respected Anglican moral and pastoral theologian, so he is felt to be a valuable ally in criticism of the doctrine. John Taylor, on the other hand, labours under the double disadvantage of having been both a Dissenter and an 'Arian', whose views on the subject of the Trinity and the person of Christ proved to be a half way stage to the Unitarianism that ultimately prevailed in his and many other Presbyterian congregations. Consequently, even when his opinions anticipate those of modern Christians, they are treated as tarnished with heresy. He is entitled to a less prejudiced assessment of his achievement.

A well-known tactic, in theological as in political controversy, is to associate the views one wishes to denigrate with some more extreme position more likely to cause revulsion. Thus in our own day any expression of social concern by a church body will be denounced in some quarters as 'Marxism'. In the theological controversies of the eighteenth century, terms which carried progressive degrees of opprobrium were 'Arian', 'Socinian' and 'Deist'. Each has been applied to Taylor, the first with some plausibility, the second with very little. The third term, Deist, could hardly have been directly applied with any credibility at all, but the suggestion that his teaching tended towards Deism, or carried some taint of it, was too handy a weapon to be neglected. Thus Wesley, in the Preface to his treatise on Original Sin, says 'it may be doubted whether' Taylor's teaching 'is not far more dangerous than open Deism itself.'[1] The sincerity of this judgement is not open to doubt; it is only another way of describing the doctrine as 'Dr Taylor's poison'. But it carries the suggestion that Taylor was at heart, but not openly, inclined to Deism; that his teaching was a sort of crypto-Deism, 'old Deism in a new dress', in Wesley's words again. But what does this language mean, and is it applicable in any sense to Taylor?

The term 'Deism' came into use to indicate a movement of thought beginning in the previous century with Lord Herbert of Cherbury (1583–1648), and developed by several writers with varying degrees of departure from orthodoxy. Its most radical expression is found in J. Toland's *Christianity not Mysterious*

(1696), which dismisses altogether any notion of revelation and the supernatural. The whole movement was powerfully influenced by the world view encouraged by Newtonian cosmology. The creation came to be seen as a marvellous but perfectly rational system, in which the Creator no longer needs to interfere. There is no place for miracle; and reason, not revelation, is the guide to truth.

That brief summary makes it obvious at once that it is absurd to call Taylor a Deist, and even 'a leading Deist'.[2] He himself, in *A Scheme of Scripture Divinity*, the outline of his teaching at Warrington, writes:

> Guard your minds well against Deism on the one hand, and Popery on the other. The Deist will persuade you revelation is unnecessary, and consequently that Scripture is no revelation from God, but a fallacy and a cheat . . . He racks his invention to start any difficulty or objection to prove that the Bible is not sufficient to the purposes of revelation.[3]

More insidious is the suggestion that though he himself was no Deist, his teaching set his pupils' feet on the slippery slope that landed them in that position. His great-grandson quotes an allegation that 'Dr Taylor admitted, but wondered at, the fact, that "most of his pupils turned Deists"'. He points out the absurdity of this canard in that the good man did not live to see any of his pupils complete their course![4] His extensive writings, especially by way of exposition of the Scriptures, and that on prayer, afford a total refutation of the allegation of Deism. So does the detail about his personal faith given by Harwood:

> With what holy joy and transporting triumph did he speak of the second coming of our blessed Lord; and with what religious rapture would he anticipate that blessed and happy day! Death had no terrors for him . . . Death would introduce him into a glorious and blessed immortality, where *God would wipe away* all tears from his eyes.[5]

On some important doctrines he clearly moved away from

what continues to be regarded as orthodoxy among the great majority of Christian churches. Two and a half centuries later, however, one cannot but ask how Taylor's position compares with that of many who remain comfortable with membership, and even a teaching role, within the traditional churches. Now that 1 John 5:7, the text Mr Sloss found so attractive, has been universally recognized as a late interpolation, it is impossible to maintain that the New Testament bears unequivocal testimony to the later, fully developed doctrine of the Trinity. There are statements and expression in those books that are far from supporting unambiguously the orthodox doctrine of the relation between the three persons. On his own premise, that Scripture *alone* is the source of sound Christian doctrine, Taylor's position, and that of Samuel Clarke, is hard to refute. Most even of those who accept the complex antitheses of the so-called Athanasian Creed now deplore its uncompromising imprecatory clauses, as did Wesley.[6] Many uncritically orthodox but undogmatic clergy, such as the diarist Francis Kilvert, have expressed their dislike of it, and would probably have found themselves in more congenial company with Taylor than with Sloss. What Taylor's works do reveal is the insufficiency of Scripture *alone* to establish Nicene orthodoxy. Protestants as well as Catholics do in fact, whether they fully recognize it or no, accept a development in the mind of the church. A wish to avoid following Taylor in his anti-trinitarianism, then, should not close our eyes to the value of some of the other conclusions to which his careful study of the Scriptures led him.

Pelagianism is one of the heresies of which he stands accused, and of which he cannot be cleared. But how heretical was Pelagius, and is Taylor? Wesley, when not engaged in controversy with Taylor, could hazard the opinion that Pelagius was perhaps 'one of the holiest men of that age, not excepting St Augustine himself', and add: 'I verily believe, the real heresy of Pelagius was neither more nor less than this: the holding that Christians may, by the grace of God, (not without it; that I take to be a mere slander,) "Go on to perfection;" or in other words, "fulfil the law of Christ".' He adds in parenthesis that Augustine could be 'as full of pride, passion, bitterness, censoriousness, and as foul-mouthed to all that contradicted him as George Fox himself'.[7] Unhappily, in the heat of controversy he himself is quite unfair to Taylor, though without descending to the scurrility he censures in Augustine. Taylor, like Pelagius, sought to press upon his hearers and readers the duty of moral effort, against what he saw as the morally debilitating effect of the Calvinist doctrines of election and irresistible grace. 'Antinomianism', the view that since the elect will be saved by the irresistible grace of God, they need not concern themselves with obeying his law, is an aberration of which Calvinism has always been in danger. Taylor did not deny the need for the grace of God: indeed, there is appended to the fourth edition of his treatise on Original Sin a most perceptive and painstaking note on the Scripture meaning of the word. But he saw a real danger in the Calvinists' determined denial of any place for human effort. If we can do nothing at all but sin, and are entirely at the mercy of irresistible grace or reprobation, what is the point of trying or exhorting others to try? If it is all God's work, leave it to him! Like Pelagius, Taylor exhorted Christians to cultivate virtue, with the help of God. If that be heresy, a good deal of everyday preaching and piety is heretical. Wesley himself, when looking in another direction, and alarmed by the insidious seductions of Antinomianism, could be similarly suspect. The truth is, Augustine's emphasis is one extreme, and Pelagius' alleged position is the other; each in its extreme form is defective, Augustine's no less than its opposite. The truth lies between; and some Christian writers emphasize one side of it, some the other, often in reaction to each other's overemphasis.

Moral earnestness is evident in all Taylor's writings. His chief aim is to ensure that Christian belief is expressed in virtuous lives. He was impatient of the abstruse and complex theologizings that fascinate some minds, and were much engaged in by many of his contemporaries. This is evident in his treatment of that central doctrine, the atonement. We have seen that even such a fervent admirer as Harwood could judge that in this he 'failed most egregiously', and without concurring in that extreme view, we may agree that his short book on that subject does not advance a very convincing elucidation of the central mystery. Nevertheless, in two respects, here also he anticipates some modern insights. In the first place, he was undeniably right to expose the misunderstanding of the Old Testament sacrificial system that is associated with the then prevalent theories of 'penal substitution'. Second, in opposition to that type of theology, he anticipates some modern approaches by looking for the *moral* effect of the atonement. He seeks its rationale in the need to secure the forgiveness of sin without encouraging indifference to it. In this he is akin to proponents of 'moral influence' theories.

As a biblical scholar and expositor, Taylor was both of his time and ahead of it. He was of his time in his unqualified acceptance of the whole Bible (in its shorter, Protestant form) as the inspired word of God. Though often shrewd in his critical judgements, he did not anticipate the advances of the next two centuries. On the other hand, he was ahead of his time, or at least of many in his time, in his insistence that if we are to understand the Scriptures aright, we must not approach them through doctrinal schemes which predetermine the interpretation to be put upon the text. He would certainly have rejected Barth's proposal to read the Scriptures through spectacles whose lenses are Calvin and Luther. He insisted that the sense of any passage must be elucidated by reference to other, related passages. To this end, he devoted those long years of meticulous labour on his Hebrew Concordance. It is the inevitable fate of such compilations to be superseded in the course of time, but his stands, in its century, a landmark in its field, and an achievement for which alone he would deserve to be remembered with honour.

Though for him, the Scriptures were supreme, Taylor held very strongly the importance of reason. In this respect, he was closely in tune with the progressive mind of his day, and was anathema to the more conservative. At the extremes stood the Deists on the one hand, who denied a revelation, and sought to establish some sort of religion by reason alone; and the dogmatists on the orthodox side who might echo Milton's 'Down, Reason, then'. But Milton's immediate qualification, 'At least, vain reasonings down', exhibits the perennial difficulty of deciding when reason is sound and when it is 'vain'. It is impossible to deny reason any place whatever in the elucidation of Christian belief; Richard Baxter had strongly maintained the importance of reason for religion, pointing out that it can only be by reasoning that people who do not already accept the authority of Scripture can be brought to do so. He was at one with his friend Tillotson, who became archbishop, in the view that the greatest harm must be done to religion if it be maintained that there is no reason for belief.[8] But among the dogmatists, if a man's reason led him to question orthodox teaching, it would be dismissed as 'carnal reason': reasoning that manifested the corrupting influence of the fall and original sin.[9] Taylor himself could write: 'Nature and Reason, in their most pure and perfect State, may be sufficient to direct in the Way of Duty, yet when Nature is corrupted, and Reason obscured, or almost quite extinguished, they are by no means sufficient to restore and recover themselves to Knowledge and Obedience to the Truth.'[10] Revelation, then, is necessary, and it is given in Scripture, which is 'infallible'; but reason is also necessary to establish the authority of Scripture, and for the understanding of it. There is an obvious difficulty here. Professor Alan Sell points out the circularity in this account of the relation of reason and revelation: '. . . revelation restores and supplements warped reason, but the deliverances of revelation must be commendable to reason, which, however, is incompetent to weigh them apart from revelation'.[11] 'The majority of Divines were,' he adds, 'despite the pitfalls, inclined to agree with . . . Richard Baxter, that reason is the porter which may admit revelation to the understanding, and the porter must not be negligent.'[12]

In all this, Taylor was influenced by the strong movement of thought known as the 'Enlightenment', which, despite the criticisms to which it is now subject, has irreversibly changed the way educated members of modern Western society, and many all over the world who share their education, now view the world and reason about it. Not only was he influenced by it: in the realm of biblical scholarship and theological thought, his writings contributed to it. The sale catalogue of Schleiermacher's library in Berlin in April 1836 lists a German translation of Taylor's treatise on Original Sin. That book was widely read on the continent, along with translations of other works by writers of similar outlook.[13] When we contemplate the avalanche in biblical and theological studies that occurred in Germany in the following century, we may reflect that such writers were among those whose boldly venturesome footsteps helped to loosen the snow and set it in motion.

Of all Taylor's controversial works, by far the most important is that one that drew down upon him so much vituperation, and provoked such vehement opposition: his demolition of the doctrine of Original Sin. This doctrine was developed by St Augustine from hints in earlier writers, but it was blown up to monstrous proportions on the basis of half a dozen texts, some mistranslated, and all misinterpreted. It had lain like a blight upon Western Christendom. Modified somewhat in the later Middle Ages, it had been revived in full vigour by the Reformers. The Council of Trent continued the process of modification in a more reasonable direction, and thus made it possible for Protestants who questioned the Calvinist doctrine to be accused of inclining to 'Popery'. Williams maintains that it cannot claim to fulfil the criteria of the Vincentian Canon; it has not been believed *semper, ubique, et ab omnibus,* for it was never incorporated into Eastern Orthodox theology. Among Protestants, doubts about it were beginning to be voiced from the time of Arminius, and as we have noted, Jeremy Taylor was humane enough to draw upon himself suspicion as to his soundness on the subject when he reached conclusions that anticipate many of those of John Taylor. But the latter's treatise is the first thoroughgoing broadside attack, and it was devastating. Despite all the heavy artillery that was deployed in the counter-attack, the doctrine expressed in the Westminster Confession and the Thirty-Nine Articles was shattered; and it remained only for the scientific advances of the next century, especially Darwinian anthropology, to sink the wreck. In the twentieth century, we find it either quietly abandoned by theologians, or reinterpreted in terms very like those that are vehemently anathematized by the Reformation formularies.[14]

The problems that the doctrine purported to answer still confront the theologian, namely the evil in human behaviour and the suffering inherent in human experience, to say nothing of 'Nature red in tooth and claw'; and attachment to traditional language is so strong that the expression 'original sin' is still often heard. But as used by a modern theologian, preacher or novelist, it means no more than the observed fact of humanity's disposition to evil, and the way sin becomes endemic in society from generation to generation. It is no longer possible for educated people in the post-Enlightenment culture to maintain with any intellectual integrity that the universality of sin is the *result*, and that all suffering, disease and death, of animals as well as humans, are the *punishment*, of the sin of the first human pair recorded in the first three chapters of Genesis. That doctrine is dead, and for this deliverance considerable credit must be accorded to John Taylor. *of Patkinson and Peacocke.*

The importance of this relief should not be underestimated. So long as the doctrine held sway, its effect on marriage and the family, on pastoral practice, and on the understanding and control of human behaviour, was pernicious. N. P. Williams, after quoting some of Augustine's more appalling passages, rightly says: 'It is, perhaps, better not to speculate with regard to the amount of unhappiness which these ideas must have brought to sensitive souls between the time of their first promulgation and that of the final eclipse of Augustinianism by Darwinism in the twentieth century.'[15] Even the most devoted members of the Prayer Book Society must surely feel that it was grossly inappropriate to begin the baptismal service with the words: 'Dearly beloved, forasmuch as all men are conceived and born in sin'. The shadow such teaching must have cast upon marital relations, if taken seriously, is obvious enough; and the more vigorous and consistent of its exponents, following Augustine's lead, took care that it did indeed have that chilling effect.[16] No less disastrous was its influence upon the care and nurture of the child. We have seen the sharp contrast between Taylor's view and that of the believers in Original Sin, as to 'the ideas most proper to be instilled into the mind of a child'. He must be accorded his share of the credit for the vast improvement in the understanding and management of childhood that has come about since his day.

Of his dealings with young people in the more turbulent adolescent years, we have conflicting impressions. On the one hand, the affection with which he was so long remembered in Norwich supports the documentary evidence that he had a successful ministry among the young; on the other, the students at Warrington seem to have found him dictatorial and demanding. But by that time he was crippled with rheumatism, and had reached the age at which many begin to find the gap between themselves and the young becoming difficult to bridge. As we have seen, there was enough of 'the old Puritan in him' to make him very wary of exposing young people to the temptations of 'alehouses, taverns, gaming, girls, idle company, frolics, vice'.[17] In Warrington or Ormskirk, he feared, the young academicians would quickly succumb. But according to his theology, that did not indicate a corruption of their nature: rather the danger of contagion by the wickedness of the world. So even in that place of variance and contradiction, his freedom from the oppressive doctrine of Original Sin must have enabled him to take a more tolerant view of his young charges than prevailed where it exercised its baleful influence. The Rules of Kingswood School, for example, which Wesley established, chiefly to care for the sons of his itinerant preachers, are remarkable for their hostility to family affection and their total want of understanding of childhood and youth. They would now be regarded as too harsh even for juvenile offenders in a detention centre.[18] The philosophy behind that Spartan regime was obviously based on the belief that only an iron discipline could keep fallen human nature under control. Warrington Academy, despite Taylor's own experience, must have been a happier place for youngsters.

The overall impression of John Taylor, then, is one of humanity and good sense. His estimate of human nature was no doubt too optimistic – at least until he encountered the 'variance and contradiction' of those last unhappy years. Despite his strongly

Puritan fear of the lures of vice, he may be thought to have under-estimated the power of sin and its prevalence in the world. Himself of the 'once-born' type, he was well suited for ministry to a settled congregation of well-educated and self-respecting citizens such as that of the Norwich Octagon. For the evangelistic task among the unchurched masses undertaken by such as Wesley and Whitefield, neither he nor his theology would have been effective. We may suspect that if he had a fault, it was a certain complacency and over-confidence in his own judgement, and an intolerance of opposition, despite his many protestations of openness to correction. Those comments on his congregation at Kirkstead, justified though they may have been, perhaps presage his difficulties at Warrington. But in both those situations there was good reason for his dissatisfaction; and when he found himself in the setting where his great gifts could flower, he sustained a highly successful and devoted ministry, and at the same time produced works which would have been a remarkable achievement for an academic with no such demanding pastorate. He corresponded with such privileged scholars on equal and cordial terms, for example with Kennicott the Hebraist, and Dr Hunt, Professor of Hebrew and Arabic at Oxford. His heterodoxy on the subject of the Trinity and the Person of Christ did not preclude friendship with dignitaries of the established church, including the Bishop of Norwich, or their commendation to their clergy of some of his writings, as we have seen. *Odium theologicum* led to his demonization by those who felt threatened by his writings. It operated more viciously in his day than is usual in theological controversy now that even the firmest believers have to be more sensitive to the questions that modern scientific and biblical studies pose for faith. The respect in which, for example, a later scion of a distinguished family in the Norwich congregation, James Martineau, was held by his trinitarian contemporaries, notwithstanding his Unitarianism, suggests in what light Taylor might have been viewed had he lived two or three generations later. He was a man of his time, and it is unrealistic to expect him to have been right about everything; but he was trenchantly right about some things, and it is time to acknowledge this.

'In lapidary inscriptions, a man is not upon oath'; nor do we expect to hear in a funeral oration a full exposure of all its subject's faults. If John Seddon heard or read Dr Harwood's funeral sermon, no doubt he made some mental reservations. But even allowing for the demands of the occasion, Harwood's testimony to the Doctor's character is very impressive; especially when we remember that, though he had previously admired him, profited by his writings, and corresponded with him, it was only when Taylor moved to Warrington that they met face to face, and their personal friendship began. It was thus during the time when Taylor's character might have been expected to appear in the least favourable light that Harwood became intimate with him; yet this is his testimony:

Nothing could be further from that haughty and supercilious air, and mien, and gait, which other great men insensibly contract, and by which they are publicly known and distinguished from the rest of the species. He was never known to browbeat modest virtue, but to encourage it by every honest art . . .

When I say he was no bigot, I am sensible that I shall be accused of great partiality by some, and of great heresy by others. But if I know anything of good Dr Taylor, this I can with truth affirm concerning him, that he loved good persons of all parties and denominations, however widely they might differ from him; and would frequently repeat it again and again, 'that Christians of all parties are agreed in the great fundamentals of religion, and only differ about some few trifling distinctions; that to embrace the same set of notions as he, or any other fallible man did, was not at all material with regard to man's happiness or salvation.'[19]

Splendid! But as with Wesley's similar sentiments in his sermon on 'The Catholic Spirit', the difficulty arises when we ask which are the 'great fundamentals', and which the 'trifling distinctions'. To orthodox Christans of many denominations, the doctrine of the Trinity is certainly among the former, and the person and work of Christ can by no means be relegated to the latter

<u>class</u>. Harwood himself does not appear to notice the tension, even the contradiction, between what he has just said and what follows:

> If ever he expressed an uncommon warmth and honest indignation against any thing, it was against *Athanasianism*, which he thought one of the greatest corruptions of pure and genuine Christianity, as this doctrine entirely subverts the unity of God, the great and primary foundation of all religion, natural and revealed.

Nevertheless it does seem that, at least until he became involved in 'variance and contradiction' at Warrington, Taylor exhibited the tolerant and peaceable spirit his principles required, and in which his opponents were too often strikingly deficient. Though he was a doughty controversialist, and could attack what he saw as false teaching in trenchant style, he did not descend to personal abuse, or presume to consign to eternal damnation those who differed from him. He did not wish to excommunicate them or withdraw from fellowship. The association of Dissenting ministers he worked hard to form in his last years at Norwich was open to all in the region, regardless of doctrinal differences. He was intolerant only of intolerance.

'I never saw a man's countenance that was a truer index of his mind, than Dr TAYLOR'S', says Harwood. 'There was something placid and ingaging in his air and features, that most powerfully commanded respect and love.' The two most easily accessible portraits accord well enough with that description. One is the engraved plate prefixed to some copies of the second folio of the Hebrew Concordance. The other is a black-and-white drawing in the possession of Harris Manchester College.[20] Both depict a reverend gentleman in clerical gown and bands. He has a high forehead and slightly 'roman' nose. The expression is calm and serious, but by no means forbidding.

His first biographer, writing early in the following century, is obviously echoing the funeral sermon, but he is also able to draw upon the testimony of old people who remembered their minis-

ter of half a century before, and with their tribute we may take
our leave of 'that great man, Dr Taylor of Norwich':

Perhaps there never was a minister more universally respected,
admired, and beloved than Dr Taylor. To this day, those of his
Norwich Congregation who are alive to bear testimony to his
many virtues never mention him but in terms of the highest
esteem and respect. His deportment was never haughty or
supercilious, his conversation never pedantic, but on the
contrary kind and affable, and entirely without the conceit and
self-importance that great men sometimes contract. Yet not
all this liberality on his part could preserve him from being
branded with the terms of 'heretic, deist, worse than deist' . . .
Such was the treatment which Calvinistic bigotry and intolerance gave to one of the most pious and sincere Christians that
ever lived.[21]

A faint biography.

Appendix I

The 'Catholicity' of Baxter, Taylor and Wesley

Both Taylor and Wesley claim to be 'catholic' Christians. In view of Wesley's sharp rejection of all that Taylor stood for, it is instructive to examine just how each understood the term. Neither, of course, used it in a sense very common today, that is, as a label for a distinctive type of church and churchmanship associated with vestments, incense, etc.; nor in the sense in which 'catholics' of that school have maintained an exclusive right to it, as in the claim of the papacy to define the only 'catholic' church, all others being in varying degrees schismatic, if not heretical. Both Taylor and Wesley understand catholicity in the inclusive sense in which Baxter had defined it a century before, in his sermon printed as *The True Catholic and The Catholic Church Described*. In his *Autobiography*, he says of that publication:

> It is for Catholicism against all sects; to show the sin and folly and mischief of all sects that would appropriate the Church to themselves, and trouble the world with the question, Which of all these parties is the Church? as if they knew not that the Catholic Church is *that whole* which containeth all the parts, though some more pure and some less . . . For I apprehended it a matter of great necessity to imprint true Catholicity on the minds of Christians, it being a most lamentable thing to observe how few Christians in the world there be that fall not into one sect or other . . . and how lamentably love is thereby destroyed . . . and the leaders of most sects do not stick to persecute those that differ from them.[1]

It was in this spirit that he offered his suggestion to the committee appointed under Cromwell's government to define the 'fundamentals' of the Christian religion, within which there was to be liberty of worship and church government:

> Therefore I would have had the brethren to have offered the Parliament the Creed, Lord's Prayer and Decalogue alone as our essentials or fundamentals, which at least *contain all* that is necessary to salvation, and hath been by all the ancient Churches taken for the sum of their religion. And whereas they still said, 'A Socinian or a Papist will subscribe all this,' I answered them, 'So much the better, and so much the fitter it is to be the matter of our concord.'[2]

By 'the Creed' Baxter means the 'Apostles' Creed'. Would Taylor have been comfortable with those 'fundamentals', or as Baxter preferred to call them 'essentials'? And would Wesley have found them sufficient? There is, of course, one hugely important difference between them and Baxter: Baxter's aim was a 'comprehension', an inclusive *national* church that would accommodate all who could accept his few 'essentials'; by Taylor's time, he and Baxter's spiritual heirs had settled for mutual toleration across a permanent plurality. So too, *in practice*, did Wesley.

A century after Taylor, in a preface to *The History of the Octagon Chapel, Norwich*, its Unitarian minister, J. Crompton, laments that as a result of controversy, Unitarianism has become

> dogmatic rather than spiritual in its manifestations. The fundamental idea of its system is the pure and perfect one of seeking for the facts and uncontroverted truths of religion as the centre of union for all forms and shades of church and doctrine. That popular exposition of belief which has vulgarly received the name of the 'Apostles' Creed,' contains nearly all the principles adopted into that theology, and around it all faith and feeling in devotion is left to be wound by the individual conscience of everyone for himself.

That Taylor himself understood the term 'Catholic' in this very broad and inclusive sense we have seen evidence in his sermon at the opening of the Octagon.

Both Taylor and Wesley would be familiar with Baxter's writings. In *The Reformed Pastor* (1656), Baxter had censured the factious, partisan spirit shown by many of the ministers:

> It is a great and common sin through the Christian world to take up religion in a way of faction, and instead of a love and tender care of the universal Church to confine that love and respect to a party . . . Of the multitude that say they are of the Catholic Church it is too rare to meet with men of a catholic spirit.[3]

Was this the source of the phrase that gives Wesley the title and theme of his sermon on *The Catholic Spirit*?[4] It was first preached in September 1749, and was published in 1750, six years before Taylor's sermon at the opening of the Octagon. The similarity of sentiment to Taylor's at some points is striking, but so also is the divergence. Wesley, like Taylor, maintains that difference in opinions or modes of worship should be no barrier to unity of spirit and mutual love between Christians. Indeed, in his *Letter to a Roman Catholic*, published in Dublin in 1749, he pleads movingly for mutual goodwill, understanding and help even between Protestants and Roman Catholics.[5] At that same period, in this sermon he says:

> Though we cannot think alike, may we not love alike? May we not be of one heart, though we are not of one opinion? Without all doubt, we may. Herein all the children of God may unite, notwithstanding these smaller differences. These remaining as they are, they may forward one another in love and in good works.

But in applying the words from his text, 'Is thy heart right with my heart?', he introduces a number of doctrinal restrictions which severely limit the scope of the 'catholic spirit' and the realm of 'opinions' in which we can afford to be tolerant:

Dost thou believe in the Lord Jesus Christ, 'God over all, blessed for ever'? . . . Dost thou know Jesus Christ, and him crucified . . . Having absolutely disclaimed all thy own works, thy own righteousness, hast thou 'submitted thyself unto the righteousness of God,' which is by faith in Jesus Christ?

– and so forth. Finally, in part III, he attacks various kinds of 'latitudinarianism', 'speculative' and 'practical':

For . . . a catholic spirit is not speculative latitudinarianism. It is not an indifference to all opinions: this is the spawn of hell, not the offspring of heaven . . .

A man of truly catholic spirit has not now his religion to seek. He is fixed as the sun in his judgement concerning all the main branches of Christian doctrine . . . Observe this, you who know not what spirit ye are of: who call yourselves men of a catholic spirit only because you are of a muddy undertanding . . . Be convinced that you have quite missed your way . . . You think you are got into the very spirit of Christ; when, in truth, you are nearer the spirit of Antichrist. Go, first, and learn the first elements of the gospel of Christ, and then shall you learn to be of a truly catholic spirit.

It is not easy to reconcile this with the eirenic sentiments expressed in the first part of the sermon. But Wesley had already met Taylor's disciples at Shackerley, and felt it necessary to make it clear that his 'catholic spirit' did not extend to such 'silver-tongued Antichrists'. It may – it must – seem strange that he could address such affectionate paragraphs to a Roman Catholic, yet be so vitriolic in his language towards a fellow Arminian Protestant, and moreover such a godly, kindly man as Taylor. But he obviously saw Taylor's radically rationalist views as a threat to the heart of the gospel he preached; a threat so serious that the 'catholic spirit' could not extend to him. He was wrestling with the problem faced by all advocates of toleration within a 'broad church': how broad is 'broad'? Baxter, and even Taylor, draw the boundary *somewhere*. It is easy to say, 'Unity in

essentials, liberty in non-essentials'; the difficulty is to decide
which is which. Clearly, on the principles expressed in the two
sermons, Taylor would have been able to offer Wesley 'the right
hand of fellowship', but Wesley's understanding of 'the catholic
spirit' would not have allowed him to extend it to Taylor: and so
it proved. Probably Baxter would not have been entirely happy
with either of them. Taylor seems to have enlarged the entrance
gate, while Wesley, for all his catholicity of spirit, sounds less
likely to have echoed Baxter's 'So much the better'. The problem
is a perennial one. There has to be *some* minimum of agreement.
There must be at least a few 'fundamentals' that constitute the
sine qua non of Christian profession. But what are they? In this
twenty-first century, even to agree on Baxter's triad requires
toleration of differences between 'liberals' and 'conservatives'
over such matters as the virginal conception, the nature of the
resurrection, and the expectation of the 'second coming'; and a
church that desires to be comprehensive finds itself driven
beyond even Taylor's wide understanding of 'catholic'.

Wesley! fear,
did not display the
'Catholic Spirit'
much when he
was on the attack!

Appendix II

The Exposition of Romans 5:12–21

If the doctrine of Original Sin has any scripture warrant at all, it must be found in this paragraph of the Epistle to the Romans. Even those who claim to find evidence of it everywhere in the Bible, like Henri Blocher with his 'ear finely attuned to Scripture',[1] must admit that it is by this passage that their ear is tuned. If the keynote is not sounded clearly and unmistakably here, it is not so sounded anywhere. How this passage is interpreted is therefore of cardinal importance. This both Taylor and his critics clearly saw, and it is this passage that he submits to his longest and most detailed examination. How well does his exposition bear scrutiny, and how does it compare with modern analyses of the paragraph?

In one fundamental respect, Taylor and his critics alike proceed upon ground which is foreign to most modern commentators. Taylor is quite categorical: 'The Word of God is infallible.' By this he means the Word recorded in Scripture. It was this conviction that made the mastery of the original languages of the Bible central to the education of all would-be expositors. It is no less important for their modern successors, and they have the advantage of two centuries of discovery and research in those languages; but for most of them, the search for the writer's meaning is not identical with the search for 'the Word of God', and they are willing to recognize that when they have done their best, certainty often eludes them. Furthermore, once it is admitted that the biblical writers did not respond like a keyboard to the finger of God, it becomes possible to see that there are different, and sometimes inconsistent, teachings within the Scriptures, possibly even within the epistles of St Paul. This insight was precluded by the view of Scripture Taylor shared with his opponents, so for him it is doubly important to establish the precise meaning, and to show that it does not support the doctrine he attacks. To this passage, therefore, he devotes many pages.

Against the usual assumption that the death that Adam incurred was something more than the death of the body – a 'spiritual' death of alienation from God – Taylor contends, with reference to Romans 5:12, 14, 15:

> No man can deny, or doubt, that the Apostle is here speaking of that DEATH which we all die . . . Of that DEATH, and of no other . . . He is still discoursing upon the same subject, and therefore *evidently*, *clearly* and *infallibly* means the same DEATH in all these places.[2]

The penalty, then, that Adam incurred, and in which he involved all his descendants, was not some corruption of his nature that made it inevitable that they would all sin, but simple mortality. He and they became mortal:

> By *Judgment to Condemnation*, or a judicial Act of Condemnation, ver. 16, 18, it appeareth evident to me, he means the being adjudged to the forementioned DEATH. He means the Sentence of DEATH, of a general Mortality, pronounced upon Mankind in consequence of *Adam's* first transgression.

Taylor pays, and demands of his reader, very close attention to the text; not only to the meaning of words, but to the construction of the argument. He contends that throughout this passage, Paul makes parallel statements; thus:

> In the 19th verse, where he concludes the whole Argument, I think any Man, who duly attends, may see that these Words, *As by one Man's Disobedience many were made Siners* [sic], are of the same Signification with those Words in the following Verse; *As by the Offence of one, Judgment came upon all Men to Condemnation* . . .

Therefore it follows, that by these Words, *By one Man's Disobedience many were made Siners*, means neither more nor less, than that by one Man's Disobedience, *The many*, that is, Mankind, were made subject to DEATH, by the judicial Act of God.

This is the context of his contention that the Hiph'il of *rasha'* does not mean that the human race were made sinful by nature, and must inevitably sin, but that all were involved in the penalty of mortality that Adam brought upon himself and all his race:

Further, let it be well considered, that the Apostle was a *Jew* ... that (though he wrote his letter in *Greek*, yet) he often uses such ways of speaking as are peculiar to the *Hebrew* Language. Now, according to that Language, *Being made Siners* may well signify, *Being adjudged or condemned to Death*. For the Hebrew Word ... which signifies *to be a Siner*, in the Conjugation *Hiphil* signifies to *make one a Siner* by a judicial Sentence, or to *condemn*; and so it is often used.

In support of this claim, fourteen passages from various Old Testament books are cited, such as Deuteronomy 25:1; 1 Kings 8:32; Isaiah 50:9. The Book of Job yields many: 9.20; 10.2; 15.6; 32.3; 34.17; 40.8. On one especially telling example, Taylor comments: 'Job xxxiv.17 *And wilt thou condemn him that is most just?* Make him a Siner by a *judicial* Act, by judging him such?' He concludes:

And you see, according to this way of speaking, how these two Expressions do exactly agree in Signification, and that they might have been expressed by the very same word in *Hebrew*. *By the Offence of one Judgement came upon all Men to Condemnation*; and, *by one Man's Disobedience many were made Siners*. For *Condemnation in Judgment, and making one a Siner*, by a judicial Act, by an Act of Judgment, are the very same thing in the *Hebrew* Language.

He now puts his finger unerringly upon the fallacy at the core of the orthodox Augustinian scheme. Any unindoctrinated person rejects the notion that unborn generations are *made sinners* in any literal sense by the action of a remote ancestor long before they were even conceived. Thus Taylor:

> But besides all this, it is here expressly affirmed, that *the many, i.e.* Mankind, *are made Siners*, not by their *own Disobedience*, but by the Disobedience of *another* Man. Now any one may see, there is a vast Difference between a Man's making *himself* a Siner by his *own* wicked Act, and his being made a Siner, by the wicked Act of *another,* of which he is altogether guiltless. They who are *made Siners* by the Disobedience of *another,* without their own Knowledge or Consent, surely *can* be Siners in no other Sense, but as they are *Sufferers.*

This conviction is the very heart and centre of Taylor's position, and here he is most likely to find the modern reader on his side. No matter how strong a case may be made for the influence of heredity and environment, and the 'solidarity in sin' of any human community, we know in our heart of hearts that we cannot be guilty of a sin that was committed before we existed, and that it is only when we personally assent to and unite ourselves with the sin of others that we become personally guilty. Without this, we may suffer the dreadful consequences of others' sin, whether our ancestors' or our contemporaries'; but if this be called being 'made sinners', it can only be in the paradoxical sense that we are caught up in the penalty of the sin. So, Taylor remarks, Lot would have been, if he had remained in Sodom; and even Christ, according to Paul in 2 Corinthians 5:21, could be 'made Sin for us, who knew no Sin': a paradox which can surely only mean he was *treated as* a sinner, not that he actually became one.

> It seems then confirmed, and cleared to me, beyond all Doubt, that, *By one Man's Disobedience many were made Siners,* the Apostle means neither more nor less, than that by *Adam's* Offence, *the many,* that is, Mankind, were made subject to Death by the Judgment of God.

A long exposition of the whole passage follows, with a discussion of Paul's emphasis that the benefits bestowed in Christ far exceed those lost in Adam, and so forth. In this context, Taylor makes a very telling point:

> For as the word רשע in *Hiphil* signifieth *to be made a Siner,* by a judicial Act, as I have shown before; so the word צדק, *to be righteous, to be justified,* in the same conjugation *Hiphil* signifieth *to be made righteous* by a judicial Act, i.e. *to be acquitted, absolved.* And thus, as it ought to do, it standeth directly opposite to *being made a Siner* by a judicial Act.

A score of pages of all this close linguistic analysis thus lies behind the conclusion Taylor now reaches as to the meaning of ἥμαρτον in verse 12:

> NOTHING more, I think, wants to be explained in this Passage but that Expression, ver.12, *And so Death passed upon all Men, for that all have sined,* namely, *in Adam.* For the Apostle doth not here intend to affirm, that Death passed upon all Men, by their *own Sins.* The whole of his Discourse plainly shows, that he understood and believed, that Death came upon all Mankind by *Adam's* ONE Offence . . . Death therefore must be understood to have passed upon all Mankind, not *for that they all have sined* really, properly, and personally; but *they have sined, are made Siners,* are subjected to Death, through the ONE OFFENCE of ONE MAN, that is, of *Adam.*
>
> THEREFORE the Apostle's Argument constrains us to take these Words, *For that all have sined, in the same,* or *nearly the same Sense,* with those, *Are made Siners,* ver.19.

The fourteen years' labour that was to result in his *magnum opus,* the Hebrew Concordance, was only just beginning, but already we see clear evidence of the minute attention to the language of the Old Testament that was to yield such a splendid harvest.

It is in a footnote on the same page as the above that Taylor deals with the construction of ἐφ᾽ ᾧ. In accordance with the grammatical rule which he takes to be most naturally applicable here, he maintains that it must be referred to the nearest preceding noun to which it is possible for the relative pronoun ᾧ to refer. This is the masculine noun θανατος, so the translation is 'unto which (death) all sinned', which, as we have seen, he takes to mean 'unto which penalty, death, all were condemned'. In the *Paraphrase*, we find:

> . . . let it be observed, That by one Man, *Adam*, Sin entered into the World; he begun Transgression; and thro' his one Sin, Death also entered into the World; and so, in this Way, through his one Sin, Death came upon all Mankind, as far as which all Men are Sufferers, thro' his Disobedience.

How his contemporaries reacted to all this we have seen; but how does it compare with modern understanding?

The meaning of ἐφ᾽ ᾧ receives diverse interpretations by modern commentators. C. E. B. Cranfield, in the International Critical Commentary, lists four possible constructions of the syntax, which yield half a dozen different interpretations of the sense. The first in his list is the strictly grammatical construction, which Taylor regards as the obvious one; but Cranfield rejects it. He says that though it yields 'a sense . . . which is not inconsistent with Paul's argument, this interpretation . . . is difficult and forced', and adds: 'It seems perverse . . . to explain it as a relative clause adjectival to ὁ θάνατος, when other explanations . . . are possible.' He finds it 'much more natural' to understand it as 'a conjunctional expression, as did a number of Greek interpreters'. This is the conclusion of W. F. Moulton: 'With a pres. in 2 Cor. 5.4 and an aor. in Rom. 5.12, the meaning is essentially the same ("in view of the fact that").'[3] Taylor is vindicated to this extent, however: that hardly any modern commentator supports Augustine's interpretation. That was based on the Latin translation *in quo*, which was taken to refer back to the 'one man', Adam, and was supposed to yield the meaning Augustine required, viz. 'in him all sinned'. As against this interpretation of the Greek, Cranfield is typical: 'ἑνὸς ἀνθρώπου is too far away to be a natural antecedent, ἐν rather than ἐπι would be appropriate if this were the meaning'. Even Father S. Lyonnet SJ,[4] who upholds the Tridentine doctrine, finds no support for the translation 'dans lequel'. On the evidence of occurrences in the papyri, in the context of treaties or agreements, he finds the phrase used in the sense of 'on condition that', often with the meaning that the condition of the contract, treaty or agreement has been fulfilled, so the transaction is completed. J. D. G. Dunn, in the *Word Biblical Commentary*,[5] finds this concluding statement in verse 12 'a vague and subsequently much disputed clause'. He comments:

> The point often missed in exegeting such ambiguity is that it would probably have been ambiguous to the first hearers also ... So it is best to retain the vagueness in our own translation – 'in that all sinned' ... All that Paul seems to want to say is that this epoch of human history is characterised and determined by the fatal interplay of sin and death – as evidenced by the fact that everyone sins and everyone dies – a partnership first established in power at the beginning of the epoch, through the one man Adam.

Since the 'broad stance' of the *Word Biblical Commentary* is that its contributors write from an 'evangelical' standpoint, with a 'commitment to Scripture as divine revelation, and to the truth and power of the Christian Gospel', what is remarkable is the enormous difference between the modern exegesis, even though from an evangelical viewpoint, and that of such interpreters as Jennings and Edwards, who believed they could establish their doctrine clearly and indisputably upon Paul's words. Sharing their belief in the inerrancy of Scripture, Taylor is equally constrained by Paul's teaching, and labours to show that it does *not* bear that meaning. Thus, though he is of his own time in his attitude to Scripture, his rejection of the Augustinian understanding of this phrase points in the direction of the moderns.

It is perhaps not surprising that his paraphrase of πάντες

ἥμαρτον by 'all men are Sufferers' hardly finds modern support. Even if Paul, with his Hebraic background, was influenced by a memory of the Hiph'il of *rasha'*, it is difficult to think that such a connection would spring to the mind of many of the Greek-speaking hearers of his letter. Taylor's interpretation is not to be dismissed as a mere eccentricity, though. In the strange world of thought in which we are moving here, there is a clear correspondence between *being justified* (treated as righteous) *in Christ*, and *being condemned* (treated as sinners) *in Adam*. Taylor is surely right to emphasize the parallelism of the two statements. Since the former does not mean that we actually performed Christ's righteous work *in Christ*, it is perverse to maintain that in some incomprehensible way we all ate the forbidden fruit *in Adam*.

Taylor is nearer to modern expositors than are his contemporaries in recognizing a problem as to the meaning of 'all sinned', and its relation to the statement that 'death came upon all men'. Does Paul mean that we all die because we all personally sin? That would be very hard to apply to newborn infants. Or is he, after all, looking in the direction of Original Sin, and saying that in some transcendental sense we 'all sin' just by being part of the human race? It is at this point that Dunn makes his happy suggestion that the listeners to the reading of the letter in Rome would be as uncertain as we are, and that perhaps even Paul did not pause to think out clearly what he meant. He wonders whether 'Paul has sacrificed precision of language for rhetorical effect', and asks how close is 'the parallelism of the "all men" in v. 18 and "the many" in v. 19. Does the language of v. 18 mean that Paul looked for everyone without exception to share in the life of the new age ("universalism")?' Dunn gives reasons why not, but nevertheless entertains 'the possibility that Paul, enthused by the epochal sweep of his vision, cherished the hope of such a universal salvation'. We recall Taylor's insistence on the close parallel between the two occurrences of 'all' in verse 18. Here again, Taylor finds more support than do his opponents in the work of a modern commentator.

Morna Hooker, in *From Adam to Christ*, Part II, examines closely the language of Romans, chapter 1, and the Septuagint of the Genesis story, and concludes that the latter is always in Paul's mind as he describes our human condition. Thus the story of the fall of Adam is central to his thought throughout. For her 'it is perhaps a measure of our distance from Paul's way of thinking that many commentators have found themselves puzzled by verses 12 to 19 of Romans 5', finding them 'the most peculiar verses in all the Epistle' (Anders Nygren), 'a theological digression' (Kenneth E. Kirk), and even 'a pleasant excursion' (Luther). On the contrary, she maintains:

> they are the key to Romans, summing up the argument of the previous chapters in terms of the contrast between Adam and Christ. Throughout the early part of Romans, Paul demonstrates how man lost his relationship with God, how he forfeited the divine glory and came under the wrath of God; in chapter 5 he declares that man is restored to a right relationship with God . . . and can be assured of salvation from the wrath to come. Paul reaches his triumphant conclusion in verses 9 to 11: having been reconciled to God by Christ's death, we shall certainly be saved by his life. The opening 'therefore' of verse 12 introduces the final QED of Paul's argument . . . *therefore* everything which happened to man in Adam is paralleled, or rather reversed, by what has happened to man in Christ.[6]

But of course, for Professor Hooker herself, the Genesis story is not literal history: was it so for Paul? However that may be, her view of the earlier chapters is very different from Taylor's, who resolutely refuses to find references to Adam where he is not specifically mentioned. That is because he is concerned to oppose the doctrine of Original Sin which the orthodox theologians found lurking in every such reference. Hooker's exposition certainly does not reinstate *that*. Like her, Taylor recognizes that the passage is the important conclusion of Paul's argument, and he is meticulous in his exposition of it. But his view that the effect of Adam's sin, from which Christ has delivered us, is only death in its literal sense, finds no support from Professor Hooker.

This small selection from among the innumerable studies of Romans, and this passage in particular, certainly supports Taylor's contention that it affords no proof for the traditional doctrine of Original Sin. On the contrary, 'The difficulty of explaining these verses satisfactorily – a difficulty . . . which can be realised at once by a glance into the various commentaries on the passage – renders it precarious in the extreme to base any arguments upon it, and impossible to prove any doctrine from its contents.'[7] Most modern readers would probably be content to take the whole paragraph in some such sense as C. H. Dodd does in the *Moffatt New Testament Commentary* on Romans:

> It is enough for him and for us to recognise that the wrong-doing of an individual is not an isolated phenomenon, but part of a corporate, racial wrongness which infects human society as we know it, and affects the individual through heredity and environment. This is the fact that Paul has in mind when he says **sin came into the world by one man** . . . He is not really concerned about origins, but about the facts as they are: **in Adam** humanity is corporately sinful.

Even since that was written, developments in the understanding of genetics have sharpened the question just how 'heredity' can be supposed to transmit 'racial wrongness' in any *moral* sense. Nevertheless if this is the general sense of the passage, it expresses a truth to which Taylor, with his strong emphasis on individual freedom and responsibility, does not give enough weight. But he deserves credit for freeing his contemporaries from the constraints of the traditional interpretation of the passage, and for showing that it provides no firm foundation for the huge structure of the doctrine of Original Sin.

Appendix III

The Afterlife of Original Sin

A full account of the later history of this doctrine lies outside the scope of a study of John Taylor, but a short note on the subsequent fortunes of what so many so long regarded as fundamental is perhaps not out of place. Our study of his life and writings has led us to the conclusion that on this subject, in his own day, Taylor had the better of the argument. It must be conceded that his view of human nature was too optimistic, and that he appears insufficiently sensitive to the depth of human wickedness. Nevertheless, in our view, his critique of the traditional doctrine left it in ruins. The determined attempts of his opponents to defend it were based on misunderstandings of Scripture, unsound reasoning, and indefensible notions of justice. But even had they succeeded, it could only have been for a time: the next century brought a transformation of the understanding of the origins both of the world and of mankind which made it impossible for educated men to base a doctrine on the literal understanding of the story of the fall, unless they were willing to commit intellectual suicide. That to this day there are many so determined is unhappily true, and it is regrettable when the faith is represented to young Christians as requiring this.

For a generation or two, into the early nineteenth century, orthodox writers managed to keep the doctrine afloat. In view of Wesley's determined defence of it, it was perhaps inevitable that the earliest Methodists would continue to sustain their founder's position. Thus Richard Watson (1781–1833), author of the first systematic formulation of Wesleyan theology,[1] upholds the traditional interpretation of the Eden story as 'clearly revealed truth', though he wisely discards the more extravagant claims for Adam, such as that he was endowed with knowledge of 'the deep philosophy of nature', when he named the animals. But all that was written a generation before Darwin; the same position maintained half a century later begins to look like England's wooden battleships in the age of the steamer. William Burt Pope's treatment of the subject in his massive *Compendium of Christian Theology*, published in 1877, now has just that appearance.[2] *The Origin of Species* had been out for eighteen years, and *The Descent of Man* six, but for Pope the story of Eden and the fall is literal fact: 'the narrative is true, and every circumstance in it real', even though every item and event in the story is also highly symbolic. 'All were emblems as well as facts.' So the story provides a firm foundation for the traditional doctrine:

> The effect of the Fall upon the posterity of Adam is described in Scripture as the universal diffusion of death as a condemnation, and of a bias of human nature towards evil. The Scriptural doctrine finds its expression in the theological term Original Sin; the hereditary sin and hereditary sinfulness of mankind derived from Adam its natural head and representative ...
>
> *In sin did my mother conceive me*, is the confession of one for all.

Pope's work thus 'marks the end of an era', but even at the end of the nineteenth century, John Scott Lidgett evidently means to restate the doctrine in a reasonable form when he writes:

> Thus ... beneath the special sins which men committ, there is a sinful disposition. Moreover, according to the laws of heredity, sin has become organic in the race; and in consequence of the solidarity of mankind, the society which is composed of sinners becomes itself sinful. Hence heredity, intercourse, the social atmosphere, perpetuate and, left to themselves, intensify the common sin ...[3]

– and so on. Some of this is obviously true; but the questionable part is precisely the element in the traditional doctrine which its advocates so vehemently maintained: that we can be made sinners by 'the laws of heredity'. Those laws have become very much better understood since 1897. We cannot now suppose that the *sinfulness* of ancestors is *genetically* transmitted to their descendants, though instinctive behaviour patterns may be.

By that date the critical understanding of the Scriptures was at least as important as the changes in scientific thought in finally eliminating reliance on the first three chapters of Genesis as literal history, upon which an explanation of the human predicament could be built. Moreover, F. R. Tennant showed, in three important works[4] in the early years of the twentieth century, that the doctrine in its traditional form was neither securely based in Scripture nor true to reason and experience. N. P. Williams made the doctrine the subject of a magisterial study in his Bampton Lectures of 1924, *The Ideas of the Fall and Original Sin* (1927), in which he shows that while there were adumbrations of a doctrine of a fall before Augustine, it is to him, and to his misinterpretation of scripture texts, that we owe the baleful dogma that took root in the West. By the time the epoch-making one-volume *Commentary on the Bible* edited by A. S. Peake brought the results of modern biblical scholarship to twentieth-century preachers and teachers, the doctrine had been 'quietly abandoned'.[5] Other Methodist scholars were quite explicit in their abandonment of it. C. Ryder Smith, for example, subjects the myth of Eden, and the interpretation that had been put upon it, to rigorous scrutiny, and finds:

> The belief that the story does teach 'original sin' is supposed, of course, to be Pauline. It will be argued later that this is a mistake; but whether this is so or not, it is clear that to find ground for the doctrine in the story of Eden is to find in it a meaning of which the Hebrews of Old Testament times were quite innocent.[6]

As a loyal and distinguished Methodist minister engaged in training the ministry, Ryder Smith would certainly regard himself as in the Wesleyan theological tradition. He was probably not thinking of Taylor's book at all; yet the fact is that using Taylor's method of meticulous study of the Scriptures, he arrived at Taylor's conclusion: that the doctrine of Original Sin is simply not to be found there.

The language of 'Original Sin', nevertheless, continues to be used long after the doctrine, in the uncompromising sense of the Westminster Confession, has ceased to be believed. Parents with a folk-memory of the traditional language will murmur 'original sin', more than half in jest, when their children misbehave or begin to show sexual curiosity. We and they may do well to reflect on the vast difference between their light-hearted remark, and the doom-laden sense in which their sixteenth-century ancestors might have used the same words – a difference closely reflected by the contrasting practice in the care of infants and the education of growing children.

Some novelists are interested in the subject. Its use by P. D. James, a firm Anglican, has been noted (p. 82). David Lodge, whose familiarity with Roman Catholicism is manifest in his novels, began a lecture on 'Happiness and the Novel'[7] with the remark: 'There seems to be a connection between narrative and original sin. A steady state of complete contentment, such as Adam and Eve enjoyed in Paradise, could not itself generate a story.' Such usage, of course, carries no necessary implication of belief in the doctrine as Augustine or the Reformers taught it. To the extent that the term is used seriously, it expresses the well-founded perception that human beings do behave very badly – all of us sometimes, and some of us almost all the time; and that however hard we try, we seem unable to avoid doing so. In the context of any serious consideration of the atrocities of which human beings have shown themselves capable, it may appear to approach its traditional theological use.

Has it, then, a place in theology after all? Without doubt, the experience of two world wars of extreme ferocity, and of the atrocities associated with Nazism, Stalinism and kindred ideologies, led to a reaction against liberal theology and any optimistic view of human nature. In the decade after the First World War the memory of that horror and the growing signs of evil to come began to reawaken the sense of man's ingrained sinfulness. The climate was favourable for a revival of the doctrine of Original Sin, and even of something like the Augustinian understanding of the story of the fall. It was in the shadow of Hitler's rising power in Germany in the winter of 1932—33 that Dietrich Bonhoeffer delivered a series of lectures in the University of Berlin, published in 1937, on *Creation and Fall: A Theological Interpretation of Genesis 1—3*.[8] The immense prestige attaching to his name, and the death he died, make it difficult to be objective in assessing these lectures. The date and circumstances of their delivery and then of their publication give his interpretation of the Bible story a prophetic status that almost puts them beyond criticism. He himself certainly uttered a 'word of the Lord' in that dreadful situation; but did he really find it in those chapters, or did he read it into them? In doom-laden prose, he reasserts the Augustinian understanding of the story:

> The Fall of man . . . is defection, it is the fall from being held in creatureliness. This defection is a continual falling, a plunging into bottomless depths, a being relinquished, a withdrawal ever farther and deeper. And in all this it is not simply a moral lapse, but a destruction of the creation by the creature. The Fall affects the whole of the created world which is henceforth plundered of its creatureliness as it crashes into infinite space, like a meteor which has torn away from its nucleus. It is of this falling-fallen world that we must now speak.

But is all that *really* found in Genesis 1—3? However that may be, Bonhoeffer's story is a terrible reminder that sin can certainly not be treated lightly; it must obviously be a major subject of theological thinking. So even in modern theology we sometimes meet again the term Original Sin. But is it the same animal that Taylor hunted to death? It may at first appear to be, but in fact, some degree of repudiation of the traditional doctrine is always involved, for reasons that are similar to those alleged by Taylor two centuries earlier.

A study of Arminianism[9] published in 1937 opens with a confident claim that at that time that theological tendency had triumphed over strict Calvinism even in its heartlands; but the concluding paragraphs of its final chapter note the rising of the cloud, considerably larger than a man's hand, represented by Karl Barth. Barth's monumental theological commentary, *The Epistle to the Romans*, marked an emphatic rejection of nineteenth-century liberal theology, in favour of something closer akin to the Reformation Confessions. Here if anywhere, surely, we may look for a full-blooded reassertion of the doctrine of Original Sin? Instead we find something that neither Taylor nor his opponents would recognize:

> The doctrine of Original Sin, as it has been generally understood in the West, would not have been to Paul an 'attractive hypothesis' (Leitzmann); it would have been just one of the many historical and psychological falsifications of his meaning. The sin which entered the world through Adam is, like the righteousness manifested to the world in Christ, timeless and transcendental. It is the disposition and relation to God of men who stand facing the old with their backs to the new.[10]

Karl Barth and Emil Brunner sounded the trumpet notes the church needed to hear in the terrible years when the horrors of totalitarianism, genocide and war shattered any surviving optimism about human nature. The title of one of Brunner's books, *Man in Revolt*, signals a diagnosis of the human condition that, on the face of it, looks like a return to the traditional doctrine. Yet here too, on closer inspection, we find huge qualifications. The fall is not a historical event:

> The whole historic picture of 'the first man' has been finally and absolutely destroyed for us today. The conflict between the teaching of history, natural science and palaeontology, on the origin of the human race, and that of the ecclesiastical doctrine, urged on both sides with the passion of a fanatical concern for truth, has led, all along the line, to the victory of

the scientific view, and to the gradual but inevitable decline of the ecclesiastical view ... Thus today we are confronted by the fact ... that the average man of today knows or believes about the origin of man only that which remains in his memory from his instruction in natural history about the 'origin of man'. The ecclesiastical doctrine of Adam and Eve cannot compete with the impressive power of this scientific knowledge.[11]

The guilt of an individual, Adam, cannot be fastened upon his descendants, nor can sin be transferred by natural inheritance. Surely, then, whatever Brunner's doctrine of Original Sin is, it is not that of the Confessions and the Articles, and to continue to use the same label is misleading.

Neo-orthodox theologians, however, seem to be too fascinated by the monster to free themselves from it. For example, Reinhold Niebuhr, we are told,[12] 'was fond of quoting the assertion of the ... *Times Literary Supplement*, "The doctrine of original sin is the only empirically verifiable doctrine of the Christian faith"'. What he and its author meant by this statement, presumably, was that the depravity of the human race is manifest in the wars, genocide and crime of our century. But with due respect to them both, that is the *problem*, not the *doctrine*. The doctrine is not a mere description of the fact, but an attempt to account for it, and that is something that cannot be 'empirically proved': it can only be convincing or unconvincing, successful or unsuccessful. So how does Niebuhr restate the doctrine of Original Sin? Not in any form in which the Westminster divines or Edwards or even Wesley would recognize it. For him, as for any sensible modern theologian, the story in Genesis is a myth or a folk tale, not literally or historically true, however much it may express, depict or mythologize profound truth. The universality of sin is

a deep mystery ... which has been simply resolved in modern culture. It has interpreted man as an essentially virtuous creature who is betrayed into evil by ignorance, or by evil economic, political, or religious institutions. These simple theories of historical evil do not explain how virtuous men of another generation created the evil in these inherited institutions, or how ignorance could give the evil in man the positive thrust and demonic energy in which it frequently expresses itself. Modern culture's understanding of the evil in man fails to do justice to the tragic and perplexing aspect of the problem.

This is reminiscent of Wesley's question, 'How came wise and good men . . . not to train up their children in wisdom and goodness . . .?' So are we back to Wesley's solution? By no means:

Orthodox Christianity . . . has frequently given a dogmatic answer to the problem, which suggests mystery, but which immediately obscures the mystery by a dogmatic formula. Men are evil, Christian orthodoxy declared, because of the 'sin of Adam' which has been transmitted to all men. Sometimes the mode of transmission has been allowed to remain mysterious; but sometimes it is identified with the concupiscence in the act of procreation. This dogmatic explanation has prompted the justified protest and incredulity of modern man, particularly since it is generally couched in language and symbols taken from a prescientific age.[13]

Whatever the term 'Original Sin' is to be reinterpreted to mean, then, it is *not* going to be the dogma against which Taylor gave early expression to modern man's 'justified protest and incredulity'.

Another theologian very influential in mid-century, Paul Tillich, likewise seems to be about to lead us back to the old doctrine of Original Sin, but in fact does no such thing. The story of Eden is, of course, a myth. It symbolizes a 'Fall', but a very different one from what the Westminster divines or Jonathan Edwards would have recognized:

The state of dreaming innocence drives beyond itself. The possibility of the transition [from essence] to existence is experienced as temptation. Temptation is unavoidable because the state of dreaming innocence is uncontested and undecided. It is not perfection. Orthodox theologians have heaped perfection after perfection upon Adam before the Fall, making him equal with the picture of the Christ. This procedure is not only absurd; it makes the Fall completely unintelligible. Mere potentiality or dreaming innocence is not perfection. Only the conscious union of existence and essence is perfection . . . The symbol 'Adam before the Fall' must be understood as the dreaming innocence of undecided potentialities.[14]

Another point to Taylor. Allowing for the very different terms in which Tillich expresses his theology, this is much more like Taylor's notion of 'Adam before the Fall' than that of his orthodox critics who poured such scorn upon it. So what about Original Sin?

Tillich seems to be about to rehabilitate the doctrine of Original Sin: 'When Augustine spoke of a *massa perditionis*, a "mass of perdition," he expressed the insight, in opposition to Pelagius, that man in his estrangement is a social being, and cannot be isolated into a subject able to make free decisions.' He speaks of 'the universal destiny of man to be estranged from what he essentially is'. This universal destiny, it seems, is unavoidably involved in the transition from essence to existence. But this is very different from the orthodox doctrine. Such a 'Fall' cannot be located in one man, or one generation of mankind; it is a 'universal destiny':

. . . the transition from essence to existence is not an event in time and space but the transhistorical quality of all events in time and space. This is equally true of man and of nature. 'Adam before the Fall' and 'nature before the curse' are states of potentiality. They are not actual states. The actual state is the existence in which man finds himself along with the whole universe, and there is no time in which this was otherwise. The notion of a moment in time in which man and nature were changed from good to evil is absurd, and it has no foundation in experience or revelation.

Theology must clearly and unambiguously represent 'the Fall' as a symbol for the human situation universally, not as the story of an event that happened 'once upon a time'.

On the subject of 'Concupiscence', Tillich recognizes that Augustine, 'never overcame the Hellenistic and especially the Neo-Platonic devaluation of sex'. The Reformers failed to eliminate 'the remnants of this tradition', and

> do not always clearly reject the un-Protestant doctrine that 'hereditary' sin is rooted in sexual pleasure in the act of procreation. If 'concupiscence' is used in this limited sense, it is certainly unable to describe the state of general estrangement, and it would be better to drop it completely.

Any use of 'the terms "original" or "hereditary" with regard to sin', therefore, calls for reinterpretation:

> But in this case reinterpretation may demand the rejection of the terms. Both point to the universal character of estrangement, expressing the element of destiny in estrangement. But both words are so much burdened with literalistic absurdities that it is practically impossible to use them any longer.

There is not much left of the doctrine as the Westminster Confession taught it, or of Article IX '*Of Original or Birth-sin*'!

In truth, as these random samples illustrate, twentieth-century restatements or rehabilitations of the doctrine of Original Sin usually turn out, on close inspection, to reject the vehement insistence of the formularies that it is *not* a matter of influence or example: that 'Original Sin standeth not in the following of *Adam*, (as the *Pelagians* do vainly talk;) but it is the fault and corruption of the Nature of every man, that naturally is ingendered of the offspring of *Adam*'. This hard core of the doctrine really makes no sense in the light of modern genetics. There is a sort of Lamarckism in Augustine's notion: sin is an instance of 'the transmission of acquired characteristics'! This simply will not do; but what is substituted is precisely what the older statements reject: mutual influence, solidarity in sin, the pervading pressure of social institutions, and so forth. We can all agree about that; but it is not what the term 'Original Sin' meant to its exponents and critics in the eighteenth century.

The tendency among some Methodist theologians to attempt to accommodate Wesley's theology on this subject, must be held to fail precisely on this score. A clear example is Thomas C. Oden,[15] who contends that the classic doctrine anticipates the modern recognition of the 'sociality' and 'intergenerational transmission' of evil. Wesley, he says, 'thought of himself merely as defending the received faith against crypto-Arians of his time, as represented by a leading deist [*sic*!], John Taylor'. 'Intergenerational transmission' is an ambiguous expression. Wesley would have taken it to include transmission through natural generation, as Augustine and the Reformers held. But does Dr Oden mean more by it than transmission through family influence, example, social pressure and the like? This is much closer to what Taylor meant by 'education', an explanation Wesley vigorously rejected.

Let it not be supposed, however, that the doctrine of Original Sin is no more. It has been slain many times, but like the fabled un-dead Count Dracula, it will not lie quiet in its grave. The Vatican, having once made a mistake, may soften its tone, but cannot relinquish a dogma: the Faith is *semper eadem*. As a Catholic scholar remarked in a newspaper article, anticipating the publication of *Veritatis Splendor*, there has been 'a long line of dogmatic statements: loud, confident, and wrong'. 'The doctrine' [of Original Sin], he continues, 'was invented by Augustine of Hippo in the early fifth century out of an incorrect translation in the fifth chapter of St Paul in the Romans. The eastern churches, which didn't need their Greek New Testament translated, never made the same mistake, and have got along pretty well without it.'[16]

On this subject, conservative Catholics find Protestant allies, especially in the Reformed tradition, and in the Conservative Evangelical camp, and that not exclusively among fundamentalists. A recent short study from that quarter by a French professor of theology offers a good example. Henri Blocher eschews fundamentalism, though he says that he would feel obliged to bow to the authority of Scripture if a doctrine were found there, 'however offensive to modern taste'.[17] He clings to the historicity of Adam and Eve, though he locates them 40,000 rather than 4000 BC, and is a good deal less positive than Jenner or Hervey would have been:

> Though we feel uncomfortable with all the uncertainties when we try to correlate scientific data and the results of a sensible interpretation of Genesis 1—4, therefore, we may *maintain as plausible the hypothesis* that the biblical Adam and Eve were the first parents of our race, some 40,000 years ago, and *we may posit* an initial period of fellowship with God in their lives before they apostatized.[18] (*Our italics*)

But is a 'plausible hypothesis' and a 'posited' state to be the foundation of a doctrine so momentous? The professor has 'an ear finely attuned to Scripture', which is able to 'detect distinct echoes' of the Eden story all over the Bible,[19] where they are by no means audible to our duller hearing. Though he recognizes that 'virtually no-one today follows Augustine in viewing the procreative act as sinful *per se* (in our fallen condition)', he seems to come pretty near it. He countenances the association of sex with 'dirt', quoting in a footnote, without apparent revulsion, Augustine's sick remark that we are born *inter faeces et urinam*, and hints that in an unfallen world there might have been some different arrangement. Would this sanitized parturition avail for all the mammals and birds too? Something more like the mating of fish, perhaps? The question is 'impossible to answer'![20] However that may be, Blocher is sensitive to the many objections that have been raised against the traditional doctrine. He recognizes that there have been 'fanciful exaggerations of the privileges of innocence', but, as we have seen, he can 'posit' a time of unclouded fellowship with God before the fall. He recognizes the tendency of evangelical preachers to use exaggerated rhetoric on the subject of human sinfulness 'out of apocalyptic zeal; the more we condemn the world, the more prophetic we feel, or are considered'.[21] The uncomfortable subject of the bearing of Augustine's doctrine upon the unbaptized, especially innocent babes, is simply ignored. In short, the confident dogmatism of the Westminster Divines has been considerably modified in recognition of the damaging criticisms it has undergone, but the fundamental doctrine remains. Original sin is something passed on from generation to generation in some mysterious fashion, so that we are *born* – indeed, *conceived* – sinners:

> We underline the fact that original sin . . . is not only potential but *actual*, from the start, as is foetal and infant life itself. The will, though undeveloped, does exist, and its anti-God tendency already constitutes a wilful exercise . . .
>
> We should exclude the fantasy about a 'sin gene' or sin as a chromosomic aberration . . . But could there be a far more subtle disorder of the genetic formula and of its expression, a disorder which would correlate to spiritual deformation? Might we imagine, for instance, that spiritual integrity could support protective or restorative mechanisms against detrimental mutations – mechanisms which were lost?[22]

'Could there be', and 'might we imagine', are a long way from the downright dogmas and anathemas of his spiritual ancestors. The corpse of Augustine's doctrine has been disinfected, embalmed, clothed in modern dress, and given the mortician's cosmetic treatment; and in this grisly guise, it is *un-dead*, ready to rise and make us all, as Taylor said, 'sinners, we know not how, and that we must be guilty, and repent of, we know not what'.

Appendix IV

Taylor's Opposition to Hutcheson's Moral Philosophy

There can be no doubt that disagreement over the teaching of moral philosophy was a major factor in setting Taylor at loggerheads with Seddon and the Trustees. The system to which Taylor was strongly opposed was that of Francis Hutcheson (1694–1755), the very professor at Glasgow one of whose favourite pupils John Seddon is said to have been. Thus when Taylor felt compelled by increasing physical weakness to suspend for a time his course of lectures in this field, he was deeply incensed to find that Seddon was filling the gap. Worse still, when a new tutor was appointed, who would take over the teaching of this subject, Taylor tried to prescribe what scheme of moral philosophy was to be taught, and was told peremptorily that he must stick to his own province and leave the others to theirs. What were the conflicting systems that aroused such strong mutual antagonism?

Hutcheson was a native of Ireland, of Protestant stock, whose spreading reputation brought him an unsolicited invitation to the chair of philosophy at Glasgow. There, in addition to his regular course work, he gave Sunday evening lectures on the evidences of Christianity which attracted hearers from all faculties. As a philosopher, he was well regarded by David Hume. In ethics, which was his chief study, he opposed the cynical theory of Hobbes and others, who regarded all motivation as ultimately self-interested. Adam Smith was one of his pupils. His teaching prepared the ground for the 'Utilitarianism' of Bentham and Mill in the next century, and indeed he seems to have been the first to use the phrase, 'the greatest happiness of the greatest number'. Though born the same year as Taylor, he had died two years before the latter moved to Warrington. His major work, *A System of Moral Philosophy*, was published shortly after his death in 1755. Henry Sidgwick in his *History of Ethics* notes:

> Shaftesbury is the first moralist who distinctly takes psychological experience as the basis of ethics. His suggestions were developed by Hutcheson into one of the most elaborate systems of moral philosophy which we possess; and through Hutcheson, if not directly, they influenced Hume's speculations, and are thus connected with later utilitarianism.[1]

Hutcheson's distinctive teaching had already been set out in shorter works, *An Inquiry into Beauty and Virtue* and *An Essay on the Nature and Conduct of the Passions*. It is to these, not to the posthumous two-volume work, that Taylor refers in his critique, published in 1759 with the title: *An Examination of the Scheme of Morality advanced by Dr Hutcheson, Late Professor of Morality in the University of Glasgow*. In the following year Taylor published the substance of his own lectures to his pupils, *A Sketch of Moral Philosophy; or an Essay to demonstrate the Principles of Virtue and Religion upon a New, Natural, and Easy Plan*.

Leechman, who had initiated the move to confer the doctorate on Taylor the year before in recognition of his Hebrew Concordance, was Hutcheson's colleague at Glasgow. He contributed a very valuable biographical introduction to the posthumous two-volume *System of Moral Philosophy*. He tells us that his late friend had been impressed by the great progress made in 'natural philosophy' when its devotees had 'thrown off the method of framing hypotheses and suppositions . . . and had set themselves to make observations and experiments on the constitution of the material world itself'.

He was convinced that in like manner a true scheme of morals could not be the product of genius and invention, or of the greatest precision of thought in metaphysical reasonings, but must be drawn from proper observations upon the several powers and principles which we are conscious of in our own bosoms, and which must be acknowledged to operate in some degree in the whole human species.[2]

He thus gave a strong impulse to the study of the psychology of the human agent as the starting point for ethical theory, rather than abstract deduction from first principles. All of us, he finds, have, in addition to the five senses which give us our knowledge of the external world, two further 'senses', viz. an 'internal sense' by which we discern beauty and worth in that world, and a 'moral sense' which recognizes goodness.

> There is therefore, as each one by close attention and reflection may convince himself, a natural and immediate determination to approve certain affections and actions consequent upon them; or a natural sense of immediate excellence in them, not referred to any other quality perceivable by our other senses or by reasoning.[3]

These 'senses', the 'internal' and the 'moral', though instinctive and not at the command of reason, are capable of development and refinement. In the development of musical taste, we progress from 'pleasure in the simple artless tunes of the vulgar' to appreciation of 'finer and more complex compositions'; and

> As some others of our immediate perceptive powers are capable of culture and improvement, so is this moral sense, without presupposing any reference to a superior power of reason to which their perceptions are to be referred . . .
>
> This moral sense from its very nature appears to be designed for regulating and controlling all our powers. This dignity and commanding nature we are immediately conscious of, as we are conscious of the power itself.

The words 'immediate' and 'immediately' – in the sense, of course, of 'without any intermediate steps', directly, needing and finding no support from reasoning etc. – recur repeatedly, and are very expressive of Hutcheson's central conviction:

> But as we immediately perceive the difference in kind, and that the dignity of enjoyment from fine poetry, painting, or from knowledge, is superior to the pleasures of the palate, were they never so delicate; so we immediately discern moral good to be superior in kind and dignity to all others which are perceived by the other perceptive powers.

The 'moral good' which this faculty so approves is that which is manifested in affections, dispositions and actions which promote happiness, especially the happiness of others. These 'all agree in one general character, of tendency to the happiness of others, and to the moral perfection of the mind possessing them'.

Do the last ten words add anything to what has gone before? They *appear* to do so; but surely 'the moral perfection of the mind', for Hutcheson, is none other than the disposition to promote the happiness of others, and to approve action which has this tendency. Hutcheson's principle leads to the conclusion that ethical terms such as right, good, moral, etc., are all definable in variants of 'having a tendency to promote happiness'. This is vulnerable to the criticisms brought against Utilitarianism in the next century. One important objection to it is the obvious difficulty that if the moral rightness of an action depends on its effects, especially on the amount of happiness it causes, moral judgements can never be securely made, since *all* the effects of a deed, into the unlimited future, can never be known. Moreover with the lapse of time, the balance of happiness and unhappiness resulting from the action may shift, and with it the moral rightness or wrongness of the action.

Hutcheson's teaching had a wide influence, but provoked sharp criticism. Richard Price (1723–91) published in 1757 *A Review of the Chief Questions and Difficulties of Morals*. He contended that moral judgement is not a matter of feeling, but of the understanding. 'Right' and 'wrong' are 'simple ideas', not resolvable into other terms, but intuitively recognized by the rational mind. In the all-important first chapter of his book, he lays the foundation of his system by contending that *sensation* and *reflection* are not the only source of our ideas: for there to be knowledge, the *understanding* must operate upon them, and this becomes the source of further ideas. Without this, there could be no knowledge, only direct experience. He instances Newton's Laws of Motion, none of which can be established by direct sense experience, but they are perceived by the understanding. He then argues:

> 'Tis a very necessary previous observation that *right* and *wrong* denote simple ideas, and are therefore to be ascribed to some *immediate* power of perception in the human mind . . .
>
> Supposing it then clear, that we have a power *immediately* perceiving right and wrong; the point I am now to endeavour to prove, is, that this power is the *Understanding* . . .

A bewildered reader may well wonder, if both Hutcheson and Price believe that we make moral judgements *immediately*, what is the point at issue. It is, however, fundamental. Hutcheson's view may be taken to lead to the conclusion that the difference between what we adjudge right and what we hold to be wrong is discerned by a moral *sense*, akin to a *feeling*. To put it crudely, we regard an action as right because we 'feel good about it', and conversely. And we 'feel good' about actions which promote happiness, especially that of others. Against this, Price maintains that 'right' and 'wrong' are immutable qualities of actions and dispositions, and these qualities are discerned, not by a 'sense', but by the understanding or reason:

> As there are some propositions, which, when attended to, necessarily determine all minds to *believe* them; and as . . . there are some ends, whose natures are such, that, when perceived, all beings immediately and necessarily *desire* them: So it is very credible and easily to be admitted, that, in like manner, there are some actions whose natures are such, that, when observed, all rational beings immediately and necessarily *approve* them . . .

. . . morality is *eternal* and *immutable* . . .
Right and Wrong denote what actions *are*.[4]

Taylor takes a similar line. In his Preface to *A Sketch of Moral Philosophy*, he tells us that he also made free use of *An Inquiry concerning Virtue and Happiness*, which his old friend from his Lincolnshire days, Philips Glover, published in 1757. The intuitive recognition of the unanalysable meaning of terms like 'right' and 'wrong' is an operation of the understanding, and is a different matter altogether from feelings of pleasure at the contemplation of benevolent actions. Nor has it anything to do with calculation of the *effects* of our moral decisions, in increasing or decreasing happiness. Taylor emphatically rejects any notion that the *consequences* of actions form the basis for moral judgement. In the same Preface, he says:

> *These Principles* [viz. 'of Virtue and Religion'] *are here considered* simply *and* absolutely *in themselves, as the Ground, or Reason, of right Action, without attending to the Consequences of such Action, or what Good may follow from it. Just as in* Euclid, *the simple principles of Geometry are demonstrated, in a series of Propositions, without considering the Purposes, to which they may be applied.*

What offended Price and Taylor and others in Hutcheson's scheme, was its subjectivity. Reliance upon a 'moral sense' as the source of all ethical judgements makes them subjective, and therefore impotent against those who may say they simply do not experience the same 'immediate' feeling. For Taylor, it is of vital importance that morals be established upon clear and indisputable principles. His mention of Euclid reminds us of Benjamin Whichcote's claim, 'In *Morality*, we are sure as in Mathematics.'[5] In Taylor's view, moral precepts are derived by the reason from first principles, Price's 'simple ideas', which are unanalysable, irreducible and self-authenticating:

> Reason is that Faculty of the Mind, by which we perceive, or understand the Truth, or the true Nature of Things, and are

capable of considering, distinguishing, comparing and judging of their Natures Properties, Circumstances and Relations, and of discovering what is agreeable to, or inconsistent with them. Thus *Reason* is distinguished from the simple Perceptions of *Sense*.[6]

He is therefore bitterly scornful of Hutcheson's relegation of reason to a subordinate, ancillary role. 'But what province doth he assign to reason?' he asks, and answers with a series of quotations from Hutcheson's *Essay* and *Inquiry* to show that reason, in this scheme, has only a practical function: to examine what the actual results of actions are, and to discern in which direction the public good lies. 'Men have reason given them to judge, and compare the tendencies of actions, that they may not stupidly follow the first appearance of public good.' Reason is thus

imployed as an inferior quality, exercising its SAGACITY *after* the two *instincts* have proposed the end to be pursued, and fixed, or determined, the rightness, or moral goodness, of the action . . . And thus, according to him, reason hath nothing to do with the internal principles of virtue, nor those principles with reason; these being entirely distinct and separate the one from the other; a paradox, I presume, which never before made its appearance in the world.[7]

Such a dethronement of reason in the realm of morality is of course flat blasphemy to a man of Taylor's convictions. He probably saw in it a tendency to undermine his whole scheme of divinity as well as moral philosophy. His letter to Benson suggests this.[8] Did he perhaps, despite Hutcheson's overt advocacy of Christianity, fear that his teaching would tend in the same direction as Shaftesbury's, towards 'a natural theology that implied the Christian scheme to be superfluous – and hinted it to be worse'?[9]

As we usually find when strongly opposed positions are taken, antagonists tend to distort or overstate their opponents' views, and Taylor may perhaps not have been entirely just in his interpretation of Hutcheson's moral philosophy. Hutcheson himself, as we have already quoted him, speaks of the 'dignity and commanding nature' of his 'moral sense' as something 'we are immediately conscious of', as of something 'designed for regulating and controlling all our powers'. That sounds like something much more authoritative than a glow of pleasure at seeing a good deed. Moreover, Hutcheson modified his position in response to the criticisms it provoked. As we have seen, Taylor directs his attack against Hutcheson's two short early essays; but even had he followed his later developments, he would still have found the difference between them fundamental. In a nutshell, it is the difference between defining 'good' and 'evil' in terms of *instinctive reaction* to conduct etc., as against understanding them, in Price's words, as referring to 'how things *are*'.

A thoroughgoing study of Taylor's own ethical teaching, or of Hutcheson's, is beyond the scope of this note. Enough has been exhibited to account for the bitterness of Taylor's resentment of any undermining of his teaching in this field, behind which he undoubtedly detected Seddon's influence. His anxiety on this score, when he was contemplating the move to Warrington, is very clear in that letter to Dr Benson. In the course of the next few years, his worst fears were realized. The Academy to which he had given the support of his name and fame became more and more committed to a system to which he was well known to be bitterly opposed. It is small wonder that he found his position unbearable.

Appendix V

Taylor's Letters to Benson

Eighteen letters from Taylor, written between March 1742 and October 1760, are preserved in the County Library, Lancaster. All are directed to Mr or Dr Benson; those that add an address either name or imply London. They show there was a good deal of coming and going between Norwich and the capital. Most of the letters were evidently carried by someone who was travelling to London, since Letter 4 concludes with the remark, 'As this is partly a Letter of Business I send it by the Post, otherwise shd have waited an unexpensive opportunity.'

George Benson (1699–1762) was a learned Presbyterian divine, grandson of an ejected minister. He was ordained on 27 March 1723 by Edmund Calamy and others. Like Taylor, but a few years behind him, Benson had studied under Thomas Dixon, and like several other alumni of the Whitehaven Academy, he moved during his early ministry from a Calvinist to an Arminian theology. He was compelled to leave his first charge at Abingdon in 1729 'because his people would not swallow down Arminianism'. His eventual position is described as 'Socinian', but we may wonder whether the term applied any more accurately to him than to his friend. He was the author of several works on the Epistles of Paul, and of replies to deistical attacks upon Christianity. The lady to whom Taylor sends greetings at the end of each letter is Mary Kettle, whom Benson married in 1742, following the death of his first wife Elizabeth Hills two years before. Both marriages were childless. The doctorate conferred by Aberdeen University in 1744 is observed in the address of the later letters.

That the letters are addressed to a friend is evident from the first; but the tone grows more affectionate in the later ones, the 'Dear Sir' and 'Revd & Dear Sir' of the first thirteen letters warming to 'My dear Friend,' and 'My dearest Friend' in the last five. In the last two, written from Warrington, the importance of this friendship to Taylor in his distress is very evident, especially in that last appeal, 'Remember me in your prayers. I don't forget...'

Taylor's handwriting is clear and firm; but in the autograph documents he has left it varies in style so much that the employment of an amanuensis has sometimes been suspected. The same wide variation occurs, however, throughout these letters, sometimes within the same letter; and yet some persistent characteristics show that the writer is always Taylor himself. Noteworthy among these is the formation of the lower case letter *e*. Though sometimes written in the usual way, especially in his more formal hand, this letter is more often formed like a diminutive theta, ϑ, looking like a cursive *o*. This characteristic persists through a good deal of variation in the general appearance of the hand, even here and there in his most careful script, and is a clear sign of Taylor's autograph. The signature and address are always written in a large, flourished, 'copperplate' hand.

In the following transcription, Taylor's spelling and use of capitals is followed, but it is often difficult to decide whether a capital is intended, especially regarding the letters A, C and S. In two or three places, Taylor appears to have written 'Mrs' where one would expect 'Mr', but the writing is identical with the 'Mrs' where it clearly does refer to a woman, so one can only so transcribe it. In Letter 12, 'Mrs Chandler' is referred to as 'he' in the next sentence, confirming that other apparent occurrences of 'Mrs' may be similarly inappropriate, e.g. 'Mrs Fenner' in letter 1, where 'Mrs' differs very clearly from 'Mr' (Milner) in the same letter.

No attempt has been made to indicate cancellations, additions or corrections: what the writer clearly intended has been printed. Taylor constantly uses the archaic sign y (a form of Old English thorn, the letter representing th) in abbreviations of the, that, them etc. This y has been transliterated th, since that is how his contemporaries read it, and to print the letter y simply misleads modern readers. Our ancestors did *not* say 'ye' for 'the', as the contractions 'yt' and 'ym' clearly show.

Letter 1 MS 5496

To the Revd Mr Benson

Dear Sr.   Norwich Mar.30.1742.

Mr Milner having informed me that there's a call for a second edition of my <u>Further Defence</u> &c. and that you were so good as to offer to correct the proof, I have now sent the piece wth the addition of a Note p.21. and an Appendix; the addition of both which I submit to your Judgment, as also any other part of the Book you may think faulty, or proper to be altered, favouring me with a Line or two concerning any thing you judge exceptionable. I think Mrs[?] Fenner should give me something for the Edition; but that, as well as the paper and character, I refer to you and my other good Friends. Only I desire it may be well done upon good paper, and a neat Letter. I would not have it in a large Print, the Letter of the first edition I should think large enough, only it would not be amiss to omit a Line at every Break. But I refer this to your better Judgment.

I have sold the paraphrases on <u>I Peter</u> wch Mr Milner sent me, and have order'd my son to pay you 20 Shillings for the five. I thank you very kindly for that you gave me, 'tis in every respect a present I value much, and heartily congratulate you upon yr successful attempts in explaining the apostolic Writings. But when I have a little more leisure I shall make bold to send you my Thots more particularly upon the Performance. I am, wishing you the continuance of Health and every Blessing, Dear Sr.

Yr affect. Brother & humble Servt.

John Taylor

I think this Piece now will bear but a small Edition.

Letter 2 MS5497

This long letter is written throughout in neat, sloped script. (Clusters of hyphens represent small damaged sections of text in the originals.) The 'Mr Jennings' mentioned in it was the author of the first riposte to Taylor's book on Original Sin: see ch. 10, pp. 84–8. 'Dr Hunt' is clearly not 'Dr Hunt of Oxford', mentioned in Letter 7, but Jeremiah Hunt DD (Edinburgh), 1678–1744, an Independent minister in London whose sermons Benson edited and published posthumously. A note written alongside the address, obviously by Benson, reads:

<u>Mem</u>. This letter was answer'd May 6.1743. only an extract is to be made out of it, of Mrs Bond's case; which is to be given to Dr Hunt to show it to Dr Clarke.

The letter is addressed in large copperplate script:

To the Revd Mr Benson to be left at Dr Hunt's in the

Glass-House Yard Minories London

Dear Sir,   Norwch Aprl. 18. 1743

I receiv'd your Letter by Mrs Hunt's Box, wch pleas'd me very much, and shall take any Opportunity to shew you I am Sensible of the Obligations you have laid me under. I am glad to find my Book is in Dr Hunt's Hands and that he intends to give it a 2d Reading. I wish he would put down in writing any Thing he judges faulty or doubtful. Your promise to peruse it is extremely kind, Pray be quite at Leisure before you begin with it, and let nothing scape your Censure. I hope you will put your Remarks in writing. I would not have given you this Trouble, but that the Thing is of Importance, and I have great Reason to be Diffident of my own Judgment. You'll see what the Title and Design of the Thing is wn it comes into yr Hands. This is but one Part of the Work, & design'd as an Introduction to a Paraphrase & Notes upon the Epistle to the <u>Romans</u>. It did not cost me near the

Labour & Time tht I have spent upon the Paraphrase &c. which I sent up to Mr Glover about five weeks ago, & upon wch I have almost done my Best. But as for tht in <u>Dr Hunts</u> Hands I have not review'd it since it was done. Tho' if the Main of it doth not stand good, the whole of the Work must fall to the Ground.

I am impatient to see yr Ansr <u>to Xty not founded on Argumt</u>. I hope such Books will prove the Occasion of striking out new Light, & of shewing the Gospel in its true Colours.

As to the Affair of the incestuous Corinthian, the last Summer and Winter have given me my belly full of Criticism; and I have no Stomach at present to turn my Thoughts that way. And therefore I desire you would excuse my entering into that Affair. Tho' I should think <u>delivering him over to Satan for the Destruction of the Flesh</u>, that <u>the spirit might be saved in the Day of the Lord</u>, means something more than ordering the <u>Corinthians</u> to turn him out of their Church.

I expect Mr Knight at Norwich the Saturday before Whitsun week, and he'll be an exceeding welcome Guest.

My Son sends his Service to you. I thank God he's Sober and Industrious. He has succeeded in his Invention beyond my Expectations, tho' I never discourag'd him; and is at present weaving a Seat incomparably beyond what you saw, but with much more ease & Expedition. By unwearied Application and Thought, by often changing his Gears, Materials & Schemes, he seems to have made himself quite Master of the Business. Weaving is not the Trade he was brought up to; he was never concern'd in mounting a Loom till he enter'd upon this project, and therefore his Difficulties must have been the greater. But I believe he has quite surmounted them all.

The families you kindly remember'd in yours are all well, and would send Service if they knew of my Writing. Mrs Milner I hear draws near her Time, but is but in a discouraging Way. I am sorry to hear Mr Milner's Brother in the North is dead.

I heartily wish we were nearer for the Pleasure & Benefit of Conversation. Norwich is very lonely to me since Mr Scott left it.

Mr <u>Jennings</u> has disappointed me. I fully expected an Answer, and had laid a Scheme in my Head of bringing them into some order in the Debate, and of obliging them to a particular Review of every Scriptural Argument. But I suppose they'll save me that Trouble. The more I reflect upon R R's Conduct and principles the more I dislike 'em. His principles are exceeding weak, his acquaintance with the holy Scriptures very little & shallow, and his Conduct not like tht of a Friend to Truth. But I doubt not 'tis thro' meer Mistake. We have great need to look well to our Hearts, and to use much Caution & Attention in Reading the Scriptures, for our Forefathers used too little. Your Example, Sr, I hope will excite many to this, and yr very Accurate Writings will greatly assist them. May heaven bless all your Studies and Endeavours. Our service to Mrs Benson.

I have a Case to commend to your Friendly Endeavours. Tis that of a Relation of Dr Clark's, the good Physician tht was concern'd in my Son's Case. Her name is Bond, neice to the famous & Worthy Mr Pierce of Exeter, and cousin to Mr James Pierce, now Surgeon, as I understand, in London. This Woman is of exceeding good Reputation, and has had a very good Education. As I am told she came into these parts about 20 Year ago, and then Mr Finch, who knew her, & has known her ever since, says she was one of the most agreeable Women he ever saw, admir'd and esteem'd by every Body. She had £300 Fortune; and marry'd, as people judg'd, well. But her Husband has some considerable while ago fail'd, and they are reduc'd to very low Circumstances; have eight children. The eldest, a Girl, is out at Service; the other Seven are at Home. The Man works at day Labour, Hedging, Ditching, Th[r]eshing &c. & brings in 4 or 5 shil a week, which is the most they have to subsist upon, & they live in a House of 40 shil a year, and the Landlord coming upon thm for Rent, which they ---- d not pay, to save the few Goods they have, she was forc'd to come to Norwich the last week to try -- she could meet with any Succour from Friends there. (They live at Heydon about 10 -- es from here) I met with her at Mr Finch's, & so became acquainted with her Case, which affected me very much. I was glad it happen'd just at that Time to be in our Power to help her. But when I heard she was a Relation of Dr Clark's I resolv'd to communicate her Case to him, being persuaded he is a Person of so much Goodness, that if he knew of her Circumstances he would give her some Relief. Two or 3 Guineas a year would not be so much out of his Pocket & a great Help to her. But we must not prescribe. All I desire, and I believe you will be ready to do it, is to acquaint the Dr with this the first Time you see him, and give my humble Service to him. If you could call in Dr Hunt to your Aid it might be so much the better. It is a good work, an affair tht touches my Heart very much, and I wish you may Succeed. I am, dear Sir, yr much obliged Friend &

affectionate Brother

John Taylor

P.S. I find I'm mistaken. Mrs Milner was deliver'd abt a fortnight ago, but she is in a very low and dangerous Condition. Mr Wright (the Surgeon) was over yesterday, and reports, she's in a deep Consumptn. but little Hopes. I'm heartily sorry for't.

Letter 3 MS5498

The handwriting changes somewhat in the course of this long letter, beginning clear and regular, and becoming more cramped and hurried towards the end. The space at the end of the letter contains eighteen lines in shorthand, obviously Benson's notes.

To the Revd Mr Benson in London

Dear Sr   Norwich May.25.1743.

Your kind letter & 6 of your Answers I receiv'd yesterday almost at the same Time. I thank you for tht the present to me, & shall take Care to dispose of the rest. I am glad Dr Hunt thinks my MS worth a 2d Reading, & tht he will take the pains and care to put down his Remarks in writing. And I earnestly desire, Sr, you would be so good as to peruse it with all your Attention and Accuracy, and spare nothing you judge false, faulty, obscure, defective, inaccurate, redundant. I would desire too that you would take notice how any part strikes & affects your mind, were it not that you who are well versed in such things can't be suppos'd to be mov'd much with any thing I can offer. I never review'd the Key to the Apostolic writings since it was done, and therefore am uncertain how much it stands in need of Correction, in some places I am sure it doth; but the Paraphrase and notes, I have gone over several Times, and have I think almost done my best. I should be glad to have done with it and yet I must not be in haste. — I wish the affair of original Sin had been further canvass'd, and it was my Design it should; & indeed I did not question but it would. However I am ready to take any opportunity to join any Person in a Public Examination of it. If I have advanc'd anything erroneous, I should be glad to see it corrected. — As to <u>regeneration</u>, <u>begotten again</u>, <u>born again</u> I have no doubt but tht in the apostolic Writings those Phrases generally if not always signify being brought into the Christian Church & profession in opposition to <u>Heathenism</u>, and it may be <u>Judaism</u> too. Nor doth it, as you say, necessarily imply Repentance, not true Repentance even in those who need it, much less Repentance in those who need it not. But then I find that the Phrases, which are used to denote our being taken into God's Family; and interested in the privileges of his Kingdom in this World, are sometimes used in a high, emphatical and perfect Sense, and denote a right improvement of those Privileges, wch secures our final and everlasting Interest in the Grace and promises of the Covenant. So <u>sanctifiy</u>, <u>justify</u>, <u>washed</u>, <u>chosen</u>, and all except <u>called</u> are used. And I think our Saviour always uses those Expressions in the Gospels, in the high, emphatical & perfect sense. And what inclines me to think it is so to be understood Joh. 3. 3, 5. is this, that <u>Seeing the Kingdom of God</u>, relates to the full and final Enjoyment of it, for <u>to see</u>, where thus apply'd, is to enjoy, to be possess'd of, or to see in the most comfortable sense.

And how far this will not agree to <u>proselytism by Baptism</u>. —
Our Saviour's Comparison, v.8, <u>the wind blows where it lists &c</u>
manifestly leads our Tho'ts to something informal and invisible
to human Eyes. But proselytism by Baptism is a thing open and
visible. To be born of the Spirit is to be born in a Spiritual Sense.
To <u>be born of Water and of Spirit</u>, I conceive is to be Spiritually
purify'd, or refin'd into a Divine Nature, by the due Application
and Improvement of our rational Powers. I see no necessity
of confining it to Baptism. And whatever <u>Nicodemus</u>'s moral
state was, surely it must be as proper for our Saviour to discourse concerning the grand Law of Seeing God, or of obtaining
eternal Life, (v. <u>3, 15, 16</u>.) as upon any inferior Subject, when
<u>Nicodemus</u> had acknowledg'd him a Prophet sent from God, I
think there was great Propriety in his insisting upon the Terms of
Salvation, which God sent him from heaven to procure to the
World, <u>v.17</u>. Nor can I see what Point is gain'd by confining our
Saviour's meaning to proselytism by Baptism, or takeing upon a
man the Christian Profession. — I am ready to alter the whole or
any Part of what I have written when convinc'd it is not Scripture
Doc. but you must bear with me a little upon this Head, for I own
(wtever the reason may be) I do not see that this Passage is to be
understood merely of being brought into the Kingdom and
Family of God. — Mr Glover has far exceeded my Expectations
in his Sentiments of my Performance. I make allowance for the
kind Propensities & good will of a Friend. He's a good Judge of
good Sense & just Thoughts, & heartily wish he were as well
qualify'd for Criticism. I doubt not, Sir, but your abilities and
Penetration in that way will discover Defects and Errors wch
have escaped him. I thank you for your Kindness to Mrs Bond,
& shall observe your orders. — As to Archdeacon Jeffries
Prayers, 'twas wth much difficulty I procur'd one here for myself,
and now I have lost it again by lending it out. If there ever was an
Edition here, I dare say, 'tis all sold off. — I dont know what to
say yet about disposing of my Copy: I thank you for your
Friendly offer to serve me. But let's see first whether it be worth
publishing. However, I don't think it is yet fit for the Press. — We
have not I think sufficient Light to discover all the Circumstances

of <u>Alexander's</u> Case in particular, nor have we any Intimation how in general the Case of any person deliver'd over to Satan terminated when he proved incorrigible under the Rod. Possibly, like <u>Pharoah</u>, the Judgment might be remov'd for his greater obduration. I have been turning over that excellent Per[formanc]e <u>the His. of the 1st Planting of the Gospel</u>, & can't find tht you rank the 2d Epistle to Timothy among tho[se writt]en from Rome; or tht you take any notice at all of it. I have read the 2 first parts of yr Ansr. and am much pleas'd wth your Acct of Faith. But I think you have misapply'd 2 or 3 Texts <u>Rom.1.5</u> — <u>16.26</u>. <u>Acts 6.5</u>. <u>Rom. 10. 16</u>. Yo intimate the <u>obedce of Faith</u>, <u>being obedient to the Faith</u> & <u>Believing</u> in those places relate to the Obedience which is Subsequent to <u>Faith</u>, or the Fruit of it. Whereas I conceive they relate to the first act and Instance of Obedience, the Embracing the Gospel when offer'd and first preach'd. For in all those places the general Acceptance & belief of the Gospel upon the preaching of the apostles is spoken of, nor is it the writer's intention immediately to signify what further effect it had, or was to have upon the minds of those who by the first Act of Obedience receiv'd it. possibly they might receive it in vain. Of this first obedience in embracing the Gospel wn 1st offer'd to thm the Apostle speaks in his first Address to the Roman Gentile Converts. Rom. 6. 17. <u>But ye have obey'd from the Heart the Mould of Doctrine under wch ye were put</u>. They had chearfully embrac'd the Gospel Faith and Profession. This was their first Obedience. They were just under the <u>Die</u> or <u>Mould</u> & the Apostle in the whole chaptr is exhorting them to admit a firm and deep Impression, by living agreeably to their Faith & profession; this is the Subsequent Obedience. — But enough for once. Adieu, dear Sr and with courage pursue the happy Road in wch yo have made such considerable Advances, and may all your Labours meet with good Acceptance. Our service to Mrs Benson.

I am, dear Sir, yr affectionate Brother, &c

John Taylor

Letter 4 MS5499

To The Rev'd Mr Benson to be left at Dr. Hunts in the
Glass-house-yard Minories, London

Dear Sr.   Norwch. Sep. 8. 1743

    I have yrs dated Aug.18. By Inquiring, I have found the pro-
prietor of Dr. Jeffries' Prayers, and a considerable number of
Books in stock. The proprietor is Mr Thos Goddard a Bookseller
here, who sent me yesterday the following Letter. Sr. __ "I was
told by my Servant that you call'd at my Shop to know what
Number of Dr. Jeffrey's Devotions I have by me, and whether the
property be mine. I have the Copy of the Doctr. & the property
is mine. But however if yr. Friend please to take what of them I
have by me at a Guinea a Hundred in Quires I will resign my
Property to him. I know not certainly how many I have, but I
think not above two Hundred. I am with much Respect &c. Tho:
Goddard.
    Let me know what yo and your Friend think of this Affair, that
I may return an Answer to Mr Goddard, or he may write to Mr
Goddard himself.
    I sent my Pieces to London for the Benefit of Remarks, and
having been there so long I was in Hopes I should have had them
returned by Michaelmas with many Remarks. If Mr Hunt only
made a Mark with a led pencil at any Exceptionable Passage I
should take it as a great Favour. For I shall think it very hard, if
he returns it in Silence, after so long a time given for a perusal.
And, Sr, if Yr Remarks were the Shorter they might be of service
to the Work. However I must leave it to Yr Discretion. But it will
be wrong to keep it long, and do little. My Service to Dr Hunt,
and desire him to bestow a little attention upon it. If it were but
a Mark in the Margin by his Hand it would put me upon considering the passage with greater Application.
    I design to give your Explication of Joh.3. 3, 5. in yr late
Answer a careful Examination. I only want to see what is right. I

have no prejudice in favour of either Sense, and can readily alter or retract any Thing.

I wish you would review yr <u>Scrip. Doc. of Regeneration</u>. I doubt not it would be of great use.

I am greatly oblig'd, and desire thanks my be return'd for yr Critique of <u>Rom.5.12.</u> I think it is worthy of much regard and when I review my Mss will consider it more closely & particularly. At present I shall only say, That the objection which the ingenious Gentleman raises against his proper sense of ημαρτον, from αμαρτωλοι v.19. is of no weight with me Because αμαρτωλοι κατεσταθησαν & δικαιοι καταστασθησονται are phrases reducible to a Standard as I think I have shown in my Book, and are Sufficiently explained by that Standard. But I cannot say as much of παντες ημαρτον. As this is partly a Letter of Business I sent it by the Post; otherwise shd have waited an unexpensive opportunity. Service to Mrs Benson.

I am, Dear Sr, yr much obliged, & affec. Brother,

John Taylor

Letters 5 MS5500

This letter is carefully written throughout in Taylor's sloped, formal hand. The major work which is giving him problems over its publication is obviously the Paraphrase and Key to the Apostolic Writings. *In the end, this was 'Printed and Sold by J. Waugh in Gracechurch Street MDCCXLV'; but publication by subscription is here considered and rejected as both troublesome and likely to lead to difficulties with the booksellers. So it proved, as later letters show, when that method had to be used for the vastly more difficult and expensive* Hebrew Concordance.

Dear Sr   Norwch Feb.17. 1743/4

Ever since I receiv'd my Mss from London, I have been busy
in reviewing it, wch is the reason of my not writing sooner to
you. I thankfully acknowledge the kind assistance of your
Remarks, and it gave me great pleasure to meet with your hand
writing here and there in the Piece. That <u>Spirits in Prison</u>, dont
signify the <u>Gentile</u> world, I was convinc'd by the Dissertation,
annexd to your Paraphrase upon St <u>Peter</u>, which I am satisfyd
has given the true Sense of the Place. It pleas'd me very much.
You kindly offer to send me a Collection of the various Senses of
<u>Spirit</u>, which you have made; I thank you for your Goodness; but
I am in no Condition to do any Thing more at present, nor shall
I at any Time be so able to digest & settle them, as you your self,
which I heartily wish you would do. To your Observations I have
paid all the Regard which I am sure you desir'd; and have faithfully & impartially done my best, and now care not how soon the
piece is published. I have little more that I can do to it, & therefore intend to send it up Shortly. I have been imploy'd two or
three Weeks in making Indexes of Texts and Things, which are
now almost finish'd by the kind Assistance of Mr Milner's
Nephew, Mr Blackburn, who has been here with his Uncle near
a Fortnight. He is a promising young Man, and came in very
seasonably to my Relief, being greatly fatigu'd with constant
Application.

As to the manner pf publishing wt I have done, I know not
what to say, and should be glad of the Assistance and Advice
of my Friends. You were speaking of a Gentleman, one Mr
Davison, I think, who desired to be concern'd it. You are a better
Judge than I in this Case, but I have no Reason to forsake Mrs[?]
Fenner. Any honest Advantage I could make of it, would suit my
Circumstances very well, tho' I had much higher and different
Views in the Work. There is a Bookseller at Manchester, who, I
believe, would be my Best Chap, but I'm afraid dealing with him
would disgust the London Booksellers, and be a Hindrance here-
after to the Book. I would not do anything tht might hinder
the Spread of it, and would allow all proper Encouragement to

promote the Sale. Some advise to publish it by Subscription; but that I fear would be troublesome, and not so pleasing to the Booksellers; I would venture the Issue of the Sale, could I depend upon fair and honourable Usage. But I shall acquiesce in what you and my good Friends judge will be, upon the whole, for the best. And therefore I desire you would be so good as consider of it a little, & let me know the Result of your Thoughts, which I hope you will be able to do by my Son, who brings this to you. Our Service to Mrs Benson. I wish you all Success in your valuable Designs,

& am, dear Sr.

pray my service to Mr Lardner,	yr much oblig'd Friend,
with many Thanks for the Present	& affectionate Brother,
of his Sermons, which in the main	John Taylor
I think are very just and good.	

Letter 6 MS5501

This letter opens with a more formal address, and is very neatly and carefully written. It is of interest for the picture it gives of the hard work and worry involved in the publication of Taylor's great Concordance, and of the unclear relations between authors and bookseller-publishers. The comment on Buxtorf's Concordance shows how far Taylor's work was from mere dependence on Buxtorf, and how well merited was the recognition it received as his own splendid achievement. There are three lines of notes in shorthand, no doubt Benson's, at the end of the letter.

Dear and Revd Sir,   Norwch, June 3. 1751.

I got well to Norwch the Friday night after I left London, & found all as usual. With great pleasure I remember your agreeable Conversation, & friendly Offices. I heartily wish you were nearer; your Knowledg & Wisdom would be of great Service to me. Upon a Review of the Case between me and Mr Waugh, I could not agree to allow him any of the Subscriptions tht either pay'd or promised while I was at London, considering they happen'd before the proposals were publish'd, and consequently before the Booksellers could be concern'd in thm & as I was at great Expence and Trouble to prepare those Proposals, that they might come into the World in the most effective manner. In short, he has given thm up, only declining the receiving of the Money due upon promissary Subscriptions. Therefore, Dear Sr, I humbly request, if you know of any willing to pay the Subscription Money, you would be pleased to take it, giving a Receipt to my Use & Accounts. But, it will be best for them to Stay till I return to London. I shall be much oblig'd for your further Assistance. I have left Franks enough at Mr Waugh's, in Case you should have any Inclination to send Proposals to any distant Friend. I am not clear about the Affair of allowing a Book in 7. Mr Waugh informs me Dr Winder allow'd 2 in 8. But Dr Winder's Case and mine are different. He had no body but himself to provide. I have a pretty numerous and still increasing Posterity to consider, and so, have nothing to throw away. The Booksellers, I perceive, have no Rule to go by, only the getting all they can from Authors. Which puzzles me very much. A Bookseller in the Country is order'd by a Gentleman to write to his Correspondent Bookseller in London to subscribe into Mr Waugh's hands. Here are 3 Booksellers concernd, will they every one expect a 7th part of a Book? Or if I allow one Book in 7, pray wch of those Booksellers must have it? I should be glad to know in the clearest manner I am able upon what Terms this Affair is to be carried on, and what Bounds are to be set to Bookseller's Demands, especially such as only execute the Orders of Gentlemen, but procure no Subscriptions themselves. I wish Mr Waugh would consider how this is to be distinctly Settled. I am busy revising, and find I can easily keep before the Printer, having already revis'd 8 Sheets. I hope to bring it to a great Degree of Exactness, & to correct all the Faults of <u>Buxtorf</u> which I find are very numerous. But as the Book has been very little us'd, no notice has been taken of them.

My humble service to Mrs Benson, Justice Riccards & his Lady, Mr Cook, Mr Comber, Dr Lardner & all my inquiring Friends & Brethren. I wish you well suppy'd with an Assistent. All is quiet here. May the Blessing of God establish yr Health, & succeed all yr useful Labours. I am, dear Sr.

Yr much obliged and affect Brother

John Taylor

Letter 7 MS5502

My dear and worthy Friend,   Norwch June 27. 1751.

I am greatly obliged to you for your kind assistance in my troublesome affair, and wish it may be in my power to make adequate Returns — I am very free to allow the Booksellers the usual and reasonable Profit, and had, before I rec'd yrs, wrote to Mr Waugh that I wd let the Booksellers have 9s a Book, as you have explain'd it, only I do not think it reasonable to allow him 9/ a Book upon those I procur'd at London. I have not heard from him since. I hope he puts the affair forward as much as he can.

Mr Dixon is again very uneasy among us. He cannot bear any Slight, and really has not Spirit enough to endeavour to bear and rise above such Remarks and Censures as he must expect now. I do all in my power to incourage him. I am sorry yo are not only disappointed of Mr Holland, but so much at a loss for an Assistant.

I cannot help you to the Answer to R. R.

Perhaps some of the Articles, wch Mr Tozer assented to, might relate to Discipline. But they were chiefly Doctrinal in the Calvinistic Scheme.

Kircher, (as Trommius observes, if I mistake not, in the preface to his Greek Concordance,) wrote a Concordance to the Septuagint Translation, but I never heard before of his compiling a

Hebrew Concordance, much less, <u>one vastly preferable to Buxtorf</u>'s. Nor surely did Dean Prideaux, or Dr Hunt of Oxford know of any such Concordance. Nor, in the Nature of the thing, can any Hebrew Concordance be in a more natural and just method, to answer the ends both of a Concordance and Lexicon, than <u>Buxtorf</u>'s; nor can I possibly alter the Method without throwing it into Disorder and Confusion. Every man is wise in his own way, & men's Heads, you know, are in various positions.

I am glad to hear of Dr Rotheram's Recovery, & hope you find yr Health pretty well established.

I thank yo for yr kind Design with Regard to Dr Leland. I wrote to him I believe more than a month ago to the same Purpose, and hope my Letter would come in time. Mrs Crane, widow of Mr Crane, our late Assistant, expected to have had her yearly allowance from the Fund, but hearing nothing of it has desired me to mention it to some of my London Friends, and I wish you could assist her in the affair.

I do not know but you may see Mr Dixon at London shortly. One of our Friends intending for London, has offer'd to carry him thither in the hired Coach. But they stay but a week. My compliments to Mrs Benson and all Friends.

I am, Dear Sir, yr much obliged & affectionate

Brother

John Taylor

Letter 8 MS5503

This short letter is written on a half sheet, in smaller script of different appearance, but still with the marks of Taylor's penmanship. It is of interest for its evidence of the efforts Taylor made in gathering subscriptions for his Hebrew Concordance. Here he suggests interesting the Irish bishops by presenting each with a copy of his short book on the Atone-

ment: the stratagem he had already employed with the English
hierarchy. The Bishop of Clonfert, John Whitcombe, seems to
have been especially interested and helpful.

Dear Sr.   Norwch July 18. 1751

I doubt not yo will be so good as to receive to my account 3
Guineas for 2 Subscriptions from Mr Mauduit. I wrote to Mr
Waugh by a private Hand, but have receiv'd no Answer. Qu.
Whether it would not be a proper Measure to make a present of
my Book of Atonement to all the Irish Bishops? Think of it. And
consider how they may be sent. Not to <u>Smith</u> the Bookseller, but
to some other Hand, to be distributed when the Irish parliament
meets. (for that will be the most proper time) Perhaps the Bp of
Clonfert, or however Archdeacon Doyle, might be willing to
present thm in my Name, or my good Friend Dr Mann, a person
of good Repute in Lord Newports, the Lord Chancellor's Family,
would I doubt not readily do it for me. My service to Mrs
Benson. I am, dear Sr

with the sincerest Affection & Gratitude yr much obliged &c.

John Taylor

If I know the Number of the Irish Bishops I could have the
Books bound here, & sent from Hence any Week to Manchester
& so to Liverpool perhaps more readily than from London,
wthout troubling Waugh. This I think would be best.

Memorandum on the facing half of the folded sheet by Benson
or his agent:

July 23 1751
Recd 3 guineas fm Mr Israel Mauduit for the first subscriptn to
Mr Taylor's heb. concordnc. for Joshua Iremongr of Mother-
well, Hants: Esq And the Revd Mr Henry Owen, M. B.
Clergymn. Mem. Mr Taylor had given rects.

Letter 9 MS5504

My Dear Friend,   Norwich Aug.21. 1751.

I rec'd yrs of the 5th instant, and am greatly obliged for your great Kindness in promoting my Subscription; I have got 4 from Lincoln, which amount to 7 Guineas and a half, one of the Subscribers having paid the whole Subscription money, wch 7½ Guineas the Lincoln Carrier, Mr Robinson will pay to you, and I desire you would receive it to my Acct. I have order'd Mr Waugh to get 22 of my Books on At—nt bound in the same manner as those for the English Bps, and I shall observe yr Advice as to the Bp of Clonfert. I have also desired Mr Orton of Shrewsbury to pay the first Subscription for one Book to you. — I thank you for your Affidavit in Mr Waugh's Letter. As tht Article was not charg'd in any preceding Bill, I am excusable, I presume, if I am not pleas'd with it.

I have revis'd 70 sheets of the Mss, and am now giving as concise & clear an Explication of the Hebrew Roots & their several Significations as I can. For Scripture Animals I have gone thro' Bochart's Hierozoicon, and have extracted all I could find to my purpose. Tis a prodigious Mass of Learning, but a considerable part of it might have been spar'd. I hope in a Day or two to have Kercher's Concordance. It was publish'd in 1607, 25 years before Buxtorf's, but in his Preface Buxtorf takes no notice of it as a Hebrew Concordance. All tht he saith of it is this; Ante paucos annos in 70 Graecorum Versione, eximium et laboriosissimum ejusmodi opus edidit Conradus Kircherus, —, addito peculiari de Concordandiarum illarum usu, commentario. But when I see it, I shall be able to say more.

I send by the Bearer of this my little piece on Education, & I beg you would assist Mr Waugh with your Advice in printing it. I would have it done in 120 in neat manner. Our compliments to Mrs Benson, wishing you both all manner of Happiness, I am

Yr greatly obliged and most sincerely affectionate

John Taylor

Letter 10 MS5505

*In this letter Taylor exhibits the value of his Concordance,
showing there has not been any earlier one of comparable
scope and thoroughness, nor one adapted to the English Bible.
His comment on the Septuagint version is interesting, coming
from a scholar with such detailed knowledge of both the
Hebrew and the Greek.*

To The Revd Dr Benson in Prescott Street.

Dear Sr.   Norw. Sep.9. 1751.

I have yrs by Mr Ashill, & thank you heartily for all your
Goodness. I order all the money subscrib'd to me to be paid to
you, & am strongly inclin'd to wish I may prove troublesome to
you. I hope to be at London the beginning of the Year, and
should be glad to be acquainted with the Names of any persons
to whom it may be proper to apply. Or if I were acquainted with
any at present I could write to them. My Number of Subscribers
(with those I procur'd at London) amount to abt. 133.

I have had Kercher's Concordance by me about a Fortnight. Tis
a Work exactly upon the same general Plan with my own. The
Difference is, that his is adapted to the Septuagint Version, mine
to the English Bible; He follows the Edition of the Hebrew
Concordance before <u>Buxtorf's</u>, and so he only gives you the
Roots or little more; mine has the advantage of Buxtorf's
Improvements, and gives you all the Branches under every Root.
This with my own Improvements makes mine a very methodical
and compleat Hebrew Concordance; whereas his, in that view, is
very incomplete and defective, and indeed is neither Hebrew nor
Greek Concordance. For altho' he has an Index of the Greek
Words, as I have of the English, showing under what Roots every
Greek word may be found, This can no more denominate his a
Greek Concordance, than mine an English one. <u>Trommius</u> has
very well supplied his Defects in giving us a compleat Greek
Concordance, and adding an Index, showing the various Greek

Works [*sic*] by which every Hebrew Word is translated, & so hath made Kercher of much less Value, though still it is not without its use. But as an Hebrew Concordance 'tis very obscure & lame. I have examin'd & consulted it with Care, but 'tis of no manner of use to me; The Greek is often so very remote from the sense of the Hebrew, that it frequently serves only to shew how wild & extravagant a Translation the Septuagint is. I have revis'd and prepar'd for the press about 70 sheets of my Mss, reducing them I am persuaded to a perfect Truth and Exactness in the Quotations, Translations, & the just and full Number of Texts under every Hebrew Word. I have added under every Root an English Explication of its Senses natural and figurative, which gives me much Satisfaction, as I am persuaded it will be a good Guide to those tht consult it in settling the Sense of particular Texts. And I hope you and my other Judicious Friends will find that I have not bestow'd my pains to no Purpose. May God continue yr Valuable Life in the most Comfortable Circumstances, & prosper all yr good Endeavours. Our service to Mrs Benson. I am,

Dear Sr, yr much obliged, &c.

John Taylor

Letter 11 MS5506

A short note in Taylor's more careful hand. The Bishop of Raphoe was Philip Twysden.

Dear Sr.   Norwch Octob. 8. 1751.

The Bishop of Raphoe, I understand by a Letter from our good Friend the Bishop of Clonfert, is now at London, and lodges in Pall Mall. He advises me to apply to him for a Subscription. But I think it would be proper first to make him a Present of my Book as to the other Bishops. If you think this to be right, I desire you would, without saying anything to Mr Waugh, take one of my

Atonements, pay him for it, & get it bound as the rest, & send it as a Present in the Name of the Author, let me know when you have done it, & I will write to him. If you know any better way of proceeding, I shall be glad to be inform'd.

The Bishop of Clonfert wants to know whether you have published a 2d Edition of yr Commentary on the Catholic Epistles. Our most friendly respects to Mrs Benson, Service to Dr Lardner and all Friends. I am yr most affectionate

Brother, &c.

John Taylor

Letter 12 MS5507

This long letter begins in well-spaced, formal script, but becomes smaller and more cramped as the writer realizes the need to economize his space. The reference to 'Mrs Chandler' in the third paragraph clearly means 'Mr', but is equally clearly written as copied.

Reverd and dear Sir.   Norwich. Oct.25.1751.

Yrs inclosed with Mr <u>Waugh</u>'s I have received and thank you greatly for your Care in correcting the Press, for which I desire you would content your self out of the Books, in taking what Number you think fit. I thank you also for your Care & Trouble abt the Book presented to the Bp of <u>Raphoe</u>; & for the Subscriptions taken in & procured by yr kind address. In short I am under so many obligations tht I fear I shall not be able to make any adequate Returns. Mr Dixon sends his Service, and joins with me in desiring you would send the 2d Ed. of yr 1st Vol of paraphrases to us in sheets by the Norwich Carrier, Nasmith, at the Bull in Bpgate Street.

I have, since I left London, raisd the Number of Subscriptions from about 85 which I got there to 143, though I have not yet made any Application here to the Clergy or others. Mr Waugh informs me that he & Mr Vallant have got about 30. I hope by the beginning of the year I may have 200, with wch Number I shall venture to put the Book to the press, and hope I may draw off about 500. I therefore desire you would consider whether it is not time now for Mr <u>Waugh</u> to finish his Fount. If you think it is, you may let him know it as from me, and so he may proceed. I believe some of those in the 143 abovementioned, are some of yr Subscriptions wch you sent me word you had procured, & all tht paid the Subscription-money to you are included except the 4 mentioned in your last Letter, wch are not included in the 143.

I have, with all possible Diligence, improved my time since I left London, in revising the Concordance & examining every Quotation with great Exactness, giving an English Explication of all the Roots & the several Senses of the Roots, from the best Commentary I could procure, & from a Collation of all the Places in the Bible where the word occurs. Thus I have gone over 80 sheets of my Mss, and shall persue the work till I return, God willing, to London. I sh'd be glad to have the assistance of <u>Schultens</u>'s Mss Lexicon. Mrs[?] Chandler, you know, has it. Do you think he would part with it as far as Norwich? I have ventur'd to ask the Favour; wch If I cannot obtain; I doubt not but he would let me have it while I am in London. It is also, as I am inform'd, in the hands of Mr <u>Patman</u>, a Dutch Minister in London; & of Mr <u>Robertson</u>, who once was with Dr Milner of <u>Peckham</u>. I should have it as soon as possible tht I may have time to weigh wt <u>Schultens</u> advances. Tho', <u>entre nous</u>, I may tell you, I have not the same opinion of <u>Schultens</u> that Mr <u>Chandler</u> has. His Learning much exceeds his Judgment. & I find in his Comments upon <u>Job</u> & <u>proverbs</u>, which I have procur'd, Interpolations very weak & extravagant. He carries the scheme of deriving <u>Hebrew</u> words from the <u>Arabic</u> beyond all due Bounds, and makes no scruple of wresting & wrenching to bring things to his Notions. A very bad Quality in a Critic.

I purpose to be in London, God willing, the Beginning of the Year; & I wish you could help me to snugg retired Lodgings in some Court, a little remov'd from the Rumble & Noise of the

City. There was one <u>Mr Hill in Falcon Court Lothbury</u> who before I went up last to London offer'd me Lodgings in his House. If he is there still, & is willing to take me in, & you think it a proper Situation, I should like it very well. I wish I could procure any of my Brethren, tht are ordain'd, & likely to be acceptable at Norwich, to exchange with me. He might lodge at my House, & have my Horse every Day to ride out with if he pleased. God bless you, my dear Friend, & give us a happy Meeting first at London, & afterwards in the world of Glory. I am yr greatly obliged &c

Our Compliments to Mrs Benson   John Taylor
& Dr Lardner

[Postscript on the reverse of the sheet:]

Since I wrote the other side I have perused the Agreement which Mr Waugh sent inclosed with yours, and find it is defective in two Articles which I sent upon to him, & to which he told me he had no objection, but he has forgot to insert them. I have added also an article relating to the not delaying the work, and another of Mr W's own proposing relating to the Times of my being paid. I have consider'd the several Parts well over, and think it reasonable in every respect, and the only Terms on my part that I can agree to, and which I expect and hope Mr Waugh will agree to. As I pay him a price considerably advanced for printing, I may reasonably expect that it should be well corrected before it comes to me. And from this I will not recede. I would not therefore have you mention anything to him about perfecting his Fount till this Agreement is perfected, which I hope he will delay no longer.

Whether Mr Blackburn will be for coming to Norwich about the time that I shall be for going to London I know not. But his Voice is rather too weak for our place, especially in an afternoon; and his place is rather too far out of the City for me. But if I can procure no better assistance we must put up with a few inconveniences.

I shall acquaint the Bp of <u>Clonfert</u> with what you say when I write to him.

Letter 13 MS5508

*This letter is interesting for its evidence of the careful research that went into the task of establishing the precise meaning of the Hebrew roots. It also reflects Taylor's standing among the most eminent Hebraists of his day. 'Dr Hunt of Oxford' is Thomas Hunt (1696–1774), Regius Professor of Hebrew and Laudian Professor of Arabic. He is described in DNB as an 'intimate friend of Dr Richard Newton, Dr Kennicott, and Doddridge'. Taylor's great-grandsons cite Hunt along with Law and Kennicott in testimony to the high esteem in which Taylor's judgement was held, 'as may be inferred from their having given extracts from his letters to them upon the subjects treated of in their works, as adding a degree of sanction to their publication' (*The Principles and pursuits of an English Presbyterian Clergyman of the Eighteenth Century. *1843, p. vii).*

[Address on outside:] To the Revd Dr Benson in Prescott Street
Goodman's Field

Dear & Revd Sir   Norwch. Nov.9.1751

I give you a World of trouble, thts certain. In the article abt correcting, I wonder you shd not see tht I meant only the <u>common Corrector,</u> as I intended to be the <u>extraordinary</u> one myself. But I have explain'd the thing so clearly to Mr Waugh, tht I think there can now be no place left for Ambiguity. And I wish you could spare a little time in helping him thro' with the memorandum. In wch I hope there will be found no Difficulty. Pray forget not to enquire for a Lodging.

I have heard nothing from Brother Chandler. I suppose he's loth to part with his Lexicon so far. Dr Hunt of Oxford informs me "tht the Ms Lexicon is no otherwise the Work of

Schultens than as the Adversaria or Note-Book of a Scholar can be call'd the Work of the Professor, who dictated the Contents by way of Lecture. For I understand that Schultens left nothing of it in Writing, but only a few marginal Notes in his Bible, wch serv'd as so many Hints to enlarge on, when he came to read to his Pupils." This Acct Dr Hunt gives me of this Lexicon. He has one of thm himself. One Kals, a Dutch Divine, now at Oxford, one of Schultens's Scholars offer'd to send me Excerptions upon every Root from this Lexicon, & gave a Specimen of those Excerptions, shewing the primary signification of the Root upon the word כפר Caphar. But, not liking his Excerptions, I sent them to Dr Hunt with my Remarks, pointing out the Faults, wch were considerable, and withall sent the Dr wt I had done my self upon the Root & its several Senses. Schultens makes linire to smear; I make tegere, to cover, the primary Signification of Caphar. Schultens goes upon the Arabic; I upon common sense considering & comparing the several Texts where the words are used. Dr Hunt in a Letter this Week greatly prefers, commends, and confirms my primary Signification. "I cannot, saith he, but wonder how Mr Schultens came not to give this meaning the first Place in his account of the Word, especially when his Arabians might have informed him that their Verb כפר often signifies to cover or conceal, but never once to smear or daub; & tht they call'd a village כפר because it was remote & conceal'd &c. & as כפר is a covert inhabitation so is כפיר a covert - Lion & wt is sd of him Ps.17.12. tht he dwells in secret places, seems to be a Definition of his Name." But Schultens gives the Reason of the Young Lion's name to be, from his Smearing himself and the Ground with Blood; wch is evidently the Characteristic of all Lions. I believe I shall make a good shift without this same Lexicon, especially as I have Schultens upon Job & Proverbs, where he writes with Care, and may much more be depended upon, than in the Lexicon.

Our compliments to Mrs Benson. I pray God bless you, & make yr Life as comfortable, as it is useful. I am

Dr Sr yr greatly obliged

J Taylor

Letter 14 MS5509

My dearest Friend,   Norwch. Apl.16. 1754.

Glad am I, and thankful to God, you are so well recover'd
from your late Indisposition, wch gave me so much uneasiness. I
am very loth to trouble you with any of my Affairs. I wish you
would at Leisure look over the Preface. I have drawn up a kind
of Dedication, wch may be inserted, if you think it proper. The
Archbishop of Canterbury I think should first see it, lest there
should be anything in it which he dislikes. But Mr Waugh can
wait upon his Grace for that. But I would have you see it first,
and if you think it needless or improper, it shall be left out. I have
here added a list of those who have pay'd the whole Subscription.
Our Service to Mrs Benson. I purpose, when Mr Bourn comes
home, to go into Lancashire, where I have not been for several
years. When I return I should be glad to see you at Norwich &
Mrs Benson. If you have any Inclination to come, I will make all
the Haste back again, that I can. I pray God continue and establish your Health. I am,

my dear Friend, your
Sincerely affectionate
John Taylor

[At right angles, on the other half of the sheet:]

A List of such as have paid the whole
Subscription

The Bishop of London
The Bishop of Norwich
Mr Cuthbert of Cork
Revd Mr Js. Weld ⎤
Revd Adam Blair ⎬ of Dublin
Ralph Card Esqr ⎟
Rev. Ja. Clagston ⎦
Revd Steph. Sleech Provost of Eton
Revd Mr Ashton Fel. of Eton

The Library of Eton College
Dr Jos. Alwell
Dr Kennicott of Oxford
Revd Mr Hunt of Hackney
— Mr Hugh Farmer
— Phil. Furneaux
Revd Dr Hill Prebendary of York
Mat. Lee of Ebford Esqr
Judge Foster
John Cay Esqr Judge of the Marshalsea Court
paid me in Pinner's Hall Vestry, two guineas for
the first Subscription, and therefore hath but one
Guinea to pay for the Second Subscription.

Letter 15 MS5510

This cheerful letter is of especial interest for its description of the odium theologicum *Taylor's views had brought upon him, and then of a change of sentiment towards him. 'The popish cause', in the last line, is a jocular reference to orthodox Calvinists, whom Taylor regarded as practising 'Dissenting popery' (see Chapter 5). It also gives us an interesting, informal picture of a Presbyterian ordination. It is written throughout in his more careful, well-spaced hand.*

To The Revd Dr Benson

My dear Friend   Norwich Dec.5.1755.

So it happens that Ralph and I must club at a little Book. It was very much unexpected, and somewhat surprising that we should be called to an Ordination in this part of the World, and have the principal Parts of the Work assigned to us. All our Brethren in Norfolk and Suffolk were also invited, but none of the Faction, which hath hitherto prevailed, would come near us, which discouraged me very much.; so tht the night before I concluded, the whole work would be devolved upon dear Mr Milner and my Self. But lo! in the morning, when I came to Harleston, (for I lodged 2 or 3 Miles from tht place) I found a collection of 13 Ministers (with the Candidate) all able worthy men, & cordial Friends, which gave me good Spirits, & we had help enough and to spare. There was my self, Mr Bourn, Mr Nasmith, Mr Milner, Mr Whiteside, Mr Alderson, Mr Stanton of Colchester, Mr Taylor of Stowmarket, Mr Lincoln of Beccles, Mr Priestly from Needham, Mr Dickenson, & Mr Dawson from Diss (I hope Mr Dickenson, a north country man, will settle there) & Mr Smithson, a very hopeful young man. We went through the Service very comfortably, & greatly to the Satisfaction of the Audience, who were not prepossessed in our Favour, as great Pains hath been taken for many Years to render us odious all over the Country, so tht I reckon'd my reputation absolutely irretrievable. But things have taken a strange turn in more places than one. All tht were present have entertain'd a quite different opinion of us, and nothing would serve them but his Sermon and my Charge must be printed. This stun'd poor Ralph, & made him grievously uneasy; he would have excused himself, as he had no intention in composing to publish, &c. But I being a harden'd Veteran in publishing, readily admitted their plea, "that it would be of great Service in those parts" and by Degrees I comforted my dear Friend, rais'd his spirits and, though he would not consent while we were at Harleston, prevailed with him to send a fair copy of his Sermon, which I believe is a very good one. Among other Things, I told him, I should order both Sermon and Charge to be put into your Hands, and to be submitted to your perusal, which had a good Effect & made him more willing. But I desire you would detain them as little as possible, because the sooner they are published the better, while Impressions are fresh upon people's Minds. By what hath happened to us here, & in other Parts of the World, I am in hopes that the popish cause is on the decline.

Dear Sr.

yr most affectionate

John Taylor

Hasten Mr Waugh as much as you can in printing this.

Letter 16 MS5511

This important letter to his trusted friend exhibits Taylor's state of mind as he contemplates the move to Warrington. The script is careful and well spaced throughout, but unflourished, presenting a sober and thoughtful appearance. The writer is obviously thinking very seriously about the project. The formal letter inviting him to take part in it, written after the first meeting of the Trustees on June 20, has clearly not yet reached him, or he would surely have said so; but as both that letter and this one show, he is well aware that such an invitation is to be expected. It is remarkable that he still supposes the scheme to be open to modification, and he expresses marked uneasiness about some of its features. The potentiality for the trouble that ensued is clearly visible.

To the Revd Dr Benson

My Dearest Friend   Norwich June 25.1757

There is an Address to our Gentlemen, sent from Manchester, relating to the intended Academy. There is one point too partially represented; I mean, the Situation of the Academy. Only <u>Warrington</u> & <u>Ormskirk</u> are mentioned, and the Merits of each considered. But there is a third Place, wch I think is deserving of Consideration, & should have been fairly proposed; & tht is <u>Hoghton Tower</u>, a <u>Villa</u> belonging to Sr <u>Harry Hoghton</u>, one of the best Families in Lancashire, & in the dissenting Interest. It is about 6 Miles eastward from <u>Preston</u>, & a day's Journey from <u>Manchester</u> & <u>Warrington</u>, In a very retired Situation, in the midst of Sr Harry's large Estate, wch lies all about it. It stands upon elevated Ground, much like <u>Windsor Castle</u>, in a good Air, with grand extensive Prospects on every Side, & a fine River at the Foot of the Mount. It is a large Pile of costly Buildings, inclosing a spacious Area, wherein are Rooms, I suppose, to receive & lodge a hundred Students or more. K. James I, when he came from Scotland to England, lodged there, with all his Retinue. There are

Halls, I doubt not, convenient for 5 or 6 or more Professors separately to lecture in; a Chappel & Pulpit for the common, Public Exercises of the whole Academy. Here the whole Society might every night be lock'd up & secured in uno claustro; good Hours & Order well preserved; the whole College easily, at a Minute's warning, convened; few or no Avocations from Study; many great Inconveniences, (alehouses, Taverns, Gaming, Girls, idle Company, Frolics, Vice) the Nusances of large Towns, & the bane of mental Improvement, & good Morals, avoided; advantages enough for innocent Recreations; and, with Tutors and Fellow Students, enough of such Conversation, as is proper for young Gentlemen, who come only for the Cultivation of their Minds. All those Advantages both to Tutors & Students are sufficient to outweigh any lesser & trifling Inconveniences — The House is now empty, & hath been so for several years, the Family being remov'd to another Country Seat within about a Mile from Preston, whch admits of, wht the Situation of Hoghton Tower will not allow, spacious beautiful Gardens, &c. nor is there any Probability of their returning to Hoghton Tower. But Sr Harry keeps a Chaplain there who preaches to a Congregation, wch assembles there constantly; and Boards, as I apprehend, with a Farmer, who dwells in some Part of the House.

I doubt not but Sr Harry would be willing that the Academy should be erected there. And his Heir and Nephew, Mr Henry Hoghton, who studied under Dr Dodderidge, a Gentleman of a very good Character, & a hearty Friend to us, I dare say, would be pleased with the Thing. And the Favour and Patronage of such an ancient & eminent Family would surely be an Advantage.

But my Design is not to stickle for the Place, or to prejudice you in Favour of it; but to give a true Representation of it, & too leave you, & Dr Avery, or any other Person to whom you are pleased to shew it, to judge as you think fit. For the 18 years that I taught and Boarded young men in Lincolnshire, I experienced the very great Benefit of a like Situation. In such Towns as either Warrington or Ormskirk, an Academy, in any Degree numerous, will probably in no long time be infected with Vice, perhaps in several Shapes; nor will it be in the Power of the most vigilant

Tutors to prevent it; so the Academy will be as bad for the Town, as the Town for the Academy, & both very troublesome & discouraging to conscientious Tutors.

Mr Henderson & Brekel are for fixing the Academy at Ormskirk, I suppose, because it lies near them; Mr Seddon, who hath been laudably active in the affair, contends for fixing it at Warrington, probably because it [is] his own town. But the Case demands disinterested Attention, & is a Matter, not of Strife, but of the coolest & most impartial Judgment. I think it may be of very bad Consequence for neighbouring Ministers to frequent the Academy as often as they please, & interfere in its affairs. This may be the Occasion of Variance and Discord among the Tutors, & Disaffection among the Pupils. And upon the whole, I judge it would be wrong, absolutely to fix it, at first, in any one Place, before Conveniences & Inconveniences are experienced; in Relation to which, Gentlemen should have Regard to the Sense & Judgment of Tutors; for a Situation will affect them more than any other Persons, & therefore, is of much greater Importance to them than to any other. Which should be well considered. The Lancashire Ministers ought not to assume a Right to settle the Tutors where they please.

Thus, my dear Friend, I have given my Thoughts freely, honestly, impartially; & you know tht you may censure them in the same manner.

I am much pleased that they have nominated Mr Sam. Dyer, for moral Philosophy and polite Literature, as hoping that he is not in Mr Hutcheson's Scheme of Glasgow, which would by no means suit my Divinity, nor be any proper Foundation of it, but believing that he understands better Principles. I hope he will accept the useful Office. Pray my kindest Respects, when you see him.

I am glad to hear incouraging Accounts of your Health. May it be continued under every other blessing of Divine Goodness is the sincere wish of,

Dear Sir,

yr truly affectionate Brother,

John Taylor

<u>Warrington</u>, it is said, "is the properest Place for the Committee to meet at." But the Committee, at stated times, may meet where they please, & appoint proper persons to visit the Academy, wherever it shall be.

Mr <u>Frankland</u>, the first Dissenting Tutor, who had a numerous Academy for many Years, always chose to be in a Country Retirement, sometimes at <u>Katland</u>, then at <u>Calton</u>, at <u>Dawson</u> & <u>Hartborough</u>, <u>Attercliffe</u>, <u>Rathmell</u>, all small Villages in <u>Westmoreland</u> & <u>Yorkshire</u>, and 'tis well known how many Ministers of the best of Characters he sent out.

Letter 17 MS5512

Taylor has now been two years at Warrington. This letter shows that he has been uncomfortable from the beginning. He has been 'forced' to move house, and has been in some way maligned to the father of a student lodging with him, presumably with regard to the accommodation and allowances. The handwriting is very careful and regular, neither his flourished copper plate style nor his hurried workaday hand: the writing of a man setting the record straight in an important letter to an influential and close friend.

To Dr Benson

My dearest Friend,   Warrington, Octob. 25. 1759

I have carefully perused yr Chap, upon Parabols, which the oftener I read, I liked the better. Your Reflections are just & useful, nor do I see what more can be properly added. I wish you the same Success in what yet remains.

As to the Affair wch Mr Threlkald mentions, it is wholly a misrepresentation of the Case & of my Views, & but one Instance out of many of the ill Usage I have met with since I came hither.

Mr Rigby hired the largest House he could procure in the Town, wch, with attending charges, will stand in about £40 a Year, and hath fitted it up in the most commodious manner, for chambers & closets, tht could be desired. I was forced out of my former Situation much against my will, and having spared no expense to make my present Situation in all respects agreeable, it will be extremely hard to have it so represented as to disgust, & prejudice the young men against it. I had nothing in view, in advising Astley and Threlkald to lodge in the same house with me, but their Advantage; they are now with me, &, I have reason to believe, are well satisfied tht I advised them as a true & faithful Friend, desirous of doing them all the good in my power. However I am conscious to the most disinterested Integrity; & by the example of our blessed Lord, endeavour to encourage my Self in being as useful as ever I can in the Service of the Gospel, expecting no other recompence, but the reward which he will give to all his Servants, small & great. I am inclin'd to think the young men were tamper'd with; & doubt not but Mr Threlkald, if he understood the true state of things, would be sorry tht he has entertain'd such unworthy Notions of a person, who is sincerely desirous to be useful to his Son in the highest degree, & who is laboring every day, & on all occasions, in season & out of season, to be so.

As to their allowance, Mr Seddon computes it thus; £10 each upon the Foundation, 4 Guineas each given by some Gentlemen (£4:4s) & £6:6. wch each of thm must otherwise have paid to 3 Tutors. In all £20:10s Thus the Gentlemen reckon. But they attended the last year only upon 2 Tutors, which brings the allowance to what Mr Threlkald mentions. This year they will attend upon all of the 3 Tutors more or less. N.B. they paid £6 a year tutorage to Mr Ashworth.

The young minister, I recommended to yr Favor, is <u>John Wildinge of Leland, — to be left at the Legs of Man in Preston, Lancashire.</u>

Kirkstead, after having been refused by 2 Ministers to whom it was offered, is at length, I hope supply'd with a Person very suitable to the Place, Mr John Dunkley, who was 14 years Usher to

Mr Aikin at Kibworth, & by him strongly recommended. My son at Norwich interested himself very much in the affair, but he never once mentioned Mr Blackburn to me, I suppose because he & Mr Blackburn's Friends at Norwich did not think Kirkstead a proper Situation for him. And I am of the Same Opinion.

Though I am almost tired of publishing, yet here's another piece of mine for the Press, upon the same Subject with the last, but handled in a different manner. It is my own Scheme of moral Philosophy, which has for 30 Years or more been the Subject of frequent & close reflection, & the rule by which I have examined the principles of Revelation. I seem to myself to have digested thoroughly the Propositions therein advanced, & to have explained them in a method new & demonstrative. And if some good Judges are not mistaken, I have perform'd what I have attempted. You'll have the Curiosity to peruse it, & I should be glad to have your opinion of it. The principles, I apprehend, are the same with Mr Price's; but he entertains Notions of the opera-tion of the mind, wch I think are too minute & disputable; or, however, of no use in explaining the Foundations of Virtue, but rather imbarrass than clear the Subject. This makes me more indifferent, whether it be shewn to him. However, I leave it to your Judgment. I expect that Mr Price is one of the monthly reviewers.

You see I keep doing something as well as you. I wish it may be to as good purpose. Indeed, I do not now enjoy my usual calm & serene state of mind. But cannot be inactive. I endeavr to support and chear my Heart with the Divine Approbation, & the prospects of a better State, which I hope will carry you & me comfortably thro' the remainder of our Work in this World. Your most sincerely affectionate

<u>John Taylor</u>

Letter 18 MS5513

This short letter, written less than six months before his death, is full of foreboding, and shows that, in Taylor's mind, much more was at stake than trivialities about his bed, or the purchase of books for the library. He believes the whole project is being turned in a wrong direction. The introduction of prepared forms of prayer, and the pressure to follow Hutcheson's system of moral philosophy, he evidently saw as symptoms of a changing ethos and of a betrayal of the older Dissent.

To The Revd Dr Benson Goodman's Fields

Warrington Octob.7. 1760

My dearest Friend,

I have perused yr Mss several times over with great attention, but find very little matter of censure. What I have remarked you will find in the inclosed paper. You appear to me to be master of the Subject, & to have executed it in a masterly manner; especially in the 5th & concluding Section, where your reasonings, I think, are strong and conclusive. I wish you may be enabled, & hope you will, to go thro' the remaining Chapters of this important Subject with the same spirit & accuracy. — As to my own Affairs, you have an account of thm in the papers directed to Mr Pope & you; wch I think will be properly lodged in Mr Pope's hands. Since my return, I find a new scene opening in these parts; and am afraid I shall find my Self at length made the dupe of a thoughtless party, who are meditating innovations prejudicial to the Dissenting Interest, & the cause of religion. The Scheme has already, I am persuaded, infected the Academy, and, I apprehend, will affect both tht & my Self still more deeply. I pray God supply me with prudence, patience & steddiness, tht I may act an honorable part under all events, whatever becomes of my temporal Interests. I am in pretty good health, but the weakness of my limbs still continues. I cannot now have long to act upon the theatre of life. What I earnestly desire is, tht my conduct, situation & temper of mind may be such tht the hope of a better world may grow stronger & brighter as I am drawing nearer to the end of this. Remember me in your prayers; I don't forget [paper torn away]

My kindest regards to

Dr Lardner.

Notes

Preface

1. See Ch. 8, pp. 65f. and n. 7.
2. Alan P. F. Sell, *Dissenting Thought and the Life of the Churches: Studies in an English Tradition* (Lewiston, NY: Edwin Mellen Press, 1990), Ch. 7.
3. Capital initials are used in the following chapters to distinguish the *doctrine* that was such an important matter of dispute between Taylor and his critics, from the bare *fact* of the universal wrong doing of the human species which is sometimes inaccurately referred to as 'original sin'.

Chapter 1: Christians and Only Christians

1. *A Sermon preached at the opening of the New Chapel in Norwich, May the 12th, 1756*, pamphlet (London, 1756). Reprinted in *The Principles and Practice of an English Presbyterian Clergyman* (London, 1843)
2. See Appendix I, 'The "Catholicity" of Baxter, Taylor and Wesley'.
3. Wesley, *Journal*, 1 April 1757; *The Doctrine of Original Sin according to Scripture, Reason and Experience* (Bristol, 1757); *Works*, Vol. IX (1830 and 1872), p. 193.
4. *A Sketch of the Life of the late Dr John Taylor of Norwich* (From 'The Universal Theological Magazine, &c.' for July 1804) . . . Corrected and enlarged in 1813.—R.T. p. 5. Grantham Killingworth (1699–1778) also wrote in opposition to Taylor's defence of paedobaptism.
5. John MacGowan (1726–80) had been a Methodist in Warrington, and for a couple of years a local preacher, but turned Calvinist, and was for a time an Independent, then a Baptist minister in Warrington, Bridgnorth, and finally the Old Meeting House, Devonshire Square, London (*Dictionary of National Biography* hereafter *DNB*). A vigorous writer, he was over-addicted to irony and vituperation, which he turned upon the Methodists in *The Foundry Budget Opened; or the Arcanum of Wesleyanism Exposed* (1780) which is described as 'a flippant and abusive paper, quite unworthy

of the great subjects treated upon'. Richard Green, *Anti-Methodist Publications* (London: Methodist Publishing House, 1902), No. 525.

Chapter 2: Wishley though Disparing

1. *A Sketch of the Life of the late Dr John Taylor of Norwich* (1804; 1813), p. 1.

2. John Hunter, *Familiae minorum gentium*, Vol. III, Harleian Society Publications, 39 (1895), pp. 1104–5. I am indebted to Mr John Creasey of Cromer for this reference.

3. This handwritten note is attached to the copy of *A Sketch of the Life* in Harris Manchester College library.

4. *A Sermon Occasioned by the Death of the Rev. John Taylor D.D . . . By E. Harwood . . .* London, 1761, p. 43. Harwood continues: 'The great neglect of this useful literature amongst Dissenting Ministers, and their general deficiency herein, he would often say, exposed us more than anything else, to the jests and contempt of the *Clergy*, who principally study and value themselves upon their accurate and superior knowledge of it.'

5. See H. McLachlan, 'The academies as centres of learning' in *English Education under the Test Acts* (Manchester University Press, 1931).

6. In a lecture about aspects of his research for the new edition of the *Dictionary of National Biography*, Alan Rushton tells us:

Many of these divines were granted degrees by the Scottish universities, in particular the Aberdeen colleges. Aberdeen awarded five DDs at one go to London ministers in 1728, either in acknowledgement of their influence or published work. Not that all the recipients sought these honours, or even knew that they were going to be awarded. Some thought little of it. David Jennings (1691–1762), Independent minister and tutor, was sent a DD apparently by post from the University of St Andrews. He wrote to Doddridge 'it will save me from being called old Mr Jennings, in distinction from my Son, who is looking towards matrimony'. (Friends of Dr Williams's Library, Fifty-Fifth Lecture, 2001, p. 9)

For David Jennings, see below, Ch. 10.

7. Letter to Sir Harry Trelawney, August 1780, *The Letters of John Wesley*, ed. John Telford (London: Epworth Press, 1931), Vol. VII, pp. 27–8.

8. Michael Watts, *The Dissenters* (Oxford University Press, 1978, paperback 1985), p. 465.

9. McLachlan, *English Education*, p. 131.

10. British Library, rare books, shelf number: 3434 de 14. *Celeberrimi viri Georgii Buchanani Paraphrasis Poetica in Psalmos nonnullos Davidis . . .* (etc.) Per THO. HILL, A.M.V.D.M. . . . LONDINI Typis *Thomas Ilive*,

in Vico Vulgo Aldersgate Street MDCCXV. After the Psalms in Latin and Greek by Buchanan, there follow some in Greek by James Duport, a former Regius Professor of Greek at Cambridge, and then some pages of musical settings, unharmonized. The book is not autographed by John Taylor, but bears the bookplate of Philip Taylor, his grandson, who was also a minister, to whom obviously it had been handed down.

    11. John and Edward Taylor, *History of the Octagon Chapel, Norwich* (1848), p. 22.

    12. Appendix I to the collection of Taylor's writings in 'English Presbyterian Trusts', Vol. V, Harris Manchester College library, Oxford.

    13. Quoted in *Transactions of the Unitarian Historical Society*, vol. 14, p. 198, from T. S. James, *The History of the Litigation and Legislation Respecting Chapels and Charities in England and Ireland between 1816 and 1849* (1867), p. 804.

Chapter 3: Insensible of their Duty to a Minister

    1. Francis Hill, *Georgian Lincoln* (Cambridge University Press, 1966), pp. 68f.; R. E. C. Cole, *Ecclesiastical History of the Deanery of Graffoe*, Associated Architectural Society's Reports and Papers, Vol. XXV, Part II, pp. 38f.; Clive Holmes, *Seventeenth Century Lincolnshire* (Lincoln: The History of Lincolnshire Committee of the Society for Lincolnshire History and Archaeology), Vol. VII, pp. 44f.; Deanery of Graffoe Parish Magazine (1891), 'Notes and Queries'.

    2. White's *Directory of Lincolnshire* (1856), p. 742, 'Kirkstead'; Anon., *The Kirkstead Story*, an illustrated local handbook printed by F. W. Cupit (Horncastle, 1968; reprinted 1993); George Eyre Evans, *Vestiges of Protestant Dissent* (Liverpool: F. & E. Gibbons, 1897). This last publication includes a photograph of the interior taken through the keyhole! The caption reads: 'Kirkstead. Interior of Abbey Chapel, with pulpit from which John Taylor, D.D., preached. As the door of Abbey Chapel is now screwed up, and admission refused by the owner, I had no alternative but to photograph the interior through the keyhole, which I did at 6.30 a.m. on 14 August, 1896. – G.E.E.'

    3. William Turner Jr., *Lives of Eminent Unitarians* (1840), Vol. I, pp. 301f.

    4. The letter is printed in full in the above volume, pp. 302–5.

    5. Quoted as from 'a familiar letter, dated April 29, 1724', J. and E. Taylor, *History of the Octagon Chapel, Norwich* (1848), p. 25.

Chapter 4: Doctor Taylor of Norwich

1. See Appendix V, Letter 15 of 5 December 1755.
2. The Old Meeting is no longer in regular use as a place of worship. A Victorian building in Princes Street superseded it, and that congregation is now within the United Reformed Church.
3. J. and E. Taylor *History of the Octagon Chapel, Norwich* (London, 1848), p. 18.
4. Thomas Dixon, son of Taylor's former mentor at Whitehaven, was his colleague in this capacity, very briefly and evidently unhappily. See Appendix V, Letter 7, 27 June 1751.
5. *History of the Octagon*, p. 32.
6. *History of the Octagon*, p. 32.
7. *Transactions of the Congregational Historical Society*, Vol. VI, p. 150.
8. Appendix V, Letter 2, dated 18 April 1743. The second part of this letter exhibits Taylor's capacity for compassionate concern for the unfortunate. It is devoted to a plea for help for a poor woman, Mrs Bond, and her distressed family, who have come down in the world through her husband's failure in business and his reduction to miserably paid casual rural labour.

Chapter 5: Dissenting Popery

1. John Wesley, *Letters*, ed. John Telford (London: Epworth Press, 1931), Vol. VII, p. 27.
2. Different though the two books are: Robinson's is a very readable essay in theology for the thinking reader; Clarke's a painstaking compilation of scripture references bearing on the Trinity, followed by an examination of their cumulative import. The impact of Robinson's was felt simultaneously by scholars and a wide public who had been alerted by an article in the *Observer*, and were then bombarded with sermons and articles for and against. Clarke's is in far from popular style, and though it caused a furore, especially among the clergy, its influence would take much longer to percolate to the general public. It did so, however, through the ministry of men like Taylor, of whom there came to be many, in the established church as well as among Dissenters. Wesley's rule that Methodist preaching services were not to be held in 'church hours' was subject to exception where the parish clergyman preached 'Arian doctrine': evidently not an uncommon experience.
3. The primary source for the following account is the contemporary manuscript Church Book of the Castle Gate Church, now housed in the Department of Manuscripts and Special Collections, University of Nottingham.

4. Church Book, pp. 7f.

5. James Sloss, *The Doctrine of the Trinity, as it is contained in the Scriptures* . . . (London, 1736). Of the eighteen lectures, the first is devoted to establishing the authenticity of 1 John 5:7. Appended to the lectures are two letters attacking this, with Sloss's replies.

6. For example, in the chapter on 'The Arian Controversy' in the history of the church written by its minister for the celebration of the 250th anniversary of its founding: A. R. Henderson, *History of Castlegate Congregational Church, Nottingham, 1655–1905* (London: James Clarke & Co., 1905), Ch. XI.

7. Church Book, pp. 12ff.

8. A nineteenth-century marginal note corrects the spelling of the minister's name to Obadiah Hughes, and adds 1735 as the date he left; so that was when the movement towards Arianism became more marked. Obadiah Hughes was a friend of Philip Doddridge, and probably took a similarly moderate line. His ministry evidently delayed but did not ultimately prevent the movement of the High Pavement congregation towards Unitarianism. Would Doddridge's influence have been similar, if he had succeeded in getting himself 'Fixt' there?

9. James Sloss, *The True Narrative of the Case of Joseph Rawson . . . together with a Prefatory Discourse and a Plea for the Right of Religious Societies to excommunicate Heretical and Unruly Members* (London, no date).

10. Henderson, *Castlegate Church*, pp. 149–50.

11. A MS note in the margin of *A Sketch of the Life of the Late Dr John Taylor of Norwich* (1813), p. 2, reads: 'Warburton in a letter to Doddridge reprobates the conduct of the N——m people vide Nicols.'

12. Writing to his friend George Benson in March 1742, Taylor notes with satisfaction the demand for a second edition of his *Further Defence*, and gives careful instructions for its production: Appendix V, Letter 1.

Chapter 6: An Hebrew Concordance

1. Quoted in a footnote to *A Sketch of the Life of the late Dr John Taylor of Norwich* (1813), also in John and Edward Taylor, *History of the Octagon Chapel, Norwich* (1848), p. 30, where that MS is said to be of about 100 pages. Is it still in existence?

2. See Appendix V, letters 6 to 14, June 1751 to April 1754.

3. Letter 13, 9 November 1751. The whole letter is of interest for its illustration of the learned correspondence that went on between scholars, and the meticulous research that lay behind the great Concordance.

4. Letter 12, 25 October 1751, questions whether 'it may be time now for Mr Waugh to finish his Fount', then in a postscript cancels this sugges-

tion. No doubt this refers to the special fount of Hebrew characters, an expensive item.

5. 'I would venture the Issue of the Sale, could I depend upon fair and honourable Usage' (Letter 5, 17 February 1744, referring to the publication of the *Paraphrase and Key*).

6. Letter 13, 9 November 1751.

7. In Letter 6, 3 June 1751, Taylor speaks of his hope to bring his Concordance 'to a great Degree of Exactness, and to correct all the Faults of Buxtorf which I find are very numerous. But as the Book has been very little us'd, no notice has been taken of them.' How very much more than a mere revision of Buxtorf his own work became is very apparent in further letters, 7, 9, 10, 12 and 13.

8. See letters 8, 9 and 11.

9. J. and E. Taylor, *History of the Octagon Chapel, Norwich* (1848), p. 30, footnote. The initials P.T. indicate that the anecdote is attested by Philip Taylor, 1747–1831, who would be about 14 at the time of his grandfather's death.

10. Letter 14, of 16 April 1754.

11. See H. McLachlan, 'Semitics in the Nonconformist Academies', *Essays and Addresses* (Manchester University Press, 1950), Ch. 11. He protests at the patronizing assumption that because they were excluded from the universities in England, the Dissenters were ignorant and un-lettered men, and points to the great contribution they made to Semitic studies during that period. Taylor was, of course, the outstanding example.

12. At the instance of Leechman, Professor of Theology. See p. 1. He had corresponded with Taylor, and later, in 1759, he visited him in Warrington. They are described as 'kindred souls'. Their mutual regard seems not to have been affected by their differing views with regard to Hutcheson's teaching on moral philosophy, to which Taylor was sharply opposed (see Appendix V). Hutcheson was Leechman's colleague in the university. The diploma describes Taylor as possessing *'tum morum sanctimoniam tum ingenium vere liberum et in nullius sectae verba jurare addictum'* ('both moral integrity and an intellect truly free, untrammelled by allegiance to any confessional formula'), *History of the Octagon*, p. 31. The full Latin text of the diploma is printed in *The Principles and Pursuits of an English Presbyterian Minister of the Eighteenth Century* (London, 1843).

Chapter 7: Scripture Doctrine

1. A. W. Harrison, *Arminianism* (London: Duckworth, 1937), pp. 89–90.

2. John Evelyn, in his *Diary*, 28 August 1655, records a conversation with 'that renowned mathematician, Mr Oughtred', who 'said original sin

was not to be met with in the Greek Fathers, yet he believed the thing'. He adds: 'This was from some discourse on Dr Taylor's late book, which I had lent him.' Jeremy Taylor's *Unum Necessarium* had appeared earlier in that year. In ch. 6, and in a ch. 7 added in response to criticisms, Jeremy Taylor anticipates many of John Taylor's conclusions. See below, ch. 9, p. 75, and n. 5, p. 244.

3. Bishop Burnet, *History of His Own Times* (London: Dent Everyman Library edition, 1906), p. 44.

4. No. 771 of *Doctor Whichcote's Aphorisms* (London: Elkin, Mathews & Marrot, limited edition 1930, reprinted from the edition of 1753).

5. *Aphorisms*, No. 130.

6. J. and E. Taylor, *History of the Octagon Chapel, Norwich* (1848), p. 27, footnote, where the anecdote is given with the initials of P(hilip) T(aylor), on the authority of 'the late worthy Dr Mercer, of Crumlin, near Dublin, who had been some years the Dissenting pastor of Dungannon'. It is stated that an edition had been printed at Belfast, and had circulated widely and with devastating effect in Ireland, as Wesley's *Journal* also attests.

7. E. Harwood's *Sermon Occasioned by the Death of the Rev. John Taylor* (1761), p. 46.

8. See Appendix V, letters 78, 18 July; 9, 21 August; and 11, 8 October 1751.

9. Above, p. 43.

Chapter 8: Broke in the Lock

1. Appendix V, Letters 2, 3, 4 and 5.

2. Jeremiah Hunt DD: see Letter 2 of 18 April 1740.

3. 'Doddridge was not so happy with the Arian John Taylor's *Key to the Apostolic Writings* ... On 19 April 1745 he confided to Samuel Wood, "The pure uncorrupted Scriptural Gospel ... without the Aid or Incumbrance of humane Schemes ... is becoming dearer than ever to my Soul. Not the less so for a certain *Key* which *inter nos* ... seems broke in the lock."' Alan P. F. Sell, *John Locke and the Eighteenth Century Divines* (Cardiff: University of Wales Press, 1997), p. 106. Dr Sell sees a pun here on the name of Locke.

4. 'The following anecdote is communicated by Mr Edward Taylor: "One day passing through the Library at the Bishop's palace, Norwich, in company with Dr. Bathurst, he put his finger on 'Taylor on the Romans,' and said to me, 'If I understand the meaning of St Paul's Epistle, I owe it to this volume.'"' J. and E. Taylor, *History of the Octagon Chapel, Norwich* (1848), p. 28, footnote.

5. In his address at his enthronement in Norwich Cathedral in 1805, the bishop frankly professed himself a disciple of Locke and Hoadly, and rejoiced in the better relations prevailing between the Dissenters and the Church. He was on friendly terms with those in his diocese: something which the ministry of Taylor fifty years before had no doubt helped to make possible.

6. *History of the Octagon*, p. 28.

7. Adam Clarke, *Commentary* (London: 1810–26), Vol. VII of the eight-volume edition, 'Epistle to the Romans', p. xl. On p. v he introduces his lengthy borrowing from Taylor with this tribute:

> To . . . do justice to the Apostle, and set an important portion of the word of God in its true and genuine light; Dr. John Taylor, of Norwich, a divine who yielded to few in command of temper, benevolent feeling, and deep acquaintance with the Hebrew and Greek Scriptures, undertook the elucidation of this much controverted Epistle. The result was . . . 'A KEY to the Apostolic Writings . . .' This KEY, in the main, is a most invaluable work; and has done great justice to the subject . . .

Nevertheless, Clarke feels it necessary to assure his readers that his own creed is not that of Dr Taylor, 'who was an *Arian* (for he certainly cannot be ranked with modern unitarians)'; 'especially in the articles of *Original Sin*, the *Atonement*, and *Deity of Christ*'. Since such matters 'are seldom *directly* touched in this introductory Key', however, the reader need fear no threat to 'the orthodoxy of his own creed'. But evidently some did feel threatened, for a later edition of the *Commentary*, this time in six volumes, adds a further footnote at Vol. V, p. 994, quoting 'a learned and judicious friend', who writes:

> I find there is a hue and cry about Dr. Taylor. I have not yielded to my antagonists, and I will still dare to think for myself . . . If these persons . . . would attentively read and compare the texts in the Old Testament quoted by Dr. Taylor in his *Key*, it would lead them to a more clear understanding of St. Paul in his Epistle to the Romans than they ever had before . . . But the cry is, 'An Arian! An Arian!' Prejudice shuts up the mind against truth; but let truth be defended wherever it may be found. It is easy to perceive that a certain class of men would reject Dr. Taylor's *Key* because it cuts up the very foundation of their system. Go on in the strength of God, and in all things act with a single eye to his glory. Vive valeque.

13 March 1815. J.C.

Who was 'J.C.'? Dr Vickers suggests Jonathan Crowther (1759–1824), close contemporary of Adam Clarke in the Wesleyan ministry, with much in common with him. See their respective entries in *A Dictionary of*

Methodism in Britain and Ireland, ed. J. A. Vickers (London: Epworth Press, 2000). In view of the more usual tone of references to Taylor by their contemporaries, it is gratifying to find two eminent Methodists taking such an enlightened stance.

Chapter 9: Dr Taylor's Poison

1. John Wesley, *Letters*, ed. John Telford (London: Epworth Press, 1931), Vol. IV, p. 48.

2. The footnote on p. 27 of the *History of the Octagon Chapel, Norwich* (1848), which gave us the anecdote of the Irish preacher, also attests the spread of Taylor's teaching in Scotland. It quotes 'Dr. Currie's Life of Burns, and the poet's *Epistle to John Goudie*', to show that 'Dr. Taylor's work on Original Sin was one of the volumes of the scanty library of the venerable patriarch of the Cotter's Saturday Night.' In the above-mentioned satirical 'Letter to John Goudie "Kilmarnock"', 'Auld Orthodoxy' is said to be 'nigh unto death', along with 'Superstition' and 'Enthusiasm', and

'Tis you and Taylor are the chief,
Wha are to blame for this mischief.

The reference to the 'New Light', in the 'Postscript' to the 'Epistle to William Simpson' is explained as 'an expression current in the West of Scotland for Dr. Taylor's teaching'. Where Burns' own sympathies lay is evident in several places, for example in the highly satirical poem, 'The Ordination' in which he caricatures the triumph of orthodoxy over 'common sense' and the 'New Light' when a new minister is ordained to succeed a 'Moderate'.

3. P. D. James, *Original Sin* (London: Faber, 1994).

4. Reinhold Niehbuhr, for example. See Appendix III.

5. Cf. *Unum Necessarium* (1655), ch. 6, sect. I, para. 20, where Jeremy Taylor makes precisely the same point; one of his many anticipations of John. See above, Ch. 7 n. 2, p. 242.

Chapter 10: The Frowns of God

1. For the passages quoted see pp. 23, 25, 69, 120–1.

2. Appendix V, Letter 2, 18 April 1743.

3. James Hervey, *Theron and Aspasio*, 3 vols (London, 1755). The quotations are from Vol. I, pp. 210f.; Vol. II, pp. 109ff., 123, 130f.

4. See letter to James Hervey, 15 October 1756, *Letters*, Standard Edition, ed. John Telford (London: Epworth Press, 1931),Vol. III, pp. 371–

88. This letter hardly supports the statement in the *Journal*, Standard Edition, ed. Nehemiah Curnock (London, 1909), Vol. IV, p. 103, footnote, that Hervey had sought Wesley's comment. He certainly did not welcome this lengthy criticism, despite such praise as: 'In the First Dialogue there are several just and strong observations, which may be of use to every serious reader.' We can all agree with the next sentence: 'In the Second, is not the description too laboured, the language too stiff and affected?' Despite his reservations, in his own treatise written the next year Wesley quotes Hervey in support of his case against Taylor.

5. Isaac Watts, *The Ruin and Recovery of Mankind* (London, 1740). Wesley reprinted lengthy extracts in his own reply to Taylor, and all the passages quoted can be found in *Original Sin*, *Works*, Vol. IX, pp. 353, 356-7, 365-6.

6. Samuel Hebden's tracts are extensively reprinted by Wesley, *Original Sin*, *Works*, Vol. IX, pp. 396-431. For the passages quoted see pp. 399, 401.

7. Jonathan Edwards, *The Great Christian Doctrine of Original Sin Defended: Evidence of its Truth Produced and Arguments to the Contrary Answered Containing in particular A Reply to the Objections and Arguments of Dr John Taylor* (etc.). First published in New England, 1757; a new edition, Edinburgh, 1798. The passages quoted will be found at pp. 137f., 151-7, 399f.

8. See Augustine's letter to Jerome in AD 415, quoted in N. P. Williams, *The Ideas of the Fall and Original Sin* (London: Longmans, Green & Co., 1927), p. 376.

9. Quoted by Uta Ranke-Heinemann, *Eunuchs for the Kingdom of Heaven* (London: Penguin Books, 1991), p. 77; first published in the USA by Doubleday, 1990.

Chapter 11: Worse than Open Deism

1. See Geoffrey F. Nuttall, 'The Influence of Arminianism in England', *The Puritan Spirit* (London: Epworth Press, 1967), Ch. VIII; especially p. 78, where he distinguishes between the 'Arminianism of the head', characteristic of Dissenters, and the 'Arminianism of the heart', with its strong sense of mission, which is that of Wesley. See also Jeremy Goring in C. Gordon Bolam et al., *The English Presbyterians* (London: Allen & Unwin, 1968), ch. I, pp. 22-3:

The Arminianism of the English Presbyterians should not be confused with the Arminianism of the Wesleyan Methodists . . . Wesley's Arminianism was that of Arminius himself (as introduced into England before the Civil War by the Caroline divines), while the Presbyterians'

Arminianism was that of a later generation of Remonstrants (as introduced into England by Limborch, le Clerc and Locke, and reinforced by Baxter's dislike of Calvinism in its Antinomian form). Wesley might be described as a Calvinist who chose to contract out of the doctrine of Predestination, whereas the Presbyterians were thorough-going Arminians (in the contemporary Dutch sense of the term) who believed that 'it was only by relating revelation and reason that a workable theology could be formulated'. This led them not just to be '*against* particular election and redemption' but to be '*for* justification by sincere obedience in the room of Christ's righteousness'.

2. A. Skevington Wood, *Revelation and Reason: Wesleyan Responses to Eighteenth Century Rationalism* (Nuneaton: The Wesley Fellowship, 1992), p. 47.

3. It is perhaps in an incautious echo of this judgement that a modern scholar refers to Taylor as 'a leading Deist'. See Appendix III, p. 188.

4. So concludes Part I of *The Doctrine of Original Sin according to Scripture, Reason and Experience*, Wesley's *Works*, 1830 edition, Vol. IX, p. 238. In the following notes, that volume is referred to as 'Wesley, *Works* IX'; and 'Taylor, *O.S.*' refers to Taylor's *Scripture Doctrine of Original Sin*, fourth edition (1767).

5. *The Standard Sermons of John Wesley* (London: Epworth Press, 1921), Vol. II, sermon 38, 'Original Sin', p. 208; Bicentennial Edition, ed. Albert Outler, Vol. II, sermon 44. Dr Sugden's three-page introduction to this sermon gives an admirable brief conspectus of the controversy, and affords evidence of the modification of their founder's uncompromising views that had by 1921 prevailed among Methodist scholars.

6. Wesley, *Works* IX, p. 311.

7. Wesley continued to regard Taylor's teaching as a dire threat to Christianity, but after one more reference to its anaesthetizing effect, this time in Belfast (*Journal*, 6 April 1769), it becomes less prominent among his concerns. A letter to Miss March, dated 16 September 1774 (*Letters*, ed. John Telford (London: Epworth Press, 1931), Vol. VI, pp. 112–13) illustrates the way serious scholars could still use the Book of Revelation as prophesying features of their own time, especially to denigrate those of which they disapproved; but it suggests that Wesley at that date was seeing 'Antinomianism', a Calvinist aberration, as an even more serious threat than Taylor's teaching. The reference in his letter to Sir Harry Trelawney of August 1780 has already been noted (Ch. 5, p. 30). It is mistaken about Taylor's age, and his supposed unacknowledged change of opinion, which suggests that Wesley had for a long time ceased to concern himself overmuch with that opponent; but he continued to set great store by his own treatise on Original Sin, which is prominent among his *Works*.

8. Wesley, *Works* IX, p. 242.

9. Taylor, *O.S.*, p. 230.

10. Modern upholders of some form of the doctrine of Original Sin, or of the truth behind it, now recognize that this picture of Adam's condition before the fall, typified by Hervey and endorsed by Wesley, is 'absurd'. See Appendix III.

11. Wesley, *Works* IX, p. 258.

12. Wesley, *Works* IX, p. 285.

13. Wesley, *Works* IX, p. 276.

14. Wesley, *Works* IX, pp. 286, 315.

15. Taylor, *O.S.*, p. 241.

16. And, indeed, upon the whole *animal* creation. Wesley, *Works* IX, p. 389 (quoting from Isaac Watts, *The Ruin and Recovery of Mankind*, 1740): 'The misery, therefore, of the brute creation, is so far from being an objection to the apostasy of man, that it is a visible standing demonstration thereof. It is by reason of man's apostasy that even brute animals suffer . . . If beasts suffer, then man is fallen.' Cf. p. 284, where Wesley himself interprets Paul's words (Rom. 8:22) to mean that 'the whole brute creation' suffers pain because of Adam's sin. Of course, it is obviously true that human wickedness causes a great deal of suffering to animals; but this is not what Watts and Wesley mean. They mean that *all* the suffering of the whole creation is due to its having been thrown out of order by Adam's sin. To be consistent in his logic, surely, Wesley ought to maintain that the animals, as he argues in the case of children, '*suffer for*' Adam's sin, therefore are *punished* for it, and therefore are *guilty* of it! But of course, animals could not be guilty in the same way as humans, for they are not descended from Adam, and cannot have sinned 'in him', as we are supposed to have done. What a mass of tangled, self-contradictory nonsense this doctrine produces!

17. Wesley, *Works* IX, p. 316.

18. Taylor, *O.S.*, p. 241.

19. Wesley, *Works* IX, p. 284.

20. See N. P. Williams, *The Ideas of the Fall and Original Sin* (London: Longmans, Green & Co., 1927) p. 377 for a graphic illustration of this appalling teaching. He describes a woodcut of 1700, prefixed to an edition of Augustine's anti-Pelagian writings. It depicts the grief and horror of a family whose baby dies on the way to church to be baptized, contrasted with the joy of those within the church whose baby is just being immersed.

21. See Ch. 9 above, p. 81; Taylor, *O.S.*, pp. 273–4.

22. Wesley, *Works* IX, p. 313.

23. Unhappily, that dismal view of childhood and youth was also dominant when he had any say in how children were to be treated. See below, Ch. 13, p. 158, and related n. 18.

24. Wesley, *Works* IX, p. 316.

25. Wesley, *Works* IX, p. 310.
26. Ibid.

Chapter 12: A Place of Variance and Contradiction

1. See above, Ch. 2, p. 13.
2. C. Gordon Bolam et al., *The English Presbyterians* (London: Allen & Unwin, 1968), pp. 224–5.
3. In the letter to George Benson quoted more fully below. For the full text see Appendix V, Letter 15, 25 June 1757.
4. Letter 15, 25 June 1757.
5. Appendix V, Letter 17, dated from Warrington, 25 October 1759.
6. Richard Taylor, *A Sketch of the Life of the Late Dr John Taylor of Norwich* (1813), p. 5.
7. W. Turner, *The Lives of Eminent Unitarians* (1840), Vol. I, pp. 334f.
8. Richard Watson, Bishop of Llandaff from 1782 to 1816, was a deplorable bishop, never setting foot in his diocese, but living 'exactly as a layman might', 'the life of a country gentleman in Westmoreland', while also continuing to hold his Regius Professorship of Divinity at Cambridge (Charles J. Abbey, *The English Church and its Bishops, 1700–1800*, 2 vols (London, 1887), Vol. II, pp. 251–7). Commendation from such a quarter will hardly seem to add much to Taylor's credit; but Watson could be, when he bestirred himself, a doughty apologist against such scoffers as Gibbon. His critical judgement in this instance is not worthless.
9. Cf. *DNB*, 'John Taylor', p. 439, col. 2, for 'Job Orton's remark (1778) that "he had to the last a great deal of the puritan in him"'.
10. *The Scripture Account of Prayer* (1761), pp. 56–7.
11. *Scripture Account*, p. 69.
12. *Scripture Account*, p. 87.
13. A footnote to *A Sketch of the Life* quotes a pamphlet of 1762, which records that 'on Jan. 6th 1762, before a mixed company of about 23 or 24 Seceders from the Church and the Dissenters, the new Liturgy was exhibited by Mr Seddon according to previous notice by him given, at the Merchants' Coffee-House in Liverpool, but without the concurrence or approbation of his brethren in that town.'
14. Bolam et al., *The English Presbyterians*, p. 225.
15. Footnote to pp. 48–9 of the funeral sermon preached by E. Harwood, printed in 1761, where it is described as 'a very affecting letter, wrote not long before his death'. It is not stated whether Harwood was the addressee, nor is there any indication where the letter is to be found. It is reprinted in Taylor, *A Sketch of the Life*.
16. *Dictionary of National Biography*.
17. See Appendix IV.

18. C. S. Lewis, *The Abolition of Man* (Oxford University Press, 1943; Collins, Fount Paperbacks, 1978), pp. 7f.

19. H. L. Short, 'Presbyterians under a new name', *The English Presbyterians*, p. 219.

20. Appendix V, Letter 14.

21. H. McLachlan, 'Sport and recreation in nonconformist academies', *Essays and Addresses* (Manchester University Press, 1950), pp. 209–10.

22. E. Harwood's sermon of 1761, pp. 38–9. In a footnote on p. 37, Harwood gives the quotation in Greek, from the *Ajax*, lines 473–6. The version by F. Storr in the Loeb Classical Library reads:

Base were it that a man should want long life
When all he gets is long unchanging trouble.
Tomorrow, and tomorrow, and tomorrow –
What pleasure comes of that? 'Tis but a move
Forward or backward and the end – is death!

23. Appendix V, Letter 18, 7 October 1760.

24. P. O'Brien MD, *Warrington Academy, 1757–86* (Wigan: Owl Books, 1969), pp. 52–3.

Chapter 13: That Great Man

1. John Wesley, *The Doctrine of Original Sin* (1757; *Works*, Vol. IX, 1830 and 1872), Preface, para. 3. In the next paragraph, Wesley explains: 'I said, *than open Deism*: for I cannot look on this scheme as any other than old Deism in a new dress; seeing it saps the very foundation of all revealed religion, whether Jewish or Christian.'

2. John C. Oden, *John Wesley's Scriptural Christianity* (Zondervan, 1994), p. 159.

3. *A Collection of Theological Tracts*, published by Bishop Richard Watson (1785), p. 208.

4. J. and E. Taylor, *History of the Octagon Chapel, Norwich* (1848), pp. 36f.

5. Funeral sermon, pp. 40f.

6. Sermon on the Trinity, para. 3, *Works* 1830, Vol. VI, p. 200; Bicentennial edition, Vol. II, sermon 55, p. 377. This paragraph is remarkable for its admission of the scruples Wesley felt about subscription, and the curious arguments by which he was enabled to overcome them; also for its approval of Dean Swift's demolition of all attempts to *explain* the doctrine. Taylor, of course, would protest that this is to require us to *believe* what we do not *understand*.

7. Sermon on 'The Wisdom of God's Counsels', *Works* 1830, Vol. VI, pp. 328f.; Bicentennial edition, Vol. II, sermon 68, pp. 555f.

8. 'I cannot imagine how men can do greater disservice to religion than by taking it off from the rational and solid basis upon which it stands and bearing the world in hand [i.e. maintaining] that men ought to believe without reason; for this is to turn faith into credulity' (Tillotson). 'What more can be done to the disgrace and ruin of Christianity than to make the world believe we have no reason for it?' (Baxter). Quoted in C. Gordon Bolam et al., *The English Presbyterians* (London: Allen & Unwin, 1968), pp. 109–10.

9. When Simon Patrick, in his college days, found the doctrine of predestination 'very hard', and he could 'never answer the objections against it', he was 'advised by divines to silence carnal reason'. He was grateful to John Smith, the Cambridge Platonist, for 'laughing him out of' following that advice (*The English Presbyterians*, p. 103).

10. Quoted by Alan P. F. Sell, *John Locke and the Eighteenth Century Divines* (Cardiff: University of Wales Press, 1997), p. 81, from Taylor, *A Scheme of Scripture Divinity*, in *A Collection of Theological Tracts* (1785).

11. Alan P. F. Sell, *Dissenting Thought in the Life of the Churches* (Lewiston, NY: Edward Mellen Press, 1990), p. 211. In the last of Taylor's works published in his lifetime, the *Sketch of Moral Philosophy*, this circularity seems to be resolved in favour of reason, to which is accorded the responsibility of deciding how revelation is to be understood:

> Revelation is no use to us, if it is not an Address to the Understanding and common Sense of Mankind. And therefore, without a faithful Use of our own Faculties, and a proper Acquaintance with the Principles of Truth and Reason, by mistaking the Sense and Phrases of the Scriptures, we may be led to deduce from them such Doctrines as are altogether unworthy of God, and the reproach of Reason and Humanity, Which, in Fact, hath been the Case. But if the Judgment is well settled in the Principles of natural Religion, we shall be furnished with a Standard, by which to measure any Part of Revelation; a Standard of the same Authority with Revelation itself. And it must be the strongest Confirmation of any Revelation, and give the Student the greatest Satisfaction of the Truth of its Doctrines, when he sees plainly that they are all worthy of the Wisdom and Goodness of God, and perfectly consonant to all the Appearances of Nature and to the true State of Things in our World. Thus Reason, rightly directed, will assist and guide Criticism; and just Criticism will confirm the Dictates of Reason; and both will join their Forces in fixing the Judgment upon a solid basis, and in giving a satisfactory and pleasing View of the Principles of Christianity.

12. Sell, *John Locke and the Eighteenth Century Divines*, pp. 84–5.

13. J. and E. Taylor, *History of the Octagon Chapel, Norwich* (1848), p. 28.

14. See Appendix III on the Afterlife of the Doctrine of Original Sin.

15. N. P. Williams, *The Ideas of the Fall and Original Sin* (London: Longmans, Green & Co., 1927), p. 374.

16. For an extended treatment of this subject, see Uta Ranke-Heine-mann, *Eunuchs for the Kingdom of Heaven*, trans. Peter Heinegg (New York: Viking Penguin/London: Penguin Books, 1991), especially Ch. 6, 'Augustine'.

17. Above, p. 128; Letter to Dr Benson, Appendix V, Letter 16, 25 June 1757.

18. See *A Plain Account of Kingswood School*, Wesley's *Works*, Vol. XIII. The rules are set out on pp. 260f. in the 1831 edition; p. 284 in the reprint of 1872. They certainly fulfil their author's stated aim to keep the scholars 'at the utmost distance, as from vice in general, so in particular from softness and effeminacy. The children therefore of tender parents, so called, have no business here.' Parents must undertake 'That they will not take him from school, no, not for a day, till they take him for good and all.' So there were no vacations, no visits home, even for a day, during all the years of incarceration! The children rose at four for private devotions at five. 'They drink water at their meals' and 'Their food is as simple as possible; two days a week it is wholly vegetable.' When not at devotions or meals, their whole time was occupied in work:

> On fair days they work, according to their strength, in the garden; on rainy days, in the house. But particular care is taken that they never work alone, but always in the presence of a Master. This . . . prevents abundance of evil; . . . not only rudeness and ill manners, but many sins that children would readily teach each other . . . For as we have no play-days, the school being taught every day in the year but Sundays, so neither do we allow any time for play on any day. It is a wise German proverb, 'He that plays when he is a boy will play when he is a man.'

19. E. Harwood, Funeral sermon, p. 39.

20. The plate prefixed to the second volume of the Concordance in the Bodleian Library copy carries the attribution: 'Heins pinx. 1746. I. Troubraken sculp. 1754'. The portrait in Harris Manchester College is described in the catalogue of the library as 'Platinotype from crayon drawing in the possession of the donor . . . Presented by Francis Taylor Esq., M. P., Diss, June 1896.' Close inspection of the folds of the gown and other details in the two pictures reveals that they are in some way mutually related. The engraving reverses the drawing; and when one of the two is held before a mirror, the resemblance is close.

21. *A Sketch of the Life of the Late Dr John Taylor of Norwich* (1813), p. 5.

Appendix I: The 'Catholicity' of Baxter, Taylor and Wesley

1. *The Autobiography of Richard Baxter*, ed. J. M. Lloyd-Thomas (Dent Everyman Library, 1931), p. 95.
2. *Autobiography*, p. 139.
3. *Gildas Salvianus: The Reformed Pastor* (1656), ch. 3, section II.
4. *The Standard Sermons of John Wesley*, ed. E. H. Sugden (London: Epworth Press, 1921), Vol. II, sermon 34; Bicentennial edition, Vol. II, sermon 39.
5. Wesley, *Works* (1830), Vol. X, pp. 80–6; see especially the four closing paragraphs in section 17, pp. 85–6.

Appendix II: The Exposition of Romans 5:12–21

1. Henri Blocher, *Original Sin: Illuminating the Riddle* (London: Apollos, New Studies in Biblical Theology No. 5, 1997), p. 33.
2. For this and the following extracts, see Taylor *The Scripture Doctrine of Original Sin*, fourth edition (1767), pp. 29–37, 50, 53.
3. C. E. B. Cranfield, *International Critical Commentary: Romans* (Edinburgh: T. & T. Clark, 1975); J. H. Moulton, *Grammar of New Testament Greek* (Edinburgh: T. & T. Clark, second edition 1906), Vol. I, *Prolegomena*, p. 107.
4. S. Lyonnet, 'Le sens de ἐφ' ᾧ en Rom. 5.12 et l'exégèse des pères grecs', *Biblica* 36 (1955), pp. 436–56.
5. James D. G. Dunn, *Word Biblical Commentary Vol. 38A: Romans 1–8* (Milton Keynes: Word UK Ltd; copyright Word Inc., Dallas, Texas, 1988. Permission sought), pp. 288–300.
6. Morna D. Hooker, *From Adam to Christ: Essays on Paul* (Cambridge University Press, 1990), Part II, p. 28.
7. R. S. Moxon, *The Doctrine of Sin* (London: Allen & Unwin, 1922), p. 2.

Appendix III: The Afterlife of Original Sin

1. Richard Watson, *Theological Institutes* (London, 1831); Wesley, *Works*, Vol. X, pp. 390–7.
2. W. B. Pope, *A Compendium of Christian Theology*, Vol. II (London: Wesleyan Conference Office, 1877). See also the account of Pope in *A Dictionary of Methodism*, p. 276.
3. J. Scott Lidgett, *The Spiritual Principle of the Atonement*, Fernley Lecture (London, 1897), p. 244.
4. F. R. Tennant, *The Origin and Propagation of Sin*, Hulsean Lectures

(1902); *The Sources of the Doctrine of the Fall and Original Sin* (1903); *The Concept of Sin* (1912).

5. Ian Sellers, 'A. S. Peake Reconsidered', *Epworth Review*, Vol. 24, No. 4 (October 1997), p. 86.

6. C. Ryder Smith, *The Bible Doctrine of Sin* (London: Epworth Press, 1953), p. 38.

7. Lecture delivered in the University of Chicago, printed in *The Birmingham Magazine*, No. 12 (University of Birmingham, October 2000), p. 4.

8. Dietrich Bonhoeffer, *Creation and Fall: A Theological Interpretation of Genesis* 1—3 (ET, London: SCM Press, 1959), p. 77.

9. A. W. Harrison, *Arminianism* (London: Duckworth, 1937).

10. Karl Barth, *Romans* (1919; ET E. C. Hoskyns, 1932), p. 171.

11. E. Brunner, *Man in Revolt: A Christian Anthropology*, Lutterworth Press, 1939, pp. 85, 87.

12. By Henri Blocher in *Original Sin: Illuminating the Riddle* (London: Apollos, 1997), p. 84.

13. *The Essential Reinhold Niebuhr*, ed. Robert McAfee Brown (Yale University Press, 1986), p. 246.

14. Paul Tillich, *Systematic Theology*, Vol. II (London: Nisbet, 1957; copyright University of Chicago Press. Used with permission), p. 39. Further quotations are from pp. 68, 64, 46, 33, 59, 53 respectively.

15. Thomas C. Oden, *John Wesley's Scriptural Christianity* (Grand Rapids: Zondervan, 1994), p. 159; see pp. 155–76. For a recognition that Wesley's views exhibit 'a bewildering variety of elements' and change in the course of his long life, see Randy I. Maddox, *Responsible Grace: John Wesley's Practical Theology* (Kingswood Books, Abingdon Press, 1994), especially ch. 3. Maddox recognizes that there was 'a notable increase' in Wesley's assertion of inherited guilt 'during his middle (most Protestant) period, particularly in contexts responding to Enlightenment optimism', but that in his later years, in contention against Predestinarianism, he came to assert that all inherited guilt is 'universally cancelled *at birth*, as one benefit of Christ's redemption' (p. 75).

16. Michael J. Walsh, librarian of Heythrop College, University of London, 'Blunders that Started with Original Sin', *The Independent*, London (24 September 1993).

17. Blocher, *Original Sin*, p. 128.

18. Blocher, *Original Sin*, p. 42.

19. Blocher, *Original Sin*, p. 33.

20. Blocher, *Original Sin*, pp. 27, 124–5; NB footnote 4.

21. Blocher, *Original Sin*, pp. 41, 89.

22. Blocher, *Original Sin*, pp. 128–9, 125.

Appendix IV: Taylor's Opposition to Hutcheson's Moral Philosophy

1. Henry Sidgwick, *History of Ethics* (1886), p. 100.

2. Leechman's biographical introduction to Francis Hutcheson, *A System of Moral Philosophy* (1755), Vol. I, pp. xiii–xiv.

3. Hutcheson, *Moral Philosophy* Vol. I. This and the following quotations are from p. 58–62.

4. Price, *A Review of the Principal Questions and Difficulties in Morals* (1751; second edition 1769), pp. 57–8, 60, 71.

5. *Doctor Whichcote's Aphorisms* (London: Elkin, Mathews & Marrot, 1930 [1753]), no. 298.

6. Taylor, *A Sketch of Moral Philosophy* (London, 1760), p. 32.

7. Taylor, *An Examination of the Scheme of Morality Advanced by Dr Hutcheson* (London, 1759), pp. 10f.

8. See Appendix V, Letter 16 of 25 June 1757, and note the penultimate paragraph.

9. Sidgwick, in the passage cited above.

Bibliography

Reference

The Dictionary of National Biography (DNB).
A Dictionary of Methodism in Britain and Ireland, ed. John A. Vickers.
London: Epworth Press, 2000.

Taylor's works, in chronological order

A Narrative of Mr Joseph Rawson's Case or an Account of Several
Occurrences relating to the Affair of his being Excluded from Commun-
ion with the Congregational Church in Nottingham With a Prefatory
Discourse in Defence of the Common Rights of Christians. London . . .
MDCCXXXVII. Later editions change the title page: A Defence of the
Common Rights of Christians with a Narrative of Mr Joseph Rawson's
Case . . . by John Taylor D. D. London: J. Waugh, second edition 1742,
third edition 1766.
The Scripture Doctrine of Original Sin, Proposed to Free and Candid
Examination. London, 1740. Second edition: To which is added A
Supplement containing some remarks upon two books, The Vindication
of the Doctrine of Original Sin, and, The Ruin and Recovery of Mankind.
1741. (DNB records a '3rd edit. Belfast, 1746, 12mo' with 'curious list of
Irish subscribers'.) Third edition, London, 1750. Fourth edition (posthu-
mous): And now added, a Reply to the Reverend Mr John Wesley; and an
Inquiry into the Meaning of the Word Grace. London, 1767.
A Further Defence of the Common Rights of Christians etc. 1742.
A Paraphrase with Notes on the Epistle to the Romans, To which is
prefixed a Key to the Apostolic Writings, or an essay to explain the
Gospel Scheme, and the Principal Words and Phrases the Apostles have
used in describing it. London, 1745.
A Catechism, or Summary of the Christian Religion for the instruction of
children. London, 1745. Several editions, the fifth dated 1760.
A Collection of Tunes in Various Airs etc. London, 1750.

The Scripture-Doctrine of the Atonement Examined First in Relation to *Jewish* Sacrifices: and then, to the Sacrifice of our blessed Lord and Saviour *JESUS CHRIST* . . . London, 1751.

The Value of a Child, or Motives to the good education of children. In a letter to a daughter. London, 1752.

The Hebrew Concordance, adapted to the English Bible; disposed after the manner of Buxtorf. London: Vol. I, 1754; Vol. II, 1757.

A Sermon preached at the opening of the New Chapel in Norwich, May the 12th, 1756.

The Lord's Supper Explained upon Scripture principles and adapted to the use of common Christians. London, 1756; second edition 1757.

The Covenant of Grace, and Baptism the Token of it. London, 1757.

An Examination of the Scheme of Morality advanced by Dr Hutcheson. London, 1759.

A Sketch of Moral Philosophy, or An Essay to demonstrate the principles of virtue and religion upon a new, natural and easy plan. London, 1760.

The Scripture Account of Prayer, in an Address to the Dissenters in Lancashire; occasioned by a new Liturgy some ministers of that county are composing for a congregation at Liverpool. London, 1761.

A Scheme of Scripture Divinity, Formed upon the Plan of the Divine Dispensations, with a Vindication of the Sacred Writings. Originally printed only for Taylor's students at Warrington; published by Bishop Richard Watson in *A Collection of Theological Tracts*. 1785.

For the Life of Dr Taylor

A Sermon Occasioned by the Death of the Rev. John Taylor, D. D., late of Norwich, Professor of Divinity and Morality in the Academy at Warrington, Lancashire, with some account of his Character and Writings, by E. Harwood. London, 1761.

The Arians and Socinians Monitor, Being a Vision that a young Socinian Teacher lately had (etc.). London, 1761. Twelfth edition, 1883. First edition anonymous, and printed for the author, later identified as John MacGowan.

A Sketch of the Life of the Late Dr John Taylor of Norwich (From 'The Universal Theological Magazine &c' for July 1804) Corrected and enlarged in 1813 – R. T. Separate copy with manuscript marginal notes in the box of papers in Harris Manchester College library. Also item 16 of Vol. 5, 'Pamphlets', under 'English Presbyterian Trusts'.

The Revd W. Turner, Jun., M. A., *Lives of Eminent Unitarians*. London: The Unitarian Association, 1840, Vol. I.

J. and E. Taylor, *History of the Octagon Chapel, Norwich*. London:

Charles Green, Hackney, 1848. 'By the late Mr John Taylor of Norwich, continued by his son Edward Taylor, Esq. Gres. Prof. Mus.'

The Principles and Pursuits of an English Presbyterian Minister of the Eighteenth Century exemplified in a Selection from the writings of Dr John Taylor of Norwich including the Sermon preached by him in 1756 at the opening of the new Presbyterian Chapel in that City. London: Printed by Richard and John E. Taylor. Published by T. Cadell . . . 1843.

Philip Meadows Taylor, *A Memoir of the Family of Taylor of Norwich.* Privately printed, 1886 (British Library shelf number 9914 e 30). It has only one sentence on their ancestor Dr John Taylor, but is a most interesting anecdotal account of some of his illustrious descendants within the memory of the author. John Taylor's two surviving children were succeeded by an astonishingly able and versatile posterity.

For the controversy over Joseph Rawson

Church Book of the Castle Gate Church, now housed in the Department of Manuscripts and Special Collections, University of Nottingham.

For Taylor's two publications, see list of his works, above.

James Sloss, *The Doctrine of the Trinity, as it is Contained in the Scriptures* . . . London, 1736.

——— *The True Narrative of the Case of Joseph Rawson* . . . London, no date.

A. R. Henderson, *History of Castlegate Congregational Church, Nottingham, 1655–1905.* London: James Clarke & Co., 1905.

For Warrington Academy

MS Minute Book of the Trustees and Committee, preserved at Harris Manchester College, Oxford.

Henry A. Bright, *A Historical Sketch of the Warrington Academy.* Liverpool, 1843.

William Turner, *The Warrington Academy*, Reprinted from articles originally published in the 'Monthly Repository', vols VIII, IX and X, 1813–1815. Warrington Library and Museum Committee, 1957.

Transactions of the Congregational Historical Society, ed. T. G. Crippen, Vol. V. 1911–12.

H. McLachlan, *Warrington Academy, its History and Influence.* Printed for the Chetham Society, 1943.

P. O'Brien, M.D., *Warrington Academy, 1757–86.* Wigan: Owl Books, 1969.

See also: Francis Hutcheson, *An Inquiry into the Original of Our Ideas of Beauty and Virtue.* 1725.

—— *An Essay on the Nature and Conduct of the Passions and Affections.* 1726.

—— *A System of Moral Philosophy* to which is prefixed some account of the author by W. Leechman, 2 vols. London, 1755.

For the Doctrine of Original Sin

The Book of Common Prayer, services for Baptism, and the Thirty-Nine Articles.

The Westminster Confession, and Longer and Shorter Catechisms. Taylor's citations in Part II of his treatise are from The Larger Catechism, questions 22 to 29 inclusive. Among forty-four signatures to a prefatory address 'To the Christian Reader, especially Heads of Families', is that of Samuel Annesley, John Wesley's maternal grandfather.

Jeremy Taylor, *Unum Necessarium.* 1655; fourth edition, 1712.

David Jennings, *A Vindication of the Scripture Doctrine of Original Sin from Mr Taylor's free and candid Examination of it.* London, 1740.

Isaac Watts, *The Ruin and Recovery of Mankind.* London, 1740.

James Hervey, *Theron and Aspasio*, 3 vols. London, 1755.

Jonathan Edwards, *The Great Christian Doctrine of Original Sin Defended.* 1757; 'A new edition', Edinburgh, 1798.

John Wesley, *The Doctrine of Original Sin according to Scripture, Reason, and Experience.* Bristol, 1757; reprinted in *Works*, vol. 9, 1830 and 1872.

F. R. Tennant, *The Origin and Propagation of Sin*, Hulsean Lectures. Cambridge University Press, 1902.

—— *The Sources of the Doctrine of the Fall and Original Sin.* Cambridge University Press, 1903.

—— *The Concept of Sin.* Cambridge University Press, 1912.

R. S. Moxon, *The Doctrine of Sin.* London: Allen & Unwin, 1922.

N. P. Williams, *The Ideas of the Fall and Original Sin*, Bampton Lectures, 1924. London: Longmans, Green & Co., 1927.

Dietrich Bonhoeffer, *Creation and Fall: A Theological Interpretation of Genesis 1—3.* Lectures delivered in the University of Berlin, 1932–33, published 1937. ET London: SCM Press, 1959.

Uta Ranke-Heinemann, *Eunuchs for the Kingdom of Heaven*, ET Peter Heinegg. New York: Viking Penguin/London: Penguin Books, 1991.

Henri Blocher, *Original Sin: Illuminating the Riddle*, New Studies in Biblical Theology No. 5. Leicester: Apollos (Inter-Varsity Press), 1997.

Richard Holloway, 'Blaming Eve', ch. 6 in *Doubts and Loves.* Canongate, 2001.

For additional references, see endnotes to Appendices II and III.

F. Greaves
R. Williams

A. Wainwright.

General, in Alphabetical Order of Authorship

Richard Baxter, *Autobiography*, ed. J. M. Lloyd-Thomas. London: J. M. Dent, Everyman's Library, 1931; first published in *Reliqiae Baxterianae*, 1696.

C. Gordon Bolam, Jeremy Goring, H. L. Short, Roger Thomas, *The English Presbyterians*. London: Allen & Unwin, 1968.

Samuel Clarke, *The Scripture Doctrine of the Trinity*. 1712; 3rd edition, 1732.

A. W. Harrison, *Arminianism*. London: Duckworth Studies in Theology, 1937.

H. McLachlan, 'The academies as centres of learning', *English Education under the Test Acts*. Manchester University Press, 1931.

—— 'Thomas Dixon, M.A., M.D. and Whitehaven-Bolton Academy'; 'Semitics in the nonconformist academies'; 'Sport and recreation in non-conformist academies', *Essays and Addresses*. Manchester University Press, 1950.

Geoffrey F. Nuttall, 'The Influence of Arminianism in England', *The Puritan Spirit*. London: Epworth Press, 1967.

Alan P. F. Sell, *The Great Debate: Calvinism, Arianism and Salvation*. H. E. Walter Ltd, 1982.

—— *Dissenting Thought in the Life of the Churches: Studies in an English Tradition*. Lewiston, NY: Edwin Mellen Press, 1990.

—— *Commemorations: Studies in Christian Thought and History*. University of Calgary and University of Wales, 1993.

—— *John Locke and the Eighteenth Century Divines*. Cardiff: University of Wales Press, 1997.

—— *Philosophy, Dissent and Nonconformity 1689–1920*. Cambridge: James Clarke, 2003 (forthcoming).

Michael Watts, *The Dissenters*. Oxford: Clarendon Press, 1978, pbk 1985.

John Wesley, *Works*, ed. Thomas Jackson, fourteen volumes, 1829–31; includes the Journal (vols I–IV), the Sermons (vols V–VII), and the treatise on Original Sin (vol. IX). Reprinted 1872, with the same pagination as far as Vol. X, but not for some later volumes. The Bicentennial edition of Wesley's Works is in process of publication, and is already extant for the Journal, the Sermons, and the Letters as far as 1755, but not for the treatise on Original Sin. The Journal is also accessible in the Standard Edition, ed. Nehemiah Curnock, eight volumes, London, 1909 and a later reprint. To facilitate search in any of these editions, references to the Journal have been made by date only. For the sermons, see also *The Standard Sermons*, ed. E. H. Sugden, two volumes, London: Epworth Press, 1921, second edition 1935; and for the *Letters*, Standard Edition, ed. John Telford, eight volumes, London: Epworth Press, 1931.

A. Skevington Wood, *Revelation and Reason: Wesleyan Responses to Eighteenth Century Rationalism*. Nuneaton: The Wesley Fellowship, 1992.

Index

*This is
Richard Watson
the Methodist.*